*The Death and Life of
the American Quality Movement*

The Death
and Life of the
American Quality
Movement

Edited by
Robert E. Cole

New York   Oxford
OXFORD UNIVERSITY PRESS
1995

Oxford University Press

Oxford   New York
Athens   Auckland   Bangkok   Bombay
Calcutta   Cape Town   Dar es Salaam   Delhi
Florence   Hong Kong   Istanbul   Karachi
Kuala Lumpur   Madras   Madrid   Melbourne
Mexico City   Nairobi   Paris   Singapore
Taipei   Tokyo   Toronto

and associated companies in
Berlin   Ibadan

Library of Congress Cataloging-in-Publication Data
The death and life of the American total quality movement
edited by Robert E. Cole.
p. cm.   Includes bibliographical references and index.
ISBN 0–19–509206–6
1. Total quality management—United States.
2. Competition—United States.
I. Cole, Robert E.
HD62.15.D45   1995   658.'62—dc20
94–37003

1 3 5 7 9 8 6 4 2

Printed in the United States of America
on acid-free paper

Preface

This book is designed to help re-energize the quality movement in the United States. The book's title suggests that something has happened to it and we believe that it has. We also believe that the quality movement is even more important to firms now than ever before. But for too many firms the move toward quality has plateaued. Why?

To understand the reasons we must look at its beginnings. The American quality movement rose out of the deep recession of the early 1980s as American companies floundered about searching for the secret of Japanese success in American markets, especially in the manufacturing sector. Many companies had trouble acknowledging the importance of quality in customer decisions. Moreover, once they accepted the importance of quality, they had a great deal of difficulty understanding the path to quality success. Quick fixes were in vogue.

When quick results were not forthcoming, naysayers predicted a short life for the quality movement. They expected it to be another in the succession of postwar management fads that left little changed in the companies introducing them.

Despite these predictions, managers persisted and the quality movement proved remarkably durable, sinking deep roots in many companies. The market pressures and opportunities were too strong to be denied. Quality performance has improved across a broad range of industries—service as well as manufacturing. The business press has noted the declining number of Malcolm Baldrige National Quality applications, using this as a measure of the waning strength of the quality movement. At the same time, it overlooks the fact that the Baldrige Award office has distributed over one million application forms. Thousands upon thousands of companies are using them as a protocol for self-assessment and a driver for quality improvement, Notwithstanding these positive developments, managers and many companies appear confused as to how to proceed further. There are many competing ideas and proposals.

This book represents the combined efforts of many experts to point the way to the next stage in the American quality movement. It captures the evolving trends in small, medium, and large companies, and in manufacturing and service firms. It explores the issues in a variety of functions, from strategic planning to marketing. And it emphasizes the roles people play, from top executives to the shop floor. Above all, our prime concern is to identify and find solutions to the central issues that confront the quality movement of the 1990s. How, for example, should the restructuring/re-engineering movement be positioned vis-à-vis the quality focus? We must address such unsolved matters if firms are to be able to go forward in their quest for exemplary quality and business performance.

The principal criterion for soliciting participants and chapters in this volume was the authors' ability to generate new knowledge about issues facing the quality movement. Areas of concentration include the role and approach to employee participation, how to reconcile quality with downsizing, the relation of marketing to quality, what to do when top management displays only a modest understanding of what is required, intelligent corporate responses to the inevitably faddish character of tools and techniques, policy deployment, the relation between process and results orientations, the special problems and challenges facing small high tech companies seeking to operationalize quality improvement, and how to keep a focus on the customer through measuring the return on quality.

February 1995   R. E. C.
Oakland, Ca.

Acknowledgments

I am indebted to the *California Management Review* and its editor David J. Vogel for encouraging me to edit a special issue on the theme of quality. That Spring 1993 issue of the *Review* received an extraordinarily positive reception and encouraged us to create this book. Authors who participated in the original effort elaborated on their original ideas and only Noriaki Kano's article was left more or less unchanged. We also added two new articles, one by Kim Cameron on downsizing and quality, and another by Phillip Wilson describing alternatives to a full-blown quality "program." Both of these entirely new contributions fill out our initiative in important ways.

I want to thank all the authors for their cooperation and the editorial and production staff of Oxford University Press. I especially want to acknowledge Gene Ulansky for his editing of the original manuscript and Rosemary Wellner for her work on this version. We also acknowledge the sponsorship of the Air Force Office of Scientific Research, Air Force Systems Command, USAF under AFOSR Grant #F49620-92-J-0539.

Contents

Contributors

PAUL BACDAYAN is a doctoral candidate in organizational behavior at the University of Michigan School of Business. Before receiving his MBA at the Amos Tuck School of Business Administration at Dartmouth, he worked in management consulting. His current research is on total quality management and expert team leaders.

JAMES A. BELOHLAV is an Associate Professor of Management at the Charles H. Kellstadt Graduate School of Business at DePaul University. His research focuses on the role of human and technical systems in corporate strategy. He is the author of *Championship Management* as well as numerous scholarly and professional articles.

KIM S. CAMERON is a professor in the School of Business Administration and in the School of Education at the University of Michigan. He has conducted research over the past several years on quality culture and quality management practices. He teaches in several executive education programs, including Strategic Quality Management. He is currently preparing a national study of total quality management practices in colleges and universities.

JAMES M. CARMAN is a Professor Emeritus of Business Administration at the Haas School of Business at the University of California at Berkeley. He is currently involved in a large study of implementation of Continuous Quality Improvement in healthcare institutions. His recent research interests focus on services management and marketing, vertical marketing systems, and governance of strategic alliances.

E. EVA CHEN is the Vice President of Quality and Operations at WiSE Communications, Inc. Prior to joining WiSE, she was the Vice President of Quality and Customer Support at Media Vision, Inc. and E-mu Systems, Inc., respectively. Dr. Chen also served as a member of the Board of Examiners for the Malcolm Baldrige National Quality Award from its inception until 1990. She received her Ph.D. in Statistics from the University of Wisconsin in Madison.

ROBERT E. COLE is Professor cf Organizational Behavior at the Haas School of Business and Professor of Sociology at the University of California, Berkeley. His current research focuses on Japanese work organizations, organizational design, and continuous quality improvement. His most recent book is *Strategies for Learning: Small-Group Activities in American, Japanese and Swedish Industry*. He was recently inducted into the International Academy of Quality. He is currently working on a book on the American quality movement from an institutional perspective.

GEORGE S. EASTON is an Associate Professor of Statistics and Quality Management at the Graduate School of Business, University of Chicago. He was Senior Examiner for the Malcolm Baldrige National Quality Award in 1991 and an Examiner in 1989 and 1990. His recent research has focused on empirical assessment of the impact of quality management on corporate performance. He also consults widely with industry in both the quality management and statistics areas.

NORIAKI KANO is Professor and Head of the Department of Management Science, Faculty of Engineering, Science University of Tokyo. A student of the late Dr. Kaoru Ishikawa, Dr. Kano has been a leading contributor to the evolving Japanese postwar quality paradigm. He is particularly well known for his work on "attractive quality versus must-be quality" and TQC in the service sector. He has broad international experience including service as a counsellor on quality to a number of major American companies. He is a long-time member of the Deming Prize Committee and has recently been named Senior Member of the American Society for Quality Control.

PETER J. KOLESAR is a Professor in the Business and Engineering Schools of Columbia University and Research Director of Columbia's Deming Center for Quality Management. His theoretical and applied work on the deployment and logistics of police, fire, and ambulance services has gained him worldwide recognition and numerous honors. His current research and consulting activity focuses on improving the effectiveness of implementation of total quality management.

RAYMOND. E KORDUPLESKI is the Director of Customer Satisifion for AT&T, and Chair of the American Marketing Association's Second Congress on Customer Satisfaction. He has worked in the telecommunications industry for more than twenty-five years and is considered one of the experts in his field.

MICHAEL PRICE is the Vice President of Engineering at E-mu Systems, Inc. Prior to joining E-mu, he served as Vice President of Engineering at Pixar, Inc., a 3D graphics and animation company, and Valid Logic Systems, Inc., a Computer-Aided Engineering firm. He previously worked at Hewlett-Packard Co. He received his B.S. in Electrical Engineering from Carnegie Mellon University.

ROLAND T. RUST is Professor of Marketing and Director of the Center for Services Marketing at the Owen Graduate School of Management at Vanderbilt University. He has worked with numerous leading businesses and non-profit organizations, including Malcolm Baldrige National Quality Award winners AT&T and FedEx. His most recent book is *Return on Quality (ROQ): Measuring the Financial Impact of Your Company's Quest for Quality* (written with Anthony Zahorik and Timothy Keiningham).

B. JOSEPH WHITE is Dean and Professor of Business Administration at the University of Michigan Business School. He was a Baldrige Award Examiner in 1990. Prior to joining the Michigan Business School in 1987, he was Vice President for Personnel and Public Affairs at Cummins Engine Company.

PHIL WILSON is Senior Vice President of Human Resources at Oracle Corporation. He has been a consultant in The Aptos Group; Vice President of Human Resources at NeXT Computer, Inc.; Vice President of Personnel at Cummins Engine Company, Inc.; and at Princeton University, Assistant Dean of the Faculty and Assistant Professor. He has served on the Board of Directors of the Council for Continuous Improvement and has given numerous public presentations on quality and human resources management.

ANTHONY J. ZAHORIK is Assistant Professor of Marketing at the Owen School of Management at Vanderbilt University. He is co-author (with Roland Rust and Timothy Keiningham) of the book *Return on Quality: Measuring the Financial Impact of Your Company's Quest for Quality*. He has also consulted and taught executive seminars on service quality programs and marketing planning to firms in many industries, including health care and banking.

The Death and Life of
the American Quality Movement

Introduction

ROBERT E. COLE

There is a great deal of confusion about the critical ingredients of total quality management, to what extent Western firms can simply borrow Japanese practices, and how firms can implement quality practices in ways that yield strong performance outcomes. Similarly, debate rages about the status of the American quality movement. Is it already past its prime—or alive and well? While still hazy, the outlines of answers to these questions are much clearer today than they were a decade ago. In this book, we aim to provide a strong basis for understanding the critical issues in quality. In my MBA course on quality and in corporate consulting, I am continually pressed to give a step-by-step "how-to-do-it formula" for quality success. What those asking these questions fail to understand is that they need first to learn how to think about quality. Without that knowledge, all rote formulas and technique are useless, bound to founder when they get thrown up against unique and rapidly changing business situations.

This book, above all, is designed to help managers and academics pose the right questions about quality, but it is also about trying to offer the right answers. We offer no pat formulas; in fact, we pose alternatives, for example, between undertaking a full-fledged quality campaign versus a more guerrilla style up-from-the bottom approach. We recognize that "one size does not fit all." Thus, we propose different strategies for different kinds of firms. The contents of this book are clearly prescriptive in a number of fundamental areas; the authors do point firms in directions we believe will yield strong performance outcomes. We also provide a great many empirical observations about what works and what doesn't.

Doomsayers have been predicting the death of the American quality movement almost from its inception in the early 1980s. Indeed, they have been given a lot of material to work with—failed attempts at implementing quality practices are commonplace. Major factors involved in these failures include: early company efforts that simplistically grasped at quality circles to provide the whole solution; overreliance on statistical methods; underreliance on statistical methods; the bellowing of top management about quality, without any follow-through; wholesale training of employees without immediate application; unrealistically high expectations for quick results; the bureaucratization of quality efforts; quality zealots who claimed quality to be a costless solution and a cure for whatever ailed a company; the failure to redesign traditional reward structures and organizational objectives to bring them into line with the new quality initiative (business as usual, but let's add quality to what we are doing); the failure to recognize the tight linkage between quality objectives and increased employee participation; the failure to fully integrate key functions like marketing into quality improvement activities; the unwillingness to adjust quality initiatives to special circumstances relating to nation, industry, and firm-level conditions such as length of product cycle and competitive environment; the inability to move away from traditional results-oriented American management style; and the failure to build customer expectations and needs into daily organizational activities. All these factors contributed to some spectacular failures and a massive waste of resources over the last decade.

Yet, out of this seemingly blind trial-and-error learning process, we are starting to see examples of successful performance and are beginning to understand what it takes to succeed. These elements of success include:

- Sustained top-management leadership for the quality initiative and active application to their own daily management activities.
- A relentless focus on the customer, both in setting strategic objectives and building organizational routines that strongly link all units and levels in the firm as well as firm suppliers and distributors in identifying and meeting customer needs.
- Systematic improvement of the quality of all business processes from an internal and (especially) external customer perspective.
- Decentralization of decision-making responsibility to a well-trained problem-solving labor force (i.e., employee participation in decision making).
- A breaking down of organizational barriers between departments and levels so that cross-functional management becomes normal operating procedure.
- A combined emphasis on incremental continuous improvement *and* breakthrough strategies that is strongly linked to competitive objectives.
- Realignment of reward and measurement systems, both formal and informal, to support these new directions.
- A decentralized information and decision support system (management by fact) that provides data to a broadly defined set of "players."

Each of these factors in turn requires a wide range of implementation activities. Beyond these broad generic ingredients, a successful approach to implementing total quality is guided by the industry, size, technology, length of product cycle, competitive environment, type of customers, and unique history of a given organization.

The chapters in this volume treat in one fashion or another both the sources of organizational failure with quality as well as the ingredients for a successful approach. But there is no simple recipe, no turnkey solution; otherwise Western firms would not be finding the transformation so difficult.

It is useful to remind ourselves that Japanese manufacturing firms took twenty years to arrive at a mature quality movement capable of delivering sustained competitive advantage; in their service sector, the movement is only about ten years old. This is not to say that Western firms must go through the same learning cycle as the Japanese. The advantages of "backwardness," as the economic historian Alexander Gerschenkron pointed out many years ago, is that one can learn from the experiences of those who have gone before. Still, expectations for instant success are hardly realistic, and many company failures have taken place in firms that thought they were waging war but in fact had only sent reconnoitering missions into the quality field.

The quality movement, whatever its faddish element, has not stalled; à la Mark Twain, rumors of its death are greatly exaggerated. Indeed, the quality movement is gaining momentum. This momentum is occurring because the forces of competition around quality have been set in motion and will not be denied. First in the international arena and increasingly in the domestic arena, firms risk losing out to competitors if they cannot match their rapidly rising levels of quality and productivity—and if they cannot do so in a sustained fashion. Because competitors are rapidly improving quality, those firms that achieve only partial success in implementing TQM may fall further behind in the competitive struggle. No wonder many firms voice disappointment with the results of their quality initiative—they can't all be winners! Victory goes to the swift and to those that can most fully internalize and adapt the new quality paradigm to their own business environments.

Management fads have a bad name. They are seen as costly distractions that keep managers from taking responsibility for running the business. They are panic responses to severe business challenges, brought out in recent years particularly by the Japanese challenge. When a new approach doesn't yield the desired results, management often acts capriciously, moving on to another seemingly more promising approach. No one who has spent time closely observing management behavior can fail to recognize the truth of many of these observations. Yet there is a simplicity about this view that does not capture many corporate experiences. There have, in fact, been a number of quality "minifads" over the course of the 1980s embracing particular techniques and approaches. A non-exhaustive list includes: quality control circles, statistical process control, benchmarking, concurrent engineering, continuous improvement, Baldrige diagnosis, ISO 9000, quality function deployment, management by policy (hoshin planning), and business process re-engineering. Consultants will make the claim that each new technique or approach they are hawking at a given time is unique and supersedes all others. Currently, we see such specious claims by proponents of the business process re-engineering movement. The best firms will resist such claims while learning the most valuable elements in each successive quality minifad and incorporating them into their overall efforts to bring about organizational transformation. And they will do this in a way that one element builds on another. For example, early participative efforts associated with quality circles were built into subsequent approaches to statistical process control. These firms recognize that fads can be a powerful vehicle for "keeping it fresh."

The Japanese went through many fads in their quality development, but no one doubts that they built a durable and powerful movement. The Japanese Union of Scientists and Engineers (JUSE), the major promoter of the Japanese quality movement in postwar Japan, worked to identify and promote innovative quality practices. They cooperated closely with their corporate members to roll out one "product introduction" after another from the 1950s through the 1970s. Each of these new quality products was the quality minifad of its time. Because of the centralized nature of the movement in Japan, there was less tendency to drop an earlier for a later product. Instead, JUSE presented new products as essential building blocks for successful quality performance. It provided a kind of "quality control" for the quality movement that tends to be lacking in the United States with the exception of the Baldrige criteria. Ironically, in recent years, a number of Japanese quality experts complain that the JUSE pipeline is no longer full; they argue that JUSE has failed to generate the rapid flow of new products necessary to energize the Japanese quality movement for the 1990s.

The American label for the new quality paradigm is itself a faddish element. Today it is "Total Quality Management" (TQM), a term that already has negative connotations. Predictably, some firms choose different names for their new quality management system. From a motivational perspective, this can be quite useful. Others confuse terminology with substance and reject the focus on quality itself. To do so, however, is to miss the opportunity to create a common language of quality within and across firms so that organizational learning and improvement can be accelerated.

We see many firms continuing to seek solutions to their competitive problems through traditional means—i.e., by arbitrary cost-cutting solutions that ignore customer needs and penalize loyal employees. Mindless downsizing itself has become a fad. How can a company show up for its meetings with analysts without announcing its new plans for "rightsizing"? Those firms that maximize quality in the eyes of their customers while at the same time meet the needs of their employees have a far better recipe for success over the long haul. It is a recipe that elicits employee cooperation for enhanced customer satisfaction. It adds to product and service quality and not only reduces costs, but increases revenues. It is a recipe that provides a long-term approach to enhancing shareholder value by ensuring corporate survival.

In the meantime, we haven't seen the end of disappointments with quality programs. They will be loudly trumpeted. As Dr. Kano notes in his chapter, the media's treatment of this subject is quite superficial. The old newsroom slogan "If it burns or bleeds, lead with it" seems to apply. Consequently, management will be challenged to maintain the "constancy of purpose" that Dr. Deming so wisely counseled as a major prerequisite for success in improving quality.

The next chapter offers a broad overview of the quality movement in America. George Easton, relying on his experience as a Baldrige Examiner, captures the strengths and weaknesses of American companies using the Baldrige categories as his frame. He reveals with singular clarity, for example, the differences between results-oriented management and process-oriented management and the difficulty American firms have experienced in making the transition. The prototypical results-oriented manager, nourished on MBO, says to his or her subordinates: "Don't bring me problems, just solutions!" This is an abdication of management responsibility. By contrast, the process-oriented manager targets not only customer-focused objectives, but also the "how" questions. How do you meet that objective? What are the alternatives? How are you going to choose among them? Do you have the resources, expertise, and authority to proceed? Moreover, contrary to the quality zealots, those internalizing the new quality paradigm understand that the purpose of this process orientation is to get results. The whole purpose of process improvement is to generate results—and managers should have as clear an idea as possible of what they will be. In short, managers need to learn to "walk and chew gum" at the same time.

The next four chapters take up the relations among quality, competitiveness, and another critical issue. James Belohlav examines the relationship between quality, competitiveness, and strategy. He notes the dangers of a simpleminded equating of quality with competitive success, yet shows how quality can become the touchstone of a successful competitive strategy by creating choices and opportunities not available to one's competitors.

Cole, Bacdayan, and White explore the relationship between quality, competitiveness, and participation. They note participation advocates' long and unrequited courtship of managers. They examine the continuing sources of this rejection and explore point by point what a quality focus can bring to these relationships. Their answer is "a lot!" In particular, they clarify the distinctive market-in strategy pursued by Japanese firms and show how it differs from the often superficial "serve-the-customer" efforts of many American firms.

Kordupleski, Rust, and Zahorik begin with the observation that marketing often seems to be a missing partner in quality initiatives despite—or perhaps because of—marketing people's belief that the customer focus has long been their domain. The authors show how an organization must link an external customer focus to regular internal work routines ("market-in") and to measurable consumer behavior to fully reap competitive benefits. Customer-driven considerations must not be allowed to result in an exclusive external focus. Instead, success requires that one literally build the customer needs and expectations—and the meeting of these needs and expectations—into daily organizational routines. Many American companies have yet to understand this linkage. Without it, no matter how successful one is in gleaning information about external customers, the results will be disappointing.

Kim Cameron explores the relationship between quality, downsizing, and competitiveness. As is well know, downsizing policies have been central to many large American companies over the last few years as they sought to come to terms with deflation, stagnant markets, and new competitive pressures. Many companies engaged in downsizing are also companies claiming to be committed to quality improvement activities. Yet they often pursue downsizing in ways that alienate employees or fail to take into consideration customer interests. The key issues addressed by Cameron concern how firms can either pursue downsizing so that they do not jeopardize quality improvement activities or develop alternative approaches to downsizing itself.

The next four chapters deal with company experiences in implementing total quality management. Michael Price and Eva Chen explore the distinctive experiences of small high-technology companies with TQM. Many such companies see TQM as yesterday's large-company fad with no great relevance to them. This is very risky. The authors not only argue for the benefits of TQM in small high-technology companies, but discuss the adaptations necessary for implementing TQM in this particular environment. They discuss the specific challenges that loom large for small companies, such as how to push for standardization—a key element in any successful quality strategy—while avoiding bureaucratization and not stifling innovation.

Phillip Wilson examines an alternative approach to the typical quality improvement involving full-scale mobilization of company employees in a TQM program. There are many firms in which management and other key employees do not support quality initiatives, often because they have been "burned" by past failures and overblown promises. In this situation, very pragmatic "guerrilla" tactics may be called for. Specifically, Wilson examines the feasibility of an inductive approach that step by step accumulates quality improvement through project-improvement activities in critical business processes (what he calls mission-critical workflows). A key problem for those pursuing this step-by-step approach, one Wilson seeks to address, is how to develop and diffuse across the firm a common language of quality concepts and methodologies. More generally, this involves the issue of how to institutionalize quality learning and practices throughout the enterprise.

A third treatment of company experiences concerns the use of continuous quality improvement as a survival strategy. Here, James Carman details the efforts of Southern Pacific to use quality as its centerpiece initiative in a turn-around strategy. This runs counter to the conventional wisdom that the return on a quality initiative is a long-term one and not likely to yield short-term results. Yet Southern Pacific will be dead in the near term if immediate results are not forthcoming. Southern Pacific's approach is simply an extreme version of the motivating forces that drove companies like Ford Motor Company in the early 1980s to make quality their centerpiece for renovating the company. It is an example of what Dr. Kano calls "Crisis Consciousness and Leadership Makes People Sweat for Quality."

In the next chapter, Peter Kolesar describes in detail the micro processes by which top management at the Aluminum Company of America (Alcoa) came to grips with quality as a corporate strategy and how they sought to drive quality down through the organization. Those familiar with the efforts of large bureaucratic manufacturing companies in the 1980s to transform themselves through a quality initiative will recognize the characteristic paths management chose. This includes paths that led to dead ends as well as those that took more promising directions. The author provides a rich description of management thinking and action; it is a documentary of typical large-company management behavior in the 1980s and early 1990s. We need to clinically analyze such experiences and learn from them.

In the final chapter, Dr. Kano, distinguished quality expert in Japan, offers yet another perspective on the American quality movement. Using his long-term experience as advisor to many leading American firms, he shows both the problems experienced by the American quality movement as well as its growing successes. He documents not only the differences, but the many similarities between the American and Japanese quality movement.

Much confusion still surrounds the meaning and components of the new quality paradigm. We believe that the chapters in this book make a modest contribution toward a much-needed clarification of these concerns.

2

A Baldrige Examiner's Assessment of U.S. Total Quality Management

GEORGE S. EASTON

Quality began to emerge as a key management focus in the United States around 1980. This emergence was primarily in manufacturing companies that were suffering severe foreign competitive pressure, most notably from Japan. Since that time, "quality management" has coalesced into a major management movement influencing nearly every industry. "Quality management," in this context, means the recognition by senior management that quality is a key strategic issue and therefore an important focus for *all* levels of the organization. Creation of the Malcolm Baldrige National Quality Award by Congress in 1987 contributed to the national visibility of quality management and thus to the momentum of the U.S. quality management movement.

Much of the U.S. quality movement is based on tools and techniques that have been key features in the development of Japanese quality management over the last forty years. Many of these techniques, such as statistical process control, were originally developed in the United States. Japanese management approaches, such as widespread employee involvement in quality improvement teams, have also been adopted by many U.S. companies. These approaches have often required complete redevelopment as substantial changes in both methods and emphasis are necessary for successful implementation in U.S. organizations. There have also been many genuine U.S. quality management innovations. In particular, prevailing traditional U.S. management approaches have been successfully refocused to address quality management issues.

The most critical challenge facing the U.S. quality movement is the development and implementation of quality-focused corporate management systems that achieve the coherence, integration, and comprehensiveness of quality management in Japan. Such comprehensive quality-driven approaches to corporate management are becoming known in the United States as Total Quality Management (TQM). Much consensus exists about some of the key components of

TQM systems, including the necessity of a customer focus, the critical role played by leadership, and the importance of widespread employee involvement. Major differences in opinion remain, however, about both the appropriate components of TQM and the emphasis among the various components. There is also much disagreement concerning the details of implementation, even in areas of general consensus.

One of the factors contributing to the difficulty of developing in the United States the same level of unification and integration achieved by Japanese quality management systems is that few U.S. managers understand the philosophical orientation underlying Japanese management. These more subtle aspects of Japanese quality management, however, may be critically important to the success of quality management in any culture. Such nuances are difficult for U.S. managers to fully understand because mastering them requires changing unstated assumptions that are intrinsic in U.S. management thought. These misunderstandings contribute greatly to many managers' tendency to trivialize the intellectual content of TQM and to believe they have complete understanding based on superficial experience with a few quality techniques.

As a result of both the consensus and disagreement discussed above, many questions remain concerning both what U.S. TQM currently is and what it ought to be. In this chapter, I attempt to contribute to the discussion of these questions by providing a critical assessment of the current state of TQM in the United States. This assessment is primarily based on my experience evaluating companies as a member of the Board of Examiners of the Malcolm Baldrige National Quality Award between 1989 and 1992.

The assessment of TQM described here is unusual because it does not just focus on the characteristics of winning companies. I concentrate not only on the small number of winners, but on the larger group of very good companies that receive high scores in the evaluation process. Further, I present a critical evaluation of the overall state of development of the TQM systems of these companies as a group. Examination of this larger group aids in discerning patterns in the approaches taken and more accurately reflects the overall state of TQM in the United States. The sample of companies that are the basis for this assessment, and the target group of companies the assessment attempts to characterize, are described in more detail in the next two sections.

My assessment is reported in a format similar to the Feedback Reports that all Baldrige Award applicants receive. For each of the seven major categories of the award, strengths and areas of improvement are described. The strengths identify common successful approaches that high-scoring companies are taking in their development and implementation of TQM. In most cases, these approaches are quite similar to those of companies that actually win. The areas for improvement identify common difficulties, errors in approach, failures, and confusions that limit the potential of these companies' TQM programs. As with the strengths, many of these areas for improvement are also often found in winning companies. It is my hope that specific discussion of the common weaknesses in approaches will shed some light on, or at least create some discussion of, the factors limiting the continued successful evolution of TQM in the United States.

Any critical evaluation of the current status of U.S. TQM requires comparison to some conceptualization of what TQM should be. The Baldrige Award Criteria attempt to provide such a conceptualization at the level of the issues that must be effectively addressed by a TQM system. The Award Criteria, however, deliberately avoid prescribing specific approaches and allow a great deal of latitude in interpretation. Thus, they give little specific guidance.[1] As a result, the strengths and areas for improvement described here inevitably heavily reflect my own conceptualization of TQM.[2] A brief introduction to the Baldrige Award and the award's scoring process is given in the chapter Appendix.

The Sample

The assessment described in this chapter is based primarily on my experience as an Examiner and Senior Examiner with the Baldrige Award between 1989 and 1992. During that period, I was involved in the scoring and/or feedback process for 22 companies that applied for the award. For three of these companies, I participated in site visits. The 22 companies span all categories of applicants for the award: large manufacturing, large service, and small business (both manufacturing and service). Table 2.1 shows the number of companies of each type. These 22 companies form the "sample" on which this assessment is based.

This "sample" is clearly not random. It is, however, of sufficient scope to develop a very good idea of the characteristics of the population of companies that apply for the award. It should be emphasized that the population of these companies is not a representative cross section of U.S. businesses or even of companies trying to implement quality management systems. Because of self-

TABLE 2.1. Types of Companies in the Sample

Size	Manufacturing	Service
Large	5	10
Small	5	2

selection, companies that apply for the award are generally far superior to typical companies. Many more companies use the Baldrige Award Criteria for diagnostic purposes than apply or ever intend to apply for the award.

Finally, my analysis of this population of companies is largely subjective. Systematic analysis would be difficult because the award's confidentiality requirements prohibit disclosure of information concerning any applicant. In addition, the applicant's materials can only be used by the examiner during the actual scoring process. Thus, my "analysis" is based on observation and subjective assessment of common approaches and characteristics—in short, on my experience.

The Target

The assessment that begins in the next section attempts to capture the state of TQM in very good U.S. companies that are committed to quality management and have achieved considerable success. The focus is not only on exceptional companies, such as those that have won the Baldrige Award, but also on the next level of companies that score about 600 or higher out of 1000 in the Award process. While understanding the approaches that winners have used successfully can clearly be beneficial, winning companies are often quite unique in both the approaches they take as well as in their success in deploying TQM and obtaining results. To assess the overall state of the TQM movement and its potential for widespread influence on U.S. management practice requires focusing on the larger number of very good companies that are committed to TQM rather than only on the occasional unique and exceptional company. The dissemination of quality management approaches into this larger group will ultimately determine the success or failure of TQM as a management revolution in the United States. The reason is that these companies are both leaders in management thought and sufficient in number to have widespread influence. In addition, the larger number of companies in this group allows common patterns to be discerned. Baldrige winners are so few in number that even subjective inference is difficult.

While the group of companies targeted by this assessment is broader than just winners of the award, the strengths and areas for improvement identified are also typical of winning companies. Winning the Baldrige Award is often interpreted as a blanket endorsement of all aspects of the winner's quality management systems. This, however, is not the case. Winning companies are selected to be role models. What role model means in this context is that winning companies do some things exceptionally well and with exceptional results, do most things well, and do not have major flaws or omissions that veto their role-model status. Thus, winning companies generally score above the 600 level in all *key* areas, indicating overall high levels of deployment of their basic approaches. But as the following assessment indicates, many important areas for improvement exist in 600-level companies as well as many strengths. These areas for improvement are also often found in winning companies.

Assessment by Category

In this section, I describe the strengths and areas for improvement common among very good TQM companies. The assessment is given for each of the seven categories of the Baldrige Award Criteria. I also note some important differences between manufacturing and service companies.

Category 1: Leadership

STRENGTHS

- Senior management is committed to quality. Senior managers are actively involved in promoting the importance of quality and customer satisfaction and they devote a substantial fraction of their time to quality-related issues (10% or more). Their involvement includes such activities as speeches, meeting with employees, meeting with customers, giving formal and informal recognition, receiving training, and training others (e.g., new employee orientation).
- Senior management has developed and communicated a set of company quality values. The key values of TQM are emphasized, such as the importance of the customer, process orientation, continuous improvement, teamwork, management-by-fact, mutual respect and dignity, and value of individual employees and their contributions.
- The entire organization understands the importance of the external customer. The concept and importance of internal customers is also understood, and most employees feel some connection between what they do and the company's ability to respond to and satisfy the external customers.
- Elements of a quality management structure are in place, such as a senior management TQM council, division and department councils, and so on. These councils are involved in the management of the quality improvement teams, suggestion system, and recognition systems.

AREAS FOR IMPROVEMENT

- Senior management's *primary* focus is still on "strategy" and strategic business units (SBUs). Management still views the company almost exclusively in terms of financial, not operational, measures. There is only limited awareness of direct quality measures, especially on a month-to-month or day-to-day basis.

- Senior management does not systematically develop or carefully plan its leadership activities. Senior managers do not apply the concept of processes to their own functions. In addition, there is little real management-by-fact. Instead, senior management primarily relies on experience together with financial and cost measures. These measures often have limited effectiveness in guiding management decisions.

- Overall, senior management's understanding of TQM is quite superficial. While senior managers support TQM in principle, they feel that, other than to promote its importance, it is not a primary activity in their realm. As a result, the scope of senior management's involvement is limited. In addition, senior management does not have a clear conceptualization of the specific roles of lower levels of management in TQM.

- Management still has, almost exclusively, a results, not process, orientation (see box).

- In many cases, senior managers have very little specific knowledge and understanding of the company's processes or of direct customer, operational, employee-related, and supplier data. They do not routinely apply the Pareto principle, either formally or subjectively, and as a result they cannot identify the key problem areas or underlying causes. For example, they are unaware of the key types and causes of customer complaints or of employee injuries. They are also often unaware of adverse trends and have difficulty interpreting the levels and trends in the context of the variation generally present in the data.

- While some quality management structure is in place, for the most part the roles of management and supervision in TQM have not been developed. As a result, most managers are not clear about what they should do other than promote quality in general terms. They believe that TQM is primarily about attitude and motivation.

- Management often does not fully appreciate the scope of their business as viewed by the customer, focusing instead on what management perceives the product to be. As a result, the scope of the quality activities, including measurement, is often too narrow.

Results Versus Process Orientation

In a results-oriented approach, management is still primarily based on setting objectives, feedback, and creating incentives. Behind this orientation is an unspoken belief that the results belong to the individuals, and that management's role is to hire the best people and create incentives for obtaining the desired results. This presumes that the individuals will be able to figure out how to achieve the goals if left to their own devices.

In a process-oriented approach, the belief is that the results belong to the processes, and the processes belong to the organization. The role of the individuals is process operation and development including improvement of existing processes and development of new ones. The role of results is to guide process development and improvement. Thus, in TQM the emphasis is on developing methods and strategies, and approaches for implementing them, that will generate the best possible results.

At management levels, the development of methods and strategies may be directly tied to achieving particular important goals, but in addition it is focused on providing methods that will enable lower levels of the organization to develop strategies and methods for achieving their goals. The Plan-Do-Check-Act cycle, together with the associated quality tools, is an example. It is not a method for achieving a particular objective, but instead a means for enabling quality-improvement teams to solve problems and generate improvement.

Category 2: Information and Analysis

STRENGTHS

- There is excellent advanced technological support of information systems.
- The company has identified key quality measures that are tracked and often given high visibility.
- A lot of data, primarily financial/accounting data, are readily available.
- Informal benchmarking and other types of information acquisition and sharing are beginning to occur.
- Competitive comparisons are made against primary competitors.

AREAS FOR IMPROVEMENT

- The quality information is not well organized to support quality management. There is generally no coherent, articulated strategy for ensuring that the information needs of all organizational levels are met. Issues of what information is global, what is local, how local information is to be managed and analyzed, how local information is to be aggregated for higher level decision making, how aggregate information is to be analyzed, and how the results of aggregate analysis are to be disseminated, indexed, and otherwise made widely available are generally not adequately addressed.

- The data that are readily available are often developed to monitor results and assess achievement of goals. These measures tend to be downstream and financially oriented. They are often not well suited either for managing operations or maintaining customer focus (i.e., managing customer relationships and tracking satisfaction). In many cases, the cost data do not give an accurate picture of operations because they are based on inaccurate assumptions, such as arbitrary allocation of overhead, or because they merge costs from unrelated causes.

- The information systems are often inflexible and unable to support the kinds of change that are a part of both continuous improvement and evolving customer expectations.

- Competitive comparisons are often limited to immediate competitors only.

- Benchmarking is often confused with and limited to competitive comparisons. The purpose of benchmarking is to generate process innovation. Benchmarking is often most fruitful when similar processes or process steps are examined in companies in different industries. In addition, noncompetitors are usually far more willing to share information.

- Analysis outside of technical functions and production areas is limited. Analysis at management levels is not based on management-by-fact. Instead, it generally relies almost exclusively on informal brainstorming. Effective problem-solving methods are not deployed at all levels.

Category 3: Strategic Quality Planning

STRENGTHS

- Baldrige applicants usually develop some sort of written quality plan. This plan may be separate or part of the overall strategic or business plans.

- Quality-related goals are set in production-related areas of the company. Often quality goals are part of the management-by-objectives process.

- Many companies have adopted stretch goals (e.g., Six Sigma).

AREAS FOR IMPROVEMENT

- Few companies appear to have a well-developed strategic or corporate quality-planning process. When plans do exist, they are seldom derived from systematic analysis of meaningful data and information, including customer, operational, and employee data and information.

- The planning processes generally stop at setting goals and objectives and developing the budget. They do not realistically address implementation issues or deployment of the plan throughout the organization. Even in companies with a fairly well-developed planning process, failure to realistically anticipate implementation issues is common and a key reason why the planning process is ineffective. In many cases the plans lack sufficient flexibility to respond to changing circumstances or mechanisms for effective reassessment and adjustment.

- The plans are often not effectively communicated to the organization. In many areas of the company, employees are either unaware of the plan or do not understand how the objectives and activities of their area relate to the overall plans. There is often no link between the overall company plans and either approaches to deployment (most commonly individual objective setting through a management-by-objectives process) or individual performance evaluation.

- Senior management believes that creating the right incentives is key to driving change. Such incentives often have unanticipated negative side effects.

- In many cases, too many top priorities are set. As a result, overall organizational focus is lost.

Category 4: Human Resource Development and Management

STRENGTHS

- A large number of teams are focused on quality improvement projects. These teams are concentrated in production and the critical areas that directly support production. There are many examples of team projects that have been successful and have generated substantial improvements.

- There is usually a suggestion system with a required response time. A substantial percentage of employees submit suggestions.

- All employees receive basic quality training. Most employees receive a substantial amount of annual training. In the best companies, employees receive 40 to 80 hours of training per year with training expenditures around 3 to 5% of payroll.

- There is widespread employee recognition for various types of contributions, including quality.
- Substantial resources are devoted to safety.
- There are a lot of traditional benefits.
- An employee survey is used to assess employee morale.
- Human Resources measures such as turn–over, absenteeism, and injuries show identifiable improvement trends and good levels in comparison to industry averages.

AREAS FOR IMPROVEMENT

- Most teams do not effectively use team processes such as problem-solving methods or quality tools, relying instead almost entirely on informal brainstorming. As a result, many teams are relatively ineffective. It is difficult to maintain momentum once the easy problems are solved.
- The concept of empowerment is poorly understood by management, even in cases where "empowerment" is an important part of a company's quality initiatives. In some cases, employees or teams are given authority that they are not comfortable exercising because either appropriate decision-making processes have not been developed or the employees have not been adequately trained. In other cases, decisions made by "empowered" teams are routinely reviewed by multiple levels of management prior to authorization. In other companies, empowerment is limited to giving the employee authority to act on behalf of the customer.
- Most employees have only received basic quality training. The effect of this training is primarily limited to awareness, either because the training is awareness training or because the employees do not successfully integrate the training into their work. In addition, there is little formal training given in company processes outside the production area.
- The effectiveness of training is not directly measured. Measurement is limited to course evaluation forms and surveys and does not address how much was learned or how well the training is integrated into the employees' work.
- Much of the employee recognition is superficial and seems to be driven by the feeling that everyone should receive recognition (e.g., employee of the week). In other cases, it is results oriented and substantially influenced by factors beyond the employee's direct control. In many cases, the extent to which the recognition reinforces quality relative to other considerations is unclear.
- Recognition of the work of quality improvement teams, such as competitions or presentations to senior management, that focuses on the team's improvement process is not common.

- The performance evaluation system is poorly aligned with the company's quality management system or overall plans and objectives. Performance evaluation emphasizes rewarding results that in many cases are primarily driven by factors beyond the individual employee's control.
- Safety and ergonomics are not part of quality improvement activities. This is often true even when there is substantial organizational focus on safety.

Category 5: Management of Process Quality

STRENGTHS

- Many manufacturing companies have vastly improved the design and introduction of new products and services. Approaches taken include increased customer focus, cross-functional teams, joint design with suppliers and customers, design simplification, process capability considerations, simultaneous engineering, experimental design, and Taguchi methods.
- In manufacturing companies, the concepts of variation and control are understood in the context of production. Many production processes are controlled using SPC. The production processes are reasonably in control. For important processes, they are also demonstrably capable.[3]
- At least one specific approach to quality improvement has been implemented resulting in tremendous improvement. Examples of such improvement approaches include statistical process control, just-in-time production, employee involvement, work cells, self-managed teams, suggestion systems, and cycle-time reduction.
- In service companies, some degree of measurement of the service production processes has been developed. In particular, most easily quantifiable measures are made for key processes and exhibit some degree of stability.
- Production processes are improved by quality improvement teams consisting of either workers or staff employees. The levels of involvement in teams by the production workforce is high. Sometimes the improvement efforts are sophisticated, using tools such as experimental design.
- Some companies have a well-defined quality systems audit function for the production processes.
- Quality improvement teams are also active in repetitive service and business process areas.
- Many companies have extensive programs with their suppliers. These include supplier quality systems audits, supplier rating and qualification

systems, training, joint design teams, joint quality improvement teams, supplier (and supplier employee) recognition programs.

AREAS FOR IMPROVEMENT

- New product development is still primarily reactive (i.e., it responds to, rather than anticipates, customer demands) and is driven by generally available technology improvements. Quality assurance of new product development and introduction is not prevention-based, relying instead primarily on inspection and testing. The new product development process is not well defined.

- Many companies, especially service companies, have very limited new product development activity. While they frequently change and augment the characteristics of their products, they do not view these changes as new product development and have no systematic approaches.

- Processes tend not to be very well defined except when they are naturally defined by the production processes, as in many manufacturing and some repetitive service activities. As a result, processes are often not well defined in service companies and job shops, or in most companies outside of repetitive manufacturing and service activities.

- In many companies, the approaches taken to quality are limited to one or two such as statistical process control or just-in-time production. Because the company has success with the specific approaches taken, management believes that they have a fully developed quality management system.

- In many cases, there is very little understanding of the idea of driving measurement of processes upstream, the importance of variables measures, or measurement qualification. Instead, management relies exclusively on end-of-process defect rates and customer complaints.

- There is often very little correlation of process measures with customer satisfaction, or of upstream measures with downstream measures. Identification of these relationships is based on the experience and intuition of management and technical staff.

- While many service companies collect the readily available quantifiable measures of their service processes, these metrics are often not direct measures of the key attributes of the service processes. As a result, many service companies have very few direct process measures—instead, they try to control their processes using customer feedback data. While customer satisfaction is clearly the goal, customer feedback generally cannot be used to effectively control processes because the cycle time for collecting such feedback is too slow and the relationship between the process parameters and the customer's perceptions is often obscure.

- Many companies do not have a very broad scope of types of improvement teams such as workforce teams, management/technical teams, teams consisting of both management/technical staff and the workforce, and cross-functional teams. Many companies' TQM programs focus entirely on one type of team, usually workforce teams. As a result, the scope of improvement is limited.

- In many cases, improvement efforts are based on informal brainstorming and not on management-by-fact and systematic analysis. This is related to the failure of the quality improvement teams to effectively use a well-developed problem-solving process supported by analysis tools.

- Documentation of the improvement methods and activities and dissemination of the knowledge gained are often limited. Quality improvement teams do not make effective use of devices such as the QC Story.[4]

- The distinction between improvements that result from bringing a process into control and continuous improvement once the process is in control is often not understood. As a result, while many problems are solved, a state of systematic, ongoing refinement is not achieved. Because great improvement often occurs when the processes are brought into control, management believes prematurely that the company has achieved a state of systematic ongoing process refinement (i.e., continuous improvement).

- Systematic approaches to improvement are less well developed in business processes and support services than in primary production areas. This is associated with the lack of well-defined processes in these areas. Repetitive service activities (e.g., billing) are sometimes an exception.

- Many companies have essentially no quality systems audits. In addition, audits originating from senior management or including senior management involvement are very rare.

- Many companies appear somewhat heavy-handed with their suppliers. A state of cooperation and appropriate integration does not exist.

Category 6: Quality and Operational Results

STRENGTHS

- Very good companies can demonstrate high levels of quality in their products and services for a wide variety of measures relative to similar U.S. companies.

- Sustained improvement trends of at least a several-fold improvement over two to five years can be demonstrated for key product and operational areas. Sustained improvement results, but with weaker trends, can be demonstrated in most areas of the company.
- Quality results for key suppliers also show significant and sustained quality improvement.

Areas for Improvement

- For most companies, the scope of the data used by management to routinely track the results of their quality systems is inadequate. Key measures from all important processes are often not readily available. In addition, management often does not track in-process and upstream measures.
- In many companies, almost no variables-based measures are tracked. Instead, the only measures are defect rates and customer complaints. Management is unaware of levels or trends in measures such as process capabilities.
- Linkage between operational measures and key customer requirements is not established.
- In many cases, sufficient data to establish trends are not readily available. Management is only aware of the most recent measures and may be unaware of adverse trends. Sustained improvement trends cannot be established.
- Even winners are not necessarily the best in the world.

Category 7: Customer Focus and Satisfaction

Strengths

- Many companies use a large number of survey-type instruments to assess customer satisfaction and customer needs and expectations. Focus groups are also common.
- There is increasing emphasis on easy access for customers and quick response times.
- Some well-defined customer service standards are developed for such things as time to answer the telephone and response time to queries or complaints. These measures are often tracked.
- There is much motivational training for customer service representatives. There is also often extensive product training.
- Increasing attention is being given to formal complaint resolution. Complaints are aggregated by types and reported to management.

- Customer service representatives are being given increasing authority to satisfy the customer.
- Customer satisfaction levels are high in comparison to similar companies in the United States. Sustained customer satisfaction improvement trends can be established. Market share and repeat customer trends are favorable.

AREAS FOR IMPROVEMENT

- There is often little understanding of technical issues relating to the accuracy of surveys (bias, variability, accuracy, etc.).
- There is also often little distinction between determining customer satisfaction and customer needs and expectations. The methods of extracting customer requirements or identifying latent desires from customer information are usually informal.
- There is no formal approach for integrating customer data with the (new) product development process. Product design relies on the designer's intuition and customer data collected primarily for other purposes. In some companies, customer data are used to help determine product features, but are otherwise not well integrated into the product design process.
- Often, only the company's current customers are surveyed. Appropriate information about lost customers, new customers, and competitor's customers is not obtained.
- Stratification of customer data is done by attributes important to the company (e.g., account size), not the customer. As a result, the data are of limited use for identifying patterns of satisfaction and dissatisfaction among customers with similar characteristics.
- In many cases, the sales force is used as a primary source of customer information. However, sales usually has no systematic, well-defined approach for gathering and aggregating customer data and no training in these activities. Other types of quality improvement activities in sales are also minimal.
- Customer service standards are not well defined except in cases where easy and obvious measures exist. Much customer service representative training is motivational and not specific. Methods for assessing customer service performance relative to standards are generally poor.
- Customers still have difficulty reaching someone with real authority to resolve their problems. The role of Customer Service is still to "protect" management.
- Companies still seem to think that customers should be completely satisfied with replacement guarantees.

- Usually, formal complaints are the only ones tracked. There is no operational definition of what constitutes a complaint. As a result, informal or minor complaints are missed and thus are not aggregated or tracked and cannot be used for assessing customer requirements and satisfaction. In addition, complaint data are not effectively used to drive quality improvement.

- In many cases, customer satisfaction comparisons are left to third parties (e.g., industry associations) that do not use valid and reliable methods.

Discussion: Some Cross-Cutting Themes

As the above assessment indicates, the approaches of leading TQM companies include many important strengths. In many cases, these approaches have produced impressive results. But there are also many important areas for improvement. Few, if any, U.S. companies have developed quality management systems with the levels of coherence, comprehensiveness, and integration of quality management in the best Japanese companies. Underlying many of the areas for improvement previously described are a number of cross-cutting themes that appear to be limiting realization of TQM's full potential in the United States. We will now discuss these themes.

One of the most important cross-cutting themes is that the scope of the concept of "process" in TQM is not fully understood by most U.S. managers, even in companies committed to quality management. This is particularly true outside of structured, repetitive manufacturing and service activities where the basic production process is readily apparent and can be defined in specific detail. Thus, for many critical activities, processes are not defined. In fact, the higher level or more abstract the activity, the less often an appropriately defined process has been developed. As a result, the approaches taken are created on the fly by the individuals responsible. Because there is no uniformity in approach, the activities cannot be stabilized or continuously improved.

This lack of understanding of process is related to the persistent results-oriented perspective of most managers. Because of this perspective, many companies' approach to management focuses on setting goals and objectives, on trying to create the right incentives, and on feedback based on after-the-fact measures. There is little before-the-fact emphasis on strategies, approaches, or methods—process-oriented notions.

The planning process often exemplifies this problem. First, the planning process itself is often poorly defined. More important, planning often stops with the development of goals and budgets with little emphasis on developing strategies and methods for achieving the goals. In addition, there is often insufficient prevention-oriented analysis to anticipate barriers to implementation or to ensure sufficient flexibility to respond to problems as they occur. While an individual's goals may be reviewed by several levels of management, the methods to be used for achieving these goals often receive at most cursory review. As a result, consensus concerning what strategies and methods to use is not developed in advance and the actual implementation is ad hoc, often developed at quite low levels of the organization. In summary, managers do not view the development and deployment of processes and methods as the fundamental management activities that drive achievement of the goals.

In many companies, the functioning of the quality improvement teams provides another important example of the limited development and deployment of the idea of a process. In the most common case, the improvement teams have been trained in a variation of the Shewhart Plan-Do-Check-Act cycle together with a few basic quality tools. These, however, fail to be integrated into an effective team process. One reason is that the team process is not completely developed. This situation is often indicated by management's having no clear concept of exactly how the teams are supposed to function. In many cases, there is no structure or method, such as documentation through a QC Story format, to guide deployment of the team process and ensure effective analysis and use of methods such as the quality tools. Effective analysis and use of the quality tools is difficult. As a result, the teams tend to rely almost exclusively on informal approaches such as brainstorming. The quality tools are seldom used, collection of data is avoided, and root-cause analysis is not particularly effective.

A second cross-cutting theme is the lack of effective management-by-fact. In many cases, companies have relatively few direct operational and customer measures that can be stratified for effective analysis and root-cause determination. Instead, as we discussed in Category 2, the measures focus on downstream results and after-the-fact assessment of the achievement of goals. The metrics used are often indirect financial measures that aggregate effects from a variety of causes. They are difficult to disaggregate or stratify in meaningful ways that directly relate to planning and decision making.

Another important cross-cutting theme closely related to the first two is the lack of effective analysis, especially team-based analysis. The development and widespread deployment of effective analysis is a fundamental component of TQM. The lack of effective management-by-fact and well-developed analysis processes contribute to the lack of effective analysis in many U.S. companies. In particular, the identification of root causes and proposals for improvement tend to be based on intuition in the form of team brainstorming instead of on systematic analysis of data.

The failure to consistently set clear priorities throughout the organization is another important cross-cutting theme. The principle of consistently developing a small number of key priorities is pervasive throughout TQM. In many companies, however, the key priorities are unclear to middle and front-line managers and the workforce. Sometimes this is because of unclear or inconsistent communication. But often a key contributing factor is that far too many top priorities are developed. As a result, departments and individuals pick and choose among the top priorities, and a consistent overall organizational focus is lost.

A final cross-cutting theme is that in many companies the primary focus of the quality effort is on the workforce. Consequently, roles for all levels of management and technical staff in TQM are not developed. As a result, management and staff tend to believe that TQM is primarily about attitude and that their role in TQM is to promote the importance of quality and motivate the workforce. While there is often effort to involve all levels of management in promoting quality, the focus is nevertheless on supporting and encouraging the workforce as the primary generators of quality improvement. The workforce, however, cannot be the primary generators of improvement. While their contribution is very important, the vast majority of quality improvement must come from management and technical staff. Without well-defined roles for direct contribution by all levels, a company's TQM program is unlikely to achieve more than moderate success.[5]

Some Comparisons to Dr. Kano's Perspective on American TQM

The above assessment of the current state of U.S. TQM was developed independently from the perspective given by Kano in the final chapter of this book and derives from an entirely different viewpoint and set of experiences. Nevertheless, it contains a number of important common themes. This section discusses some of the key similarities and differences between the assessment previously described and Dr. Kano's perspective on American TQM and tries to integrate the two discussions.

Process

The lack of understanding of the general concept of processes and of process orientation among U.S. managers is not explicitly addressed by Kano. It is, however, an important theme underlying a number of his main points. The key issue is the application of process notions to what employees do (human activities), including both analysis and actions. In this context, words such as method, technique, strategy, tactic, or approach that address the question "how" may better capture the essence of process. Kano points out that even in manufacturing the approaches used often inadequately define the processes. In particular, he notes that while statistical process control (SPC) is one of the key methods used in many companies, it is often not linked to process standardization. My experience agrees with this observation. In addition, even in some companies that have succeeded in standardizing certain key processes, the concept of standardization is not widely appreciated as a key strategy in the development and management of processes throughout the company.

Standardization in the sense used by Kano means development and uniform deployment of the critical methods necessary in the operation of the process. Those methods must be completely developed so that they provide effective operational definitions and must be uniformly deployed so that the critical methods are executed in the same way by all employees, every time. This stability and repeatability of critical methods are crucial for obtaining statistical control, and, as Kano indicates, without it SPC is often not particularly effective. In fact, standardization is one of the most important strategies for obtaining statistical control. It can be applied to all processes, even those for which measurement and SPC are difficult.

Effective standardization of processes requires focusing on a relatively small number of critical methods. The idea of focusing on a small number of high priority issues is a key theme throughout TQM. It is also important that the standardization of the process methods be at the right level of detail. The objective is to obtain uniform execution of the critical methods. Standardization requires discipline and is part of the "sweating work" Kano mentions. It is important not to waste employee goodwill on unimportant aspects of the process or on detail that does not contribute to process control.

It is also difficult to standardize processes without involvement of the process operators in the development and continuous improvement of the methods (standards). The knowledge of the process operators is generally required to effectively align the standards with the realities of day-to-day operations. In addition, it is difficult to obtain the level of self-discipline necessary for the required level of process rigor without substantive involvement of the process operators. This is one of the reasons why employee involvement is a critical part of successful quality management.

Finally, process standards must be continually improved and kept aligned with the process' customer requirements. The word standardization tends to imply a permanence not intended by the concept. Without continuous improvement and continual alignment with the process' customer requirements, the process will quickly lose effectiveness. The overall objective is to achieve a sort of dynamic rigor. This is not trivial.

In contrast, in many companies unimportant aspects of the processes are defined in stifling detail while at the same time critical methods are not appropriately developed or deployed and not uniformly executed. In addition, the process operators are not really engaged in the operation, alignment, and improvement of the process. The processes do not operate in a state of control or only remain in control for short periods of time. Although it is a very important tool in quality assurance, SPC alone cannot effectively address these issues.

Management-by-fact and Analysis

A crucial theme in both the assessment of U.S. TQM given in this chapter and Kano's perspective in the final chapter is a lack of adequate management-by-fact. For example, Kano lists "emphasis on the use of data" as one of the key concepts of TQM and gives an interesting example relating to lightening strikes at Florida Power and Light.

It is important to note that the concept of management-by-fact is not limited in scope to just the use of quantitative data. The nature of the data is often far more important than the fact that quantitative data was collected and analyzed. In particular, many U.S. companies have an overabundance of data, particularly cost data. In response to TQM, many companies have also started collecting all sorts of easily quantifiable and readily available measures. Such data are then perfunctorily examined as a part of decision-making activities.

The problem is that, in many cases, the easily available data have little direct bearing on the issues at hand. In particular, cost data are often contaminated by arbitrary overhead factors and aggregate costs due to multiple causes. In many other cases, easily collected quantifiable data have little or no relationship to the real drivers of customer satisfaction or cost. In still other cases, the data are not scaled so as to be particularly meaningful and it is difficult to reconstruct the appropriate scaling factors after the fact. For example, scrap may be unusually low on a particular day because the process was down or high because the process was run overtime.

Thus, a key part of the management-by-fact concept is that data analyzed must have direct bearing on the root causes relating to the decisions to be made. Kano's Florida Power and Light example demonstrates this. In particular, data were clearly available relating to power outages. There was probably much other data also available, possibly including weather data indicating the presence or absence of electrical storms. The problem was that data directly relating to the strength of lightening strikes that caused outages were not available. These data were required to directly address the key issue at hand. It is easy for U.S. managers to believe that their organizations routinely conform to the principle of management-by-fact just because much data are collected and appear to be used as a part of decision-making activities. Assessment of the extent of integration of management-by-fact must include examination of the linkage between the data and information used and the key issues underlying the decisions to be made.

The lack of effective analysis may more accurately capture factors limiting U.S. TQM than just emphasis on inadequate management-by-fact. The widespread deployment of effective analysis, including problem solving, is one of the clear themes in TQM. While, as Kano points out, more use of advanced analysis techniques such as analysis of variance and multiple regression might represent a future opportunity, the key management issue in TQM is the widespread deployment of effective analysis approaches using basic methods. Analysis in this sense includes developing and deploying effective frameworks and strategies for problem solving, root-cause analysis, planning, and so on. Management-by-fact as described above, particularly the idea that the data and information used must have as direct bearing as possible on the issue at hand, is a key component of such effective analysis.

One area of analysis that appears to be a common problem in U.S. TQM is the failure to base planning, root-cause analysis, and problem solving on appropriately thorough analysis of the current situation. In particular, in the team-based problem-solving in many companies, the development of hypotheses to be tested is based on collective intuition through brainstorming rather than on systematic analysis and observation of the current situation. This kind of development of hypotheses leads to improvement by trial and error that is generally quite slow and often sheds little light on true root causes.[6] These are some of the issues associated with Kano's observation that employees often do not fully understand the nature of the problems they are addressing and his emphasis on the importance of the "5 Whats."

It should be noted that the lack of widely deployed effective analysis is also related to the lack of full understanding of process concepts. In many companies, problem solving and analysis processes are not well developed and there is little discipline in their use.

Planning

Another theme common to the Baldrige-based assessment of U.S. TQM and Kano's perspective is both the importance of planning as a critical driver of TQM and as a key area for improvement in many U.S. companies. Kano frames his discussion in terms of Management by Policy (*hoshin kanri*) and observes that there are four phases in a planning process: development of the plans, deployment of the plans, implementation of the plans, and evaluation and feedback. Many companies entirely lack a well-developed planning process or only have partially developed processes for one or two of these four phases. This lack of a well-developed planning process contributes to management's "preference for pursuing dreams" noted by Kano.

Some of the common issues relating to planning I have discussed that are also noted by Kano include the failure to base plans on effective analysis, the failure to develop a small number of priorities, and the failure to effectively implement the plans. The failure to base the plans on effective analysis is another example of lack of management-by-fact. The failure to effectively implement the plans often results from both the development of too many priorities (Kano's "chase too many rabbits") and a lack of process orientation in developing the plans. Once again, the importance of TQM's principle of developing a small number of clear priorities is apparent. As discussed above, planning often lacks a process orientation in that it stops with the development of objectives alone. The methods used to achieve the objectives do not receive the kind of serious attention by multiple levels of management they deserve or that is necessary to ensure consensus concerning the approaches to be taken. While Kano does not specifically discuss this process orientation in the development and implementation of plans, the concept is clear in his discussion concerning evaluation and feedback for the planning process. Kano indicates that both the "objectives and the methods for realizing the objectives should be evaluated." Planning also is often not prevention oriented, another clear principle of TQM, in that it does not anticipate implementation problems or incorporate sufficient flexibility to respond to changing circumstances. These issues are unlikely to be effectively addressed without the development of planning processes that incorporate specific methods to address each of them.

The Role of Senior Management

Kano describes the increasing commitment to TQM and leadership by senior management over the last decade. He gives very little explicit treatment, however, of the specific roles of senior management. A lack of clear understanding of their role is, I believe, one key factor limiting the further development of TQM in the United States.

Ultimately, senior management is responsible for both the design and deployment of the total management system, including the quality management system. This responsibility cannot be met without considerable knowledge of quality management systems and practices. This is true even when staff members are the primary developers of specific tools and processes, which is the usual case. Senior management must be able to evaluate such tools and processes, determine whether they are effectively deployed, and assess the extent to which the management systems are coherent and integrated. If senior management fails to gain the knowledge to do this as the quality management system develops, the TQM system's development will be limited. Only senior management has both the authority and perspective necessary to ensure full deployment and integration of the management system.

Thus, the role of senior management extends far beyond just promotion of TQM. While such promotion is a critical role for senior managers, they also have critical roles in management system design, in planning (including planning related to the development of the TQM system), and in assessing the management systems and deployment of the plans. Kano briefly mentions these roles in his discussion of the presidential policy, which includes soliciting input to the plan from multiple levels within the organization, and the presidential diagnosis, which includes a process-oriented evaluation of the current planning cycle and the overall management system. In my experience, the senior management of very few companies have a clear understanding of the quality management system, including the roles of all levels of management or a vision for its continued development. The lack of such understanding and vision is almost always associated with a corresponding lack of uniform understanding within the organization and a resulting lack of coherence and overall integration of the management system.

Summary

What, then, is the prognosis for TQM in the United States? Overall, the assessment is generally favorable. An increasing number of companies are actively focused on quality as a key approach to improving their competitiveness. And as the above assessment indicates, U.S. companies that are committed to quality have a large number of areas of true strength. In many cases, they also demonstrate some exceptional management innovation. Further, their efforts are yielding clear results in terms of customer satisfaction, operational improvement, and employee involvement.

While the assessment is generally favorable, these companies also have a large number of important areas for improvement. As indicated by both the assessment described in this chapter and Kano's discussion in the final chapter, these areas for improvement are not superficial or merely a matter of failure in execution. They are not simply blemishes on conceptually well-developed management systems. Instead, they are weaknesses in the fundamental approaches taken to management such as the lack of full understanding of process, the lack of emphasis on planning, the lack of effective systems to implement the plans, the reliance on incentives, failure to apply the principle of management-by-fact, focusing on results to the exclusion of processes or methods, focusing on financial measures to the exclusion of direct operational measures, and inadequate understanding of customer expectations. Senior management is not yet fully aware of the totality of its appropriate role in TQM and is often not even completely comfortable in its present role.

Thus, TQM in the United States is far from mature. It is important that TQM approaches continue to be developed, refined, and expanded, even in companies that have already achieved considerable success. Otherwise the competitive advantages that TQM promises will not be realized and many companies will be left struggling against competitive decline without any unified or coherent strategy for revitalization.

APPENDIX: The Baldrige Award

This Appendix briefly describes the Baldrige Award and the process used to evaluate applicants. It is intended to provide some background information and context for the assessment of the state of U.S. TQM described in this chapter. For additional information, a copy of the Award Guidelines can be obtained from the Baldrige Award Office at (301) 975-2036.

The Baldrige Award

The law creating the Malcolm Baldrige Award (Public Law 100-107) indicates a number of purposes. First, the award is intended to increase the awareness of quality and quality management as a critical strategic issue in U.S. competitiveness. Second, it is envisioned to develop and promote an understanding of the requirements for excellent quality management systems. The award is also intended to promote the sharing and dissemination of information about effective quality management strategies. Finally, the award should identify companies with role-model quality management systems.

Companies apply for the Baldrige Award in one of three categories: manufacturing, service, and small business. The small business category is for companies, both service and manufacturing, with 500 or fewer employees. Up to two awards can be given each year in each category, although no awards need be given if none of the applicants in that category meets the requirements for role-model status. In the first five years of the award, only three awards in the Service Category and four in the Small Business Category have been given. Two awards in the Manufacturing Category have been given every year. Previous winners of the Award are listed in Table 2.2.

Companies apply for the Baldrige Award by submitting a written application describing their quality management systems. These written applications must respond to approximately 90 "areas to address" organized into about 30 items in seven major categories. These seven categories are:

1. Leadership
2. Information and Analysis
3. Strategic Quality Planning
4. Human Resource Development and Management
5. Management of Process Quality
6. Quality and Operational Results
7. Customer Focus and Satisfaction

The written applications must be no more that 75 pages (60 pages for small businesses).

The Scoring Process

The evaluation of the written company applications begins with independent scoring of each application by four to eight examiners (in 1992, eight examiners were used). At the level of the items (28 items in 1993), each examiner independently evaluates how well the company's quality management systems, as described in the application, address the issues contained in the item. For each item, the examiner writes specific comments indicating, first, the strengths of the company's approach to that item and then the areas requiring improvement.

The evaluation of the items is based on three dimensions: the company's approach to the issues in the item, the extent to which the approach is fully and appropriately deployed within the organization, and the results that have been achieved. Not all three dimensions apply equally to each item; the examiners must make judgments about their importance based on the item and the characteristics of the company being scored.

TABLE 2.2.   Winners of the Malcolm Baldrige National Quality Award

Year	Category	Company
1993	Manufacturing	Eastman Chemical Co., Kingsport, Tenn.
	Small Business	Ames Rubber Corp., Hamburg, N.J.
1992	Manufacturing	AT&T Network Systems Group/Transmission Systems Business Unit, Morristown, N.J.
		Texas Instruments Defense Systems and Electronics Group, Dallas, Tex.
	Service	AT&T Universal Card Services, Jacksonville, Fla.
		Ritz-Carlton Hotel Co., Atlanta, Ga.
	Small Business	Granite Rock Co., Watsonville, Calif.
1991	Manufacturing	Solectron Corp., San Jose, Calif.
		Zytec Corp., Eden Prairie, Minn.
	Small Business	Marlow Industries, Dallas, Tex.
1990	Manufacturing	Cadillac Motor Car Co., Detroit, Mich.
		IBM Rochester, Rochester, Minn.
	Service	Federal Express Corp., Memphis, Tenn.
	Small Business	Wallace Co., Houston, Tex.
1989	Manufacturing	Milliken & Co., Spartanburg, S.C.
		Xerox Business Products and Systems, Stamford, Conn.
1988	Manufacturing	Motorola, Inc., Schaumburg, Ill.
		Westinghouse Commercial Nuclear Fuel Division, Pittsburgh, Pa.
	Small Business	Globe Metallurgical, Inc., Cleveland, Ohio

Once the examiner has written comments for an item, a percentage score is assigned. This score must reflect the comments. In order to help calibrate the scores, scoring guidelines have been developed that outline characteristics of quality management systems at various scoring levels for each of the three dimensions—approach, deployment, and results (see Table 2.3). The percentage scores are ultimately multiplied by the points assigned to each item in the award criteria and summed for the overall point score. The total point scale is from 0 to 1000 points.

Based on the independent scoring of each application by the examiner teams, a panel of nine judges selects the companies that will continue to the next stage of the evaluation process. For those applications not selected to continue, a feedback report is written. Every company that applies for the award receives a written feedback report.

The next step for those applications continuing in the evaluation process is the development of consensus about the scoring within the team of examiners

TABLE 2.3. Scoring Guidelines

Score	Approach/Deployment	Results
0%	• Anecdotal information; no system evident in information presented	• No data reported or anecdotal data only
10–30%	• Beginning of a systematic approach to addressing the primary purposes of the item • Significant gaps still exist in deployment that would inhibit progress in achieving the major purposes of the item • Early stages of a transition from reacting to problems to preventing problems	• Early stages of developing trend data • Some improvement trend data *or* early good performance reported • Data are not reported for many to most areas of importance to the item requirements and to the company's key performance-related business factors
40–60%	• A sound, systematic approach responsive to the primary purposes of the item • A fact-based improvement process in place in key areas addressed by the item • No major gaps in deployment, though some areas may be in early stages of deployment • Approach places more emphasis on problem prevention than on reaction to problems	• Improvement or good performance trends reported in key areas of importance to the item requirements and to the company's key performance-related business factors • Some trends and/or current performance can be evaluated against relevant comparisons, benchmarks, or levels • No significant adverse trends or poor current performance in key areas of importance to the item requirements and to the company's key performance-related business factors
70–90%	• A sound, systematic approach responsive to the overall purposes of the item • A fact-based improvement process is a key management tool; clear evidence of refinement and improved integration as a result of improvement cycles and analysis • Approach is well deployed, with no significant gaps, although refinement, deploy-	• Good to excellent improvement trends in most key areas of importance to the item requirements and to the company's key performance-related business factors *or* sustained good to excellent performance in those areas • Many to most trends and current performance can be evaluated against relevant comparisons, benchmarks, or levels

Continued

37

TABLE 2.3.   Scoring Guidelines (*Continued*)

Score	Approach/Deployment	Results
	ment, and improved integration may vary among work units or system activities	• Current performance is good to excellent in most areas of importance to the item requirements and to the company's key performance-related business factors
100%	• A sound, systematic approach, fully responsive to all the requirements of the item • Approach is fully deployed without weaknesses or gaps in any areas • Very strong refinement and integration—backed by excellent analysis	• Excellent improvement trends in most to all key areas of importance to the item requirements and to the company's key performance-related business factors *or* sustained excellent performance in those areas • Most to all trends and current performance can be evaluated against relevant comparisons, benchmarks, or levels • Current performance is excellent in most areas of importance to the item requirements and to the company's key performance-related business factors • Strong evidence of industry and benchmark leadership demonstrated

Source: Malcolm Baldrige National Quality Award 1993 Award Criteria.

assigned to the application. The approach used identifies items for which there is too much variability among the examiners' independent scores. The reasons for the divergence are then discussed. It is the responsibility of the senior examiner leading the consensus process to ensure that instantaneous majority rule does not occur. Rather, the underlying reasons for the divergence in scores should be uncovered, and their merits openly discussed and assessed.

The consensus process results in a modified set of scores and a senior examiner's report that both synthesizes the written comments made by the members of the examiner team and indicates reasons for changes in the scores occurring as a result of the consensus process. Based on the consensus scores, the judges then select the companies that will receive a site visit. In 1992, 90 companies applied for the award. Out of these, nine manufacturing, five service, and five small companies were selected for site visits.

The primary purpose of the site visit is to clarify and verify the content of the company's written application. Typically, the site visit is performed by a team of seven examiners that includes the members of the original consensus team. The site visit usually involves four days at the applicant company. To effectively conduct such a site visit requires extensive advanced planning in addition to the time actually spent with the company. For small companies, both the number of examiners involved and the length of time spent on site are likely to be somewhat less.

During the site visit, the examiners conduct extensive interviews with employees at all levels of the company and examine company documentation. The objective is to verify the key information in the company's application, assess the extent of deployment of the company's approaches, clarify vague or confusing areas, and determine the appropriateness of the company as a role model. The site visit is followed by a day during which the team synthesizes the information collected during the site visit and develops a report comprised of both an overall assessment of the company's status as a role model and a summary of key strengths and areas for improvement in each of the seven categories.

The final step in the scoring process is the selection of the winners by the judges. The judges base their decision on the information contained in the company's application, the original independent comments and scoring by the examiner team, the consensus comments and scoring, the reports generated by the site visit, and, finally, discussion with the senior examiner who led the site visit.

The scoring matrix in Table 2.3 has been developed to aid in discrimination among the companies that achieve high scores. Examination of the scoring matrix will show that companies scoring about 50% are really very good companies with quite well-developed quality management systems. In fact, the median score for companies that apply for the award is below 500 out of the total 1000 points. Figure 2.1 shows a histogram of the scores for the 1992 applicants.

Notes

I would like to thank Robert Cole, Sherry Jarrell, Harry Roberts, and William Golomski for comments that greatly improved the original manuscript. This work was supported in part by a summer research grant from the Graduate School of Business, University of Chicago.

1. This chapter does not discuss the merits of the Baldrige Award. For such a discussion, see Garvin (1991).

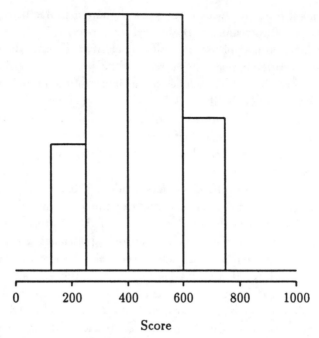

Figure 2.1. Histogram of the scores of 1992 applicants.
Source: Malcolm Baldrige National Quality Award Office

2. This discussion should be interpreted as one person's opinion and in no way as official doctrine of the Baldrige Award.
3. The extent to which the production processes can be considered in-control depends on what technical definition of in-control is used. Experience suggests that many manufacturing processes that appear to be in-control using simple control charts fail to be in-control when more rigorous definitions of in-control are used such as those based on statistical models that take into account autocorrelation [e.g., see L. C. Alwan and H. V. Roberts, "Time-Series Modeling for Statistical Process Control," *Journal of Business and Economic Statistics,* 6 (1988), 87–95]. Many of the key manufacturing processes in the target group of very good companies are likely to fail the more rigorous definitions of in-control. Nevertheless, the key processes in these companies generally are quite stable and capable, usually appearing to be in-control according to simple control charts.
4. QC Story is a team problem-solving process that, together with QC Tools, both guides team problem solving and serves as a format for documenting team improvement activities and analysis [see H. Kume, *Statistical Methods for Quality Improvement,* The Association for Overseas Technical Scholarship, Tokyo (1985)]. The term QC Story is also used to refer specifically to the story-board format Japanese QC Circles use to present the results of their improvement activities to management.

5. For further discussion of these points, see G. S. Easton, "The Role of Employee Involvement in Total Quality Management" (manuscript).

6. It should be noted that testing the hypotheses and subsequently verifying an improvement using data is a different issue than basing the development of hypotheses on data. Such testing and verification is critical to ensure that improvements are real. Provided that such testing and verification are done, improvements generated by trail and error will be genuine. The rate of improvement, however, is likely to be quite slow. For further discussion see Kume, op. cit., Chapter 10, and Easton, op. cit.

3

Quality, Strategy, and Competitiveness

JAMES A. BELOHLAV

Major business periodicals have chronicled, for decades, the many faces of corporate competitiveness. Reflecting current competitive realities, remarks of executives from a wide spectrum of American industries lament the increasingly contentious interactions with "Japan, Inc." The intensity of global competition has shown, however, that Japan is only part of the overall puzzle as South Korea and other areas within the Pacific Rim are also emerging as formidable contestants in the battle for dominance. Before the ink on many battle plans has dried, the realm of competition has continued to enlarge and many businesses wonder about the impact of the European Common Market on the bottom line. The competitive landscape seems only to get more complex for business people.

In response to the changing character of competition, the definition and scope of corporate strategy are also being revised. A common denominator in many of the discussions on competitiveness and strategy seems to involve the issue of quality. A reasonable question to ask is "How important is quality to the long-run success of the organization?" Some individuals suggest that quality needs to be a focal point for all operational activities.[1] However, before we discuss the role of quality, it is useful to examine how corporate strategy has developed.

In the classic book, *The Mind of the Strategist,* Ken Ohmae provides some cogent commentary on the evolving pattern of business perspectives. In particular, he defines the competitive potential of a company in terms of its strategic capacity. The significance of strategic capacity is that it essentially determines the fundamental framework for developing corporate strategy. The strategic capacity of any company is a product of its business portfolio: market attractiveness and company strength.[2] Market attractiveness is concerned with how much or how little growth there is within given markets, while company strength involves how a particular business is operated.

Within the contemporary business milieu, Ken Ohmae identifies a shifting point of view on the relative importance of the components constituting the business portfolio. The changing perceptions of what composes the "correct" makeup of a business portfolio has, in turn, changed what is "appropriate" corporate strategy. In the period preceding the 1970s, he notes that market attractiveness and company strength were perceived as being of relatively equal importance. Consequently, there was a balance of effort utilizing both market attractiveness and company strength as basic elements of corporate strategy.

Strategy in the 1970s

As companies entered the 1970s, however, many firms tended to see market growth as the unparalleled approach to apparently boundless corporate growth. Thus, corporate strategies tended to shift away from developing company strengths and emphasized market attractiveness as the major component of corporate strategy. Matching the shifting strategic business perspective was a shift in corporate structure to capitalize on market growth by forming conglomerate organizations. Essentially, many corporations became just a group of businesses or products that had little in common other than providing a means for continued financial growth. In general, value for the corporation came by way of external acquisitions instead of through internal business creation.

Within this same period, the strategic portfolio models concept of corporate strategy gained in ascendancy. One widely popular approach was provided by the Boston Consulting Group (BCG) with its Growth Share Matrix.[3] The popularity of the BCG model and other similar types of portfolio models of strategic management was a function of at least two factors. First, the strategic portfolio models linked marketing, financing, and operating considerations together to provide an interactive wholeness lacking in earlier formulations of the strategic management process. Second, and from a more pragmatic perspective, the BCG model of strategic management defined market attractiveness as market growth and company strength as market share relative to dominant companies within the market. Thus, the strategic portfolio views shaped as well as reflected the prevailing views on market growth and market attractiveness within the American business environment.

Strategic actions within a corporation primarily consisted of shifting resources so that the resources maximized the contribution of either growth or cash to support growth in the overall corporate entity. In the BCG Growth Share Matrix, products and businesses were defined as stars (market leaders in growing markets), cash cows (market leaders in mature markets), question marks (participants but not leaders in growing markets), and dogs (the name speaks for itself) based upon how these products or businesses were contributing cash or growth to the overall organization. The strategic portfolio presented the framework and the conglomerate structure provided the vehicle to optimize the corporation's operations.

From the strategic portfolio perspective, the scope of competitive strategy is basically an external, exogenous event to be monitored, managed, and exploited. When utilizing a strategic portfolio approach within a conglomerate structure, the measurement of success can come from the only common denominator that makes any sense within a diverse, unrelated entity—numerical or financial data.

Strategy in the 1980s

With the coming of the new decade of the 1980s, the shift in perspective continued to occur, but now it was away from market attractiveness and toward company strength. In general, this shift in outlook has been described as the "back to the basics" movement.

This reversal in strategic posture was, in large part, a function of some simple observations of the business environment. One observation was that the BCG style portfolio strategies were, in general, providing mixed results. Another, perhaps more important, reason comes from the observation that "Profit is not enough. Profit, as a goal, is insufficient even to sustain profit."[4] Illustrating the preceding comment, one only has to look at companies such as Toyota and Wal-Mart who started out in market niches perceived as relatively poor. Hindsight has shown, however, that these companies not only survived but prospered and in many respects today even dominate their respective industries.

As a result of the ideas presented in his book *Competitive Strategy*, Michael Porter became the standard for a different style of thinking on competitive strategy arising during the 1980s. Even though the earlier portfolio models and Michael Porter use similar terminology, their basic views are quite different.

For example, Michael Porter defines market attractiveness as a function of five fundamental forces that can vary from industry to industry. Taken from this standpoint, the BCG view of strategic management became, in reality, only one component of one force defining market attractiveness. Under one set of conditions, the portfolio models could be exactly correct. Under a different set of conditions, the conclusions of portfolio models might portray appropriate actions that are at best only partially accurate. Hence, the reasons for the inconsistency of results experienced using the strategic portfolio models became quite obvious even with just a perfunctory examination.

Michael Porter identifies and clarifies important aspects present in the strategic management process by literally taking a step backward from the primarily financial perspective of the earlier views of strategy. In doing so, he examines those underlying factors responsible for creating the end result.

In terms of company strength, Michael Porter widens the scope of corporate action with three basic courses of action that he refers to as generic strategies. The generic strategies identified by Porter are actions described as:

> *Overall cost leadership.* "a set of functional policies aimed at . . . aggressive construction of efficient-scale facilities, vigorous pursuit of cost reductions from experience, tight cost and overhead control, avoidance of marginal customer accounts."[5]
>
> *Differentiation.* "creating something that is perceived *industrywide* as being unique. Approaches to differentiating can take many forms: design or brand image, technology, features, customer service, dealer network, or other dimensions."[6]
>
> *Focus.* "the low cost and differentiation strategies are aimed at achieving their objectives industrywide, the entire focus strategy is built around serving a particular target very well, and each functional policy is developed with this in mind."[7]

These three generic strategies take competitive strategy from the realm of being external, primarily reactive corporate actions to endeavors that are internal, primarily active corporate actions.

To be successful, according to Michael Porter, companies must focus on and select one of these three courses of action and rigorously pursue its application. He notes: "Successfully executing each generic strategy involves different resources, strengths, organizational arrangements, and managerial style . . . Rarely is a firm suited for all three."[8] If a company does not pursue a generic strategy or executes the generic strategy ineffectively, eventually the more clearly defined competitors within an industry will end up dominating the industry and the less clearly defined companies will become mired and end up stuck in the middle. The net result of the generic strategy is that companies become focused on their customers or their industry better than companies who either are governed by strictly financial objectives or develop poorly conceived strategies. Simply put, anyone can prosper in a growing market but only well-defined, clearly focused companies can do well in mature, more competitive markets.

Strategy in the 1990s

The 1990s have seen the direction in some companies take an even greater internal perspective by emphasizing what has been popularly referred to as quality. Much of the increasing interest in quality has been attributed to the pioneering efforts of individuals such as W. Edwards Deming and Joseph Juran.[9] As a result of the work of Deming, Juran, and others, the quality movement has not only been recognized by individual firms but also by the U. S. government with its conferring of the Malcolm Baldrige Quality Award on manufacturing, service, and small-business organizations that meet its exacting standards. How does the quality movement fit into the strategic management of an organization? How quality fits into corporate strategy is not especially clear and has caused some confusion because quality is a term used in a variety of ways.

Quality has been used to describe techniques such as quality circles. It has also characterized processes such as statistical process control. More often among high performance organizations, such as Motorola, it has come to mean much more—a philosophy underlying the decisions and actions constituting their corporate strategy. Hence, quality is seen as an operational activity, part of a system, and as something related to the culture and values of an organization. It is, indeed, all these things and that is what makes it sometimes difficult to see the link between quality and corporate strategy.

If we examine quality from Michael Porter's framework, the most visible link between quality and strategy is to what Porter describes as a differentiation strategy. Differentiation is concerned with providing those factors buyers consider to be important, and quality is, after all, related to producing a better product or service for the customer. Xerox, Lands' End, and Motorola are three companies that exemplify the quality perspective well. Xerox promises to replace any product for any reason within three years of its purchase; Lands' End has products that are guaranteed, period; Motorola has the goal of Total Customer Satisfaction.

Instead of discussing quality in the abstract, it would be more illustrative to examine a particular application. In this regard, the experiences of Motorola, one of the first Malcolm Baldrige Quality Award winners, provide significant insight into the connection of quality to corporate strategy. Motorola achieves customer satisfaction, at least in part, through a process referred to as Six Steps to Six Sigma. Briefly, the Six Steps to Six Sigma consist of the following general actions:

1. Identify the product you create or the service you provide.
2. Identify the customer(s) for your product or service, and determine what they consider important.

3. Identify your needs (to provide product/service so that it satisfies the customer).
4. Define the process for doing the work.
5. Mistake-proof the process and eliminate wasted effort.
6. Ensure continuous improvement by measuring, analyzing, and controlling the improved process. [10]

At the core of Motorola's quality initiative is a vigorous attention to customer needs and satisfactions followed by painstakingly producing a product or service that fulfills customer requests in the manner that they desire.

Contrary to popular misconceptions, however, increasing quality does not necessarily lead to increasing costs. The relationship between cost and quality is often viewed to occur in a fashion similar to that depicted in Figure 3.1. The quality-cost relationship shown in the figure led in only one direction whose wisdom was described in the following manner: "The old school taught improving quality cost money! It was prudent to ship some defects, it saved money!" [11] There was the inevitable trade-off each company had to make between high quality and low cost. Over the past decade, Motorola found that this bit of

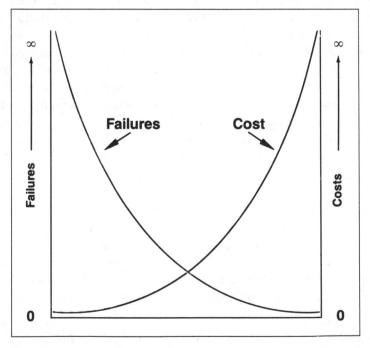

Figure 3.1.   Common business wisdom on the quality-cost relationship. *Source:* Motorola, Inc.

common business wisdom was, in fact, not very wise at all. What Motorola actually discovered was that "Improving sigma capability in both product and process results in a product which is virtually latent defect-free, and it results in the lowest manufacturing cost."[12] Common business wisdom was not only inaccurate, but led Motorola's businesses in exactly the opposite direction from where they should have been going.

The relationship of cost to quality is, in reality, a family of relationships, which is illustrated in Figure 3.2, rather than the often assumed single relationship previously presented. What Figure 3.2 shows is that the more quality increases, the more costs go down. One commentator observes, "That's because good quality reduces the so-called hidden plant: people, floor space, and equipment used for nothing but finding and fixing things that should have been done right the first time. This typically represents 25% to 35% of total production costs."[13] The reason high quality reduces costs is readily visible but not always obvious when it becomes obscured by the blinders of common business wisdom.

Consequently, the not-so-well-publicized fact is that well-organized quality initiatives are not just cost-effective but are also the most cost-effective strategies for an organization. The following commentary recounts how the quality-cost connection was indelibly etched in the mind of George Fisher, former

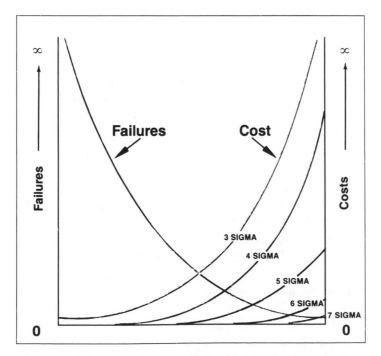

Figure 3.2.   Actual quality-cost relationship. *Source:* Motorola, Inc.

CEO of Motorola. "[The quality-cost] lesson hit home for Fisher in 1982, when he directed a pivotal push to crack the Japanese telecom market, then rigorously protected. His team developed a pager that met the exacting demands of Nippon Telegraph & Telephone Corp. It was produced to quality standards at least five times better than Motorola's U.S. pager. But it turned out to be more profitable."[14] Motorola's experience in Japan, as it turned out, was not a unique circumstance but an event that would be relived over and over.

Quality and Competitive Position

It is important to understand the relationship of quality to competitive position. So far, our discussion has centered on Motorola's individual experiences. What Motorola also found to be generally true was that while quality can affect strategy, it greatest impact was on how it influenced competitive position. Motorola discovered that quality itself was not a unidimensional concept but that distinct levels of quality are possible. Further, the level of quality attained had a direct influence on the ability to create future strategies because of the competitive position it created. From their analysis, Motorola concluded that high-quality companies are not just better than their competitors; they achieve magnitudes of difference that can be insurmountable. To understand the consequences of the levels of quality on competitive position, a somewhat more technical perspective is required.

Earlier, the Six Steps to Six Sigma process was presented as Motorola's approach to quality. The sigma in this process refers to a statistical term that is part of the mathematics of quality. If we view some statistics that Motorola provides (see Figure 3.3) to classify error or defect rates without going into too much detail, we see that an average organization tends to operate in the 4 sigma range, which creates 6210 defects per million parts or steps (ppm). In contrast, a 5 sigma organization will create 233 defects ppm and a 6 sigma organization, the best in its class, creates only 3.4 defects ppm. In addition to the "hidden plant" phenomenon, Motorola's experience has also shown that "A 4 sigma manufacturer will spend in excess of 10% of the sales dollar on internal and external repair. A 6 sigma manufacturer will spend less than 1%. A 4 sigma supplier cannot directly compete with a 6 sigma supplier and survive."[15] From Motorola's perspective, producing higher quality was not an option but a mandate. Furthermore, simply doing better would not be enough to remain competitive in the long run. If the highest levels of quality were not achieved, their direction and fate would ultimately be determined by their quality-oriented competitors, who in this case primarily tended to be the Japanese.

From just a simple observation of Motorola's analysis, it becomes obvious

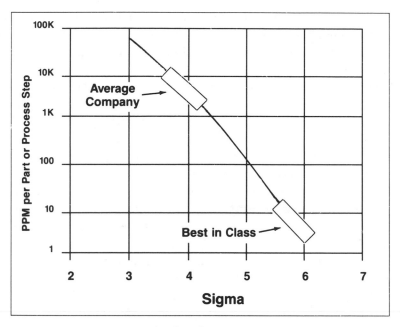

Figure 3.3.   Levels of quality. *Source:* Motorola, Inc.

that high quality not only puts a company on a much different competitive plane than its counterparts but it also makes a wider variety of strategic options accessible to the company. That is, attaining high levels of quality creates the potential to pursue not only a differentiation strategy but also a low cost leadership strategy within their markets. The competition finds that even rigorous adherence to a single generic strategy may not be enough to be competitive with a quality company. While some companies in competitive industries tend to point to lower wages, unfavorable exchange rates, and other competitive factors, many have also found the simple answer is no answer at all. The real magic formula of the seeming Japanese dominance simply lies in understanding the role quality plays in their corporate strategy.

Previously, Michael Porter was quoted as saying that only in rare instances can a company successfully pursue more than one strategy. Yet the conclusions in the preceding examination appear to run counter to his assertions. Is Michael Porter wrong? No, but his observations relate only a portion of the total story. The generic strategies, as Michael Porter observed, represent the positions of focused organizations. When this focus is interrupted, performance inevitably deteriorates. He notes this phenomenon with the following remark, "Becoming stuck in the middle also afflicts successful firms, who compromise their generic strategy for the sake of growth or prestige. . . . The temptation to blur a generic strategy, and therefore become stuck in the middle, is particularly great for a focuser once it has dominated its target markets."[16] What Michael Porter is saying is that his generic strategies require a continuing high degree of focus and discipline.

Motorola, and other quality companies, have told the rest of the story. That is, when quality companies pursue multiple strategies they are not blurring their strategic perspective but instead are fully utilizing existing advantages they have created as a result of an even higher level of focus at the overall corporate level. The quality perspective does not consider the business portfolio, market attractiveness and company strength, as an either-or situation. The quality initiative has folded the two different perspectives of the business portfolio into a single unitary dimension. This dimension might be more correctly termed the value dimension, since one is simultaneously and coincidentally concerned with the customer and with the operations that create value for that customer. Contrary to the observations of Michael Porter for businesses in general, the development of multiple strategies in a quality organization does not lead to an inferior position relative to the competitors within an industry. The advantage of the quality perspective lies in its ability to provide the potential for occupying a superordinate position within an industry.

Changing Strategic Perspectives

We have noted the relationship of quality to corporate strategy and competitive position. Ultimately, a company's position and strategy dictate how the company interprets and interacts within its environment. Perhaps an equally significant benefit of incorporating quality into the organization lies not in the fact that it provides more or better strategic alternatives but that it offers keener managerial perceptions of the environment itself. A quality focus shifts the managerial perspective from a macro to a micro viewpoint. This shift in perspective is important because a macro perspective essentially only allows a company to predict what might happen. When the environment is viewed from a micro standpoint, however, a company can exert some degree of control, and in certain instances even a significant degree of control, over its own destiny almost regardless of industry. As a result of gaining control over its immediate operating environment, the company may have a hand in shaping the course of its competitors and perhaps even the direction of the environment itself.

What are the ways quality has changed perceptions of the environment? It is probably fair to say that it has accelerated several trends already in progress. Figure 3.4 shows several of the more prominent trends.

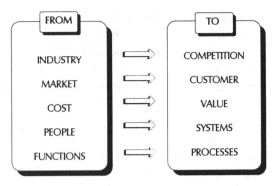

Figure 3.4. Changing views of the environment.

Industry to Competition

Instead of concentrating on the industry, the focus of a quality-oriented company turns to examining its competitors. Recognizing the importance of the competition, the quality company not only wants to know *what* products and services their competitors are providing but also *how* they are providing those products and services. Jack Shewmaker, former president, vice-chairman, and chief financial officer at Wal-Mart, offers an illustration of just how one can get more from less with the following commentary. "I visited many competitors' stores with Sam Walton. I particularly remember one visit because the competitor's store was a disaster. But Sam didn't acknowledge the store's shortcomings. All he saw was one small, but good, display in a far corner. He said to me, 'Jack, how come we're not doing that?'"[17] The change in focus from industry to competition is important because an industry perspective can obscure who the real competitors are. The quality company understands that competition comes in many forms, is not always within the same industry, and at times may not even be among the better organizations.

Reverse engineering, benchmarking, and reducing cycle time all help an organization to increase levels of performance. However, the unqualified realization is that value and quality can only come from within the organization. Once a company is the best, it also understands the necessity of continually striving to beat itself. The company itself becomes its own toughest competitor but it does so with a wary eye on the environment.

Market to Customer

While growth can be a result of external events such as demographics or technology, other fruitful avenues of growth also exist. It is not that market characteristics are unimportant to quality companies but that markets are made up of individual customers. It is the recognition that there are general needs but each individual customer also has a unique situation. Thus, while quality companies pursue and sometimes even create markets, satisfying individual needs allows an organization to reach its fullest potential for creating value.

Changing from a market to a customer focus also brings about the awareness that a product or a service by itself is a simple, static view of the operating environment. Quality companies tend to view themselves as part of a larger value chain that starts with a customer and moves back through the company to the supplier. The supplier, at the beginning of the value chain, is important for several reasons. The supplier can: (1) be the source of higher quality input, (2) influence time, human, and financial resources used in creating products or services, and (3) in reality be a partner with the company to satisfy needs the customer perhaps does not even yet realize exist.

The quality perspective moves an organization from viewing a product or service to and through the whole value chain to understand how and why the product or service is being utilized. Often businesses have the perception that they must define their customers. In fact, quality companies realize that the reality of the situation is the other way around—customers define their business.

Cost to Value

To understand why basic perceptions relating to industry and market are changing to competitor and customer, one must understand a fundamental change in perspective of the business enterprise itself. If we ask the question "What is the purpose of a business?," traditional responses would probably tend to emphasize ideas such as "maximizing profit" or perhaps "increasing shareholder value."

In general, these answers are being reconstructed by quality-focused companies. The old answers are being revised not so much because they are wrong but rather because by themselves they are inadequate. They do not serve as definitions of a business because profits and stock price are results. A company is a system and profits and stock price are the results of the operation of the system—a barometer of its effectiveness. Profits and even stock price can be altered, for example, by simply changing accounting methods. Further, when profits or stock price are paramount, the standard prescription for increasing performance has generally been to cut costs. One can change profits rather rapidly by reducing workforce, or by eliminating operating facilities, and so forth. Many companies in recent days are using a variety of cost-cutting techniques to change perceptions of their performance. In the short run, this effectively changes appearances but does not change the underlying reasons for success. That is, we can change the image of how our companies are operating without changing how they are actually operating.

Peter Drucker[18] suggests a different answer to the question "What is the purpose of a business?" His reply is to create a customer. Since the quality-focused organization's perspective is already on the customer, the only valid corporate actions are those that create value. What does creating value mean? To a world-class company, it means satisfying both the perceived and unperceived needs of their customers better than one's competitors. The first and most important step in the process is understanding what value is. The real meaning of value can only come from customers themselves. Traditional actions such as marketing research and focus groups provide the right kind of information as an input. However, creating value requires employee involvement and participation throughout the organization starting at the very beginning and going all the way to the very end.

The value-creating process is disarmingly simple. Customers tell us what they want (needs), we figure out how to do it (value). Creating value creates customers. Creating customers creates revenues and ultimately profits. The traditional answers to the purpose of a business have focused on the very end of the equation for business success. Quality-oriented companies have changed the focus to the beginning, the source of the greatest overall impact, and use value as a driving force in their operations.

People to Systems

A fourth change comes in the shifting of perspective from managing people to managing systems. When one views a system, not only do we see the parts (plants, machines, people, etc.) but also the interactions between those parts. From this viewpoint, sources of error can be eliminated from the system itself rather than making the futile attempt of rewarding or punishing people for performance that may ultimately be out of their control.

Furthermore, when defects in the system are removed, people no longer have to worry about fighting fires that continually occur because the system is defective and can turn to more productive actions. The actions of the quality company are much different from many of its competitors who are still correcting the same errors over and over within their systems. The quality organization has people able to concentrate on producing more and better ideas to improve their system. Perhaps the greatest irony that Bill Smith, Vice President of the Land Mobile Products Sector at Motorola, relates is that "the fewer the defects there are, the easier it is to detect the defects that do occur."

Functions to Processes

As companies move toward viewing their operations in terms of systems, they also move away from regarding business actions and events as incremental and isolated to viewing these actions and events as continuous and interrelated. An incremental perspective tends to focus on a company's functions (operations, marketing, etc.) and often assumes the environment to be relatively static. A continuous perspective, however, tends to focus on basic business processes that leads to a dynamic, interactive view of the environment.

In organizational terms, what does all of this mean? Using the process perspective has led quality companies to think of themselves horizontally, not vertically. Traditional functional views of a company have created what has been termed functional silos.[19] That is many companies consist of vertical, functional hierarchies with each function trying to maximize its performance. In general, the traditional functional view of a company has led to people viewing other people within the same company as competitiors. Horizontal management,[20] in contrast, views the horizontal processes across the entire enterprise (from the customer through the supplier) necessary to produce a product or service. From the horizontal viewpoint, actions such as cross-functional work teams are utilized to take into account the unique value creating capabilities of each function for developing the ultimate product or service.

Another, perhaps more widely reported, aspect of the process perspective has been continuous improvement. The quality-oriented organizations emphasize improved performance as something to be done by everyone all the time rather than as actions taken on a project-by-project basis. The idea of continuous improvement has evolved far past the point of just improving processes and decreasing costs. The current environment is rapidly moving toward the idea of the company as a learning organization.

David Garvin defines the learning organization as "an organization skilled at creating, acquiring, and transferring knowledge, and at modifying its behavior to reflect new knowledge and insights."[21] Thus, the simple idea of continuous improvement itself has been continually growing to include the transfer of individual learnings into organizational learnings, and perhaps even societal learning.

A Final Comment

Two caveats should be understood. First, high levels of quality are not necessarily synonymous with being successful or even making good strategy. The quality perspective provides the basis that reveals sustainable business advantages. The quality company elects how and when to utilize an advantage.

Furthermore, if an industry is in decline or there is a poor economy, just being high quality may not be enough to maintain competitiveness or even profitability. In addition, good quality does not make up for not understanding the dynamics of one's industry. The forces that define an industry can, as Michael Porter notes, change over time. As these forces change, they essentially define a new industry.[22] Unless these changes are understood, performance relative to competition can decrease.

Second, just as there are different levels of quality, there are also different levels of quality management. One can produce defect-free products or services, but this is not the same as total quality management. Some actions associated with total quality involve:

• Distinguishing potential future development projects.
• Paying strict attention to processes.
• Prioritizing and focusing attention on problems.
• Focusing attention on the corporate system.[23]

Total quality involves the whole organization from the top to the bottom. It does not emphasize one function of an organization over another since the functions are just different aspects within a unified process.

The relationship of quality to strategic management is straightforward. However, directly equating high quality with competitive success would be misleading. What makes quality the touchstone of competitive strategy is that it creates choices and opportunities not available to an organization's competitors. Quality provides a different perspective and the *potential* to put an organization on a different competitive plane than its competitors. From a strategic perspective, the company determines whether and in what manner the quality advantage it has created will be used. Thus, the link between quality and corporate strategy is simply that quality creates the ability for an organization to take actions that are literally impossible for its competitors.

Notes

1. See the following for a discussion of quality within the organization: Joel Dreyfuss, "Victories in the Quality Crusade," *Fortune*, October 10, 1988, p. 84; Alan P. Brache and Geary A. Rummler, "The Three Levels of Quality," *Quality Progress*, October 1988, pp. 46–51; David A. Garvin, *Managing Quality* (New York: Free Press, 1988).
2. Kenichi Ohmae, *The Mind of the Strategist* (New York: McGraw-Hill Book Co., 1982), pp. 153–154.
3. See Thomas H. Naylor, *Strategic Planning Management* (Oxford, OH: Planning

Executives Institute (currently known as the Planning Forum), 1980), pp. 59–78, for a discussion of the Boston Consulting Group Growth Share Matrix.

4. Joe Flower, *Prince of the Magic Kingdom* (New York: John Wiley & Sons, Inc., 1991), p. 262.
5. Michael E. Porter, *Competitive Strategy* (New York: Free Press, 1980), p. 35.
6. Ibid., p. 37.
7. Ibid., p. 38.
8. Ibid., p. 42.
9. Some current works by these individuals are: W. Edwards Deming, *Out of the Crisis* (Cambridge: Massachusetts Institute of Technology, Center for Advanced Engineering Study, 1986); and Joseph M. Juran, *Juran on Leadership for Quality: An Executive Handbook* (New York: Free Press, 1989).
10. "The Six Steps to Six Sigma," Motorola Malcolm Baldrige Quality Seminar, 1989, p. 8.
11. Ibid., p. 7.
12. Ibid.
13. Lois Therrien, "The Rival Japan Respects," *Business Week,* December 13, 1989, p. 112.
14. Ibid.
15. "The Six Steps to Six Sigma," op. cit., p. 6.
16. Michael E. Porter, op. cit., p. 17.
17. Jack Shewmaker, "The Master Sellers," *Nation's Business,* November 1988, p. 26.
18. A classic discussion on the basic nature of a business is provided in Peter F. Drucker, *Management: Tasks, Responsiblities, and Practices* (New York: Harper & Row, 1973), pp. 58–73.
19. For a discussion of functional silos see "Organizational Renewal—Tearing Down the Functional Silos," *Target,* Summer 1988, pp. 4–14.
20. For a discussion of horizontal management see John A. Byrne, "The Horizontal Corporation," *Business Week,* December 20, 1993, pp. 76–81.
21. David A. Garvin, "Building the Learning Organization," *Harvard Business Review,* July–August 1993, p. 80.
22. Many of the basic changes in an industry can be stated in even more basic microeconomic relationships. An excellent discussion is provided by Peter Carroll in "The Link Between Performance and Strategy," *Journal of Business Strategy,* 1982, pp. 3–20.
23. Shigeru Mizuno, *Management for Total Quality* (Cambridge, MA: Productivity Press, 1988).

4

Quality, Participation, and Competitiveness

ROBERT E. COLE, PAUL BACDAYAN, AND

B. JOSEPH WHITE

Despite years of preaching from academics and repeated assertions of the benefits associated with participatory work practices, managers have been slow to
embrace and incorporate these practices into everyday work routines in American corporations.[1] Why is this the case? Once we identify the obstacles, we can
examine the role that a modern quality improvement focus plays in eliminating
those obstacles.[2]

Employee participation can take many different forms.[3] By participation,
we mean an employee involvement in decision making that has three characteristics:

- It is *relatively formal*. It is part of official role behavior.
- It is *direct*. It involves individuals instead of, or in addition to, elected
  representatives.
- It is *relatively local and moderately open regarding decision-making access*.
  Workers have a strong input into most operational decisions directly
  affecting their work and will be delegated authority for some aspects of
  that work.

Although we will use the term "participation" (or "employee involvement"), work arrangements with such characteristics go by many names, such
as "participative decision making" and "empowerment." Each has some distinctive nuance, but for our purposes they will be treated as the same.

The central puzzle is: "Why don't managers fully embrace participation?"
Despite extensive exposure to ideas about participation and its alleged benefits,
surveys of American firms show rather superficial participation: participatory
techniques, while used in many companies, rarely affect large numbers of
employees in any single company.[4] Comprehensive reviews of the effects of
participatory practices often reveal modest short-run improvements with "a

positive, often small effect on productivity, sometimes a zero or statistically insignificant effect, and almost never a negative effect."[5] These are modest claims indeed. Historical accounts suggest a long but on-again-off-again pattern of experimentation with participation. Thus, Tom Bailey's recent overview of employee participation in the United States concludes:

> There are many positive, even enthusiastic reports of the benefits of work reform and employee participation practices and to some extent these examples are supported by systematic research that also shows positive effects. Nevertheless, the diffusion of these practices has been slow and frustrating, and many efforts do not last.[6]

On the critical issue of work standards, Professor Kano in the last chapter of this book notes that in American industry these standards are typically determined by staff departments in corporate headquarters. Consequently, workers see them as inflexible bureaucratic control mechanisms—hardly the ideal environment for ensuring continuous improvement. A more participative process would delegate work standard revisions to local workplace managers and workers.

A variety of possible explanations may account for the limited implementation of participatory outcomes. David Levine argues that the external environment of the firm is hostile to participation in the United States and leads the market to discourage participation along with related practices (e.g., encouraging employment security), "suggesting the need for public policies to overcome the current penalties suffered by initial adopters."[7] While these arguments may well be valid, they interact with internal inhibitors. Our own analysis of these internal factors attributes the low level of acceptance to the low level of managerial support—and that, in turn, to managers' perceptions of a weak connection between participation and improved productivity (or other desirable organization-level outcomes). Furthermore, an understanding of the internal factors leading managers not to support participation can also shed light on why workers don't give stronger support to participatory initiatives.

Strengths and Weaknesses of the Participation Tradition

Table 4.1 provides an overview of the strengths and weaknesses of the participation tradition in terms of its contributions to individuals and groups and to overall organizational objectives. The extensive literature on participation treats its strengths (which are primarily at the individual and small-group level) in great depth and can be summarized as follows.

TABLE 4.1. Strengths and Weaknesses of the Participative Tradition by Level of Analysis

Level of Analysis	Strengths	Weaknesses
Individual/ Small group	• Focus on motivation	• Lack of employee rewards
	• Opportunity for goal agreement	• Motivational emphasis diverts attention from process improvement
	• Emphasis on interpersonal process	
	• Human capital development	
	• Integrating interdependent tasks	
Department/ Managers	• Release for higher level activities	• Absence of managerial rewards
		• Absence of role for lower managers
System/ Organization/ Society	• Potential competitive advantage	• Flabbiness
	• Democratization	• Absence of strategic context for group activities

- *Motivational*—The participation theme highlights the important relationship between human motivation and organizational outcomes. Its premise is that participation yields its best results when it is based on a voluntary act. The enactment of participation is said to lead to self-realization and human dignity.
- *Opportunity for goal agreement*—Participation provides a way of aligning individual and organizational objectives.
- *Emphasis on interpersonal processes*—Participation provides a heavy emphasis on such human process skills as communications, teamwork, and conflict resolution, skills that improve the quality of decision making and enhance employee "buy-in."
- *Human capital development*—Participation stresses the importance of building individual and team competency through training. It thus encourages the development of human capital.
- *Integrating interdependent tasks*—Participation through team activity provides a strategy for integrating work involving highly interdependent tasks.
- *Release for higher-level activities*—Participation releases managerial and technical personnel from firefighting activities by making lower-level employees responsible for maintaining and improving their work processes.

- *Potential competitive advantage*—Participation has the potential to unleash a great force by allowing all employees to make substantial contributions to improving work performance.

- *Democratization*—Notions of self-governance and self-determination underlie approaches to participation. Some individuals, particularly scholars and labor activists, see participation as a strong democratizing force that finally brings the benefits of political democracy to the workplace.

By contrast, the weaknesses of the participation tradition are primarily at the organization level. Although less commonly discussed, they are critical because they diminish managerial and worker support for participation. These weaknesses can be summarized as follows:

- *Lack of employee rewards*—Employee rewards, including nonmonetary enhancements such as employment security, are seldom specified. Without such assurances, individuals will often withhold commitment because they see participatory initiatives that lead to productivity gains as threatening their economic security by lowering the demand for labor.

- *Myopic emphasis on motivation*—The overwhelming stress on the motivational benefits of participation tends to crowd out other necessary conditions for organizational success such as the improvement of operational processes. The simplistic idea that "if we could just get people motivated, everything would turn out all right" is an implicit assumption of much American academic literature (perhaps because of the domination of this literature by psychologists), not to speak of many American managers. Trying harder, by itself, is not enough!

- *Absence of managerial rewards*—Managerial rewards (including power and status) for supporting participative work practices are seldom well defined. Lower-level supervisors, and middle managers in particular, often regard participatory initiatives as a threat to their traditional roles and prerogatives; they see little personal benefit in supporting them. Managerial promotion criteria typically have not been tied to success in introducing and leading participatory activities.

- *Absence of role for lower-level managers*—Looking at both the scholarly literature and practitioner experience, there is a lack of clarity about the operational requirements (integrating groups and participation into the existing managerial structure). As a consequence, participatory initiatives experience high resistance from supervisors and middle managers because their role is unclear.

- *"Flabbiness"*—Participation advocates are typically unclear about the nature of participative activities as they relate to actual work operations; the emphasis is on the process of participation per se, not the elements of a systematic work improvement methodology. It is often unclear just what one is supposed to be participating in. Consequently, firms tend not to sustain participatory efforts since managers do not regard participation as tied to important organizational objectives. Participation comes to be seen as an end in itself.[8] Workers also perceive this irrelevance and withhold their support. Under these conditions, the agenda of issues in which people can participate tends to dry up.

- *Absence of strategic context for group activities*—This is the final and critical factor. The workteam is portrayed as "context-less," that is, not embedded in the work flow and not tied to a customer. Given this lack of linkage, managerial support for participation fades because participation is seen as a peripheral activity, not coupled with strategic objectives. In this context, participation comes to be viewed more as a philosophy, a parallel work process (conducted apart from the main business activities of the enterprise), and as an end in itself rather than as a means to the end of increasing organizational effectiveness.

This list of weaknesses focuses heavily on what we believe are the major organizational forces driving change or inhibiting it. As can be seen in Table 4.1, the potential advantages identified as strengths of the participative tradition are canceled at the organization level by the participatory tradition's flabbiness and the absence of strategic context for group activities. While the weaknesses are the sort of reasons that managers might give for not starting or abandoning participation, and therefore merit attention, they are unfortunately not the reasons that researchers in the participatory tradition typically have addressed.

The majority of the weaknesses identified above focus on manager's support for participation. Our intent in emphasizing this support is not to deny the need for employee cooperation and support (or union support, where relevant) in implementing participatory work practices. Instead, we wish to assert that in most cases it is management, and only management, that can initiate such activities and command resources to consistently support them. Moreover, it is managers who are in a position to provide the resources that can secure worker commitment through offering such benefits as job security, recognition, and wages. But without benefits to managers and the organization as a whole, managerial support for participation is unlikely to be forthcoming, and if it is, it is unlikely to be sustained.

A Brief Comparative Historical Note

We can contrast Japan on the one hand with America and Europe on the other in terms of the historical relationship of participation to quality. Whereas the two traditions developed separately in America and Europe, they emerged after World War II as integrated practices in Japan. Known as total quality control (TQC), this approach stresses quality improvement through the efforts of all employees and all departments. Such an approach is distinctive and original in philosophy and scope.

The Japanese integration of quality and participation provides important organization-level benefits which, when coupled with individual- and group-level benefits, foster managerial support for participation. Similarly, the historic separation of the two traditions in America and Europe has weakened managerial support for participation and stunted the development of both the quality and the participation movements. While the reasons for these different historical trajectories lie beyond the scope of this book, they relate to the unique development of the scientific management movement (Taylorism) in the United States, driven in part by a large, relatively uneducated immigrant labor force in the early twentieth century. While Taylorism spread to both Europe and Japan, in Japan the participatory theme received an early hearing.[9]

"Market-in" and Other Key Characteristics of the Modern Quality Paradigm

Table 4.2 lists the key characteristics of the modern quality approach as developed by the best Japanese firms. The following list is a brief overview of these characteristics.

TABLE 4.2.   Characteristics of the Modern Quality Movement as It Evolved in Japan

---

- "Market-In" approach provides strong external customer orientation and uses internal customer chain as connection to final user
- Quality as an umbrella theme for organizing work
- Improved quality seen as means to forge strong competitive strategy
- All-employee, all-department imvolvement a pivotal strategy for improving quality of every business process
- Upstream prevention activities key to quality improvement
- Well-defined problem-solving methodology and training activities tied to continuous quality improvement
- Integration into control system of goals, plans, and actions for continuous quality improvement
- Focus on cross-functional cooperation and information sharing

---

- The "market-in" principle—Market-in is a major focus in Japanese quality improvement activities. It means bringing customer needs into every possible part of the organization, thereby heightening uncertainty. These activities include informing production workers or front-line service employees of customer claims relevant to their work, conveying to a broad range of employees how customers use products and services, and educating as many as employees as possible on customer-desired product and service features. The market-in approach contrasts sharply with the reliance on specialized organization experts to process information about the environment and solve specific problems.

- Quality as an umbrella theme—Quality provides an overall theme for change in the organization, one that is more intrinsically appealing and less threatening than competing themes such as cost reduction or productivity improvement. It is hard to find anyone who is against quality, but cost reduction and productivity improvement often evoke fears of displacement. Quality by contrast is positive, unifying, and constructive.

- Quality's relationship to costs and productivity—Japanese manufacturers (by which we especially mean large- and medium-sized firms) saw improved quality as flowing from the elimination of waste and rework in every business process; this definition contrasts with the traditional American view of improved quality through adding more product attributes or additional inspectors, thereby leading to added cost.

- All-employee, all-department involvement—The Japanese extended the concept of quality improvement to include business processes beyond the shop floor (e.g., purchasing and design), thus broadening the scope of participation to include all employees and departments. In the best large manufacturing firms, employee involvement means that all employees, individually and in teams, are trained to engage in designing and redesigning their own work processes.

- Upstream prevention—The Japanese also recognized that upstream prevention activities, particularly in the design phase, were the primary place where large-scale quality breakthroughs could take place. While to some extent this devalued the contributions of lower-level employees, it also made it clear that traditional efforts to blame lower-level personnel for poor quality were misplaced.

- Problem-solving methodology—Japanese firms developed a simple yet powerful problem-solving methodology that was usable by workers with high school and even junior high school educations. This methodology is based on application of Shewhart's Plan, Do, Check, Act cycle (PDCA) and is used to improve the employees' own work processes. The methodology is backed up with training in a variety of problem-solving tools, including the Pareto and cause-and-effect diagrams. The solution to many problems was no longer the domain of the industrial engineering department. Simplified statistical tools became widely used among workers in all departments.

- Integration with control system—The deployment of quality improvement efforts is carefully cascaded down through the organization, starting from a long-term plan, moving to the annual plan, and then having each level (from managers down through worker quality circles) formulate quality improvement objectives that tie into these plans. Progress toward these plans is checked regularly through personal audits by top executives. By integrating quality into the control system in this way, middle managers and workers are made central to the execution of quality improvement and implicitly told that what they are doing is important. As Professor Kano shows in his chapter, the management-by-policy approach (*hōshin kanri*) resembles the concept of MBO used in American firms; in both cases managers make efforts to link lower-level activities to higher-level goals. Yet, *hōshin kanri* contrasts sharply with the usual implementation of MBO by providing many substantive activities that ensure and sustain the linkage (e.g., regular audits by top executives).

- Cross-functional cooperation and information sharing—Information about customer needs and expectations is critical to successful quality improvement because this information drives important processes such as goal setting, problem identification, and problem solving. Japanese firms are less inclined to assign customer research to one highly specialized group and they tend to widely deploy the resultant information to as many organizational actors and departments as possible. Consider the example of Quality Function Deployment (QFD). QFD is a system for translating consumer requirements into appropriate company requirements at each stage from research and development through the intermediate stages to marketing/sales and distribution. From our point of view, however, QFD is important and successful because it involves a matrix of specified activities that regularly brings members of different departments together to solve problems. Through these discussions, customer needs and competitor information are widely shared throughout the organization. Key targets for quality, cost, and delivery (QCD) are typically set by cross-functional groups.

In sum, the best large Japanese manufacturing firms—through wide sharing of customer information, "market-in," and the empowerment of decentralized work teams to act on that information—have implemented a system of broad-based, task-focused participation that has yielded quality gains at the organizational level.

Individual and Group-Level Benefits of
Quality-Participation Integration

The Japanese have also realized important individual and group-level benefits from the integration of quality with participation that we can frame as improved *information processing* and improved *motivation*. These individual and group-level outcomes contribute indirectly to the organization-level outcomes of managerial support for participation.

First, from an information processing standpoint, comprehensive and grass-roots participation in problem solving allows firms to move the "distribution of intelligence" downward in the organization. Participation brings to bear increased information and capability in local problem solving without involving costly middle managers who often contribute to information distortion. Consequently, participation can improve information processing and decision making, thereby increasing organizational effectiveness.[10]

Second, from an employee motivation standpoint, the market-in approach makes sense for two reasons. First, the process activities for meeting market requirements are based on the sound behavioral principle that those involved in work processes will more enthusiastically implement changes that they themselves have designed. In addition, quality—the act of satisfying the customer and therefore the market—provides a powerful motivational theme around which to build employee involvement and commitment.

Organization-Level Benefits of
Quality-Participation Integration

The organization-level interpretation of the benefits of merging quality with participation is the cornerstone of our answer to our original question about why managers haven't supported participation. Managers at all levels (and, to a lesser extent, workers) have lacked motivation to support extensive employee participation, particularly in the redesign of the routines that guide work. Why? As we suggested earlier, the lack of organization-level benefits is a barrier that partly explains the low managerial support for the participative redesign of routines. Another key piece of the explanation is the political dimensions of change.

Nelson and Winter explain the political difficulty of changing existing routines.[11] Organizations, and the routines by which people interact, function as "truces" among relevant power holders. Fear of breaking the existing truce (based on sunk costs and fear of losing existing power) is a powerful force holding the organization's participants on a path of relatively inflexible routines.

This is true of routines within departments, and even more true of routines for processes crossing departmental boundaries—as most important organizational processes do. Changing routines for cross-departmental processes is especially critical for quality improvement because many of the most important quality failures (such as in new product design) occur at the poorly managed interfaces between departmental and occupational fiefs.

Just how does the Japanese approach of merging quality improvement with participation decrease the fear of changing routines and increase managerial support for participatory work practices? The answer requires a closer look at the synergy between participation and the "market-in" principle.

Market-in as "De-buffering"

The idea that organizations might try to bring the market into the organization, and thus heighten uncertainty for many employees, runs counter to most social science (especially business strategy) thinking about organizations. Such thinking stresses uncertainty reduction as the normal criterion for organizational decision making. Buffers, which include inventories and specialized units to preprocess information from the environment, shield the bulk of organizational members from the direct forces of the environment.

The buffering approach to dealing with uncertainty captured a good deal of how Western firms have operated in the post-World War II period. We note the difficulty large American firms currently are having in moving beyond the popular rhetoric of "serving customers" to truly addressing customer needs. This difficulty appears closely related to an unwillingness or inability to remove implicit buffering approaches that are part of the taken-for-granted ways American firms are organized. Managers simply assume in many firms, for example, that marketing has responsibility for dealing with the customer and that all other units should receive their information through marketing.

Beyond the United States, buffering has been a explicit theme in the Swedish and German approach to group activity. Here, the strategy has been to buffer individual tasks from upstream and downstream pressures (with commensurate and expensive increases of in-process inventory). The idea was to avoid shutdowns when blockages occurred and obtain a humane pace of work that gave workers more control and autonomy over their work environment. While the short-term benefits to workers and managers are clear, the long-term benefits to management and organization-level objectives are less obvious. Recognition of these problems is increasingly leading to the redesign of major Northern European companies. The model in Sweden for example is no longer Volvo with its buffered semiautonomous work groups but Asea Brown Boveri

(ABB) with its Project T50, which stresses decentralization, customer satisfaction, a learning organization, and reduced cycle time.[12]

In contrast to the traditional Western managerial approach to uncertainty, the best Japanese manufacturers seek to heighten the pressure for change that the environment exerts on all parts of the organization. The just-in-time (JIT) system represents the most visible symbol of bringing market pressures into the firm, but the scope and depth of the market-in principle go far beyond JIT. The "pull system" driving JIT initiates production as a reaction to present demand. But market-in provides far more comprehensive coverage of market characteristics, including anticipation of future demand and of multidimensional aspects of customer needs and expectations. Similarly, it widely distributes throughout the firm knowledge about other dynamic aspects of the firm's environment such as raw materials, suppliers, labor markets, regulatory environment, and so on.

The heightening of uncertainty associated with this approach is linked directly to a motivational strategy of involving all employees in the change process. The amount of business information on performance and environment that many large Japanese manufacturing firms distribute to employees, including those at the lowest levels, is staggeringly high compared to what occurs at most American firms. American managers often restrict sharing even elementary information on a unit's performance and environment.

Moreover, the best Japanese firms supply the necessary training to ensure that employees understand the information being provided. Finally, Japanese managers empower employees to act on such information. By offering this framework in which employees are part of the improvement process, fear of changing existing routines is reduced. "Fearlessness" becomes an extraordinary asset as organizational environments become more uncertain in industry after industry. If the firm can better align itself with its environment and therefore better cope with rapidly changing circumstances, higher-level managers will be more inclined to support participation. Indeed, the market-in principle, effectively applied, can redirect fear of change into fear of statis. One of the authors saw a dramatic visual representation of this redirection at the Mazda Hiroshima transmission plant in 1988. A large banner hanging over the assembly line urged workers to FEAR ESTABLISHED CONCEPTS (*Kyofu Kisei Gainen*).

The Japanese focus on the customer and "market-in" ties work improvement efforts directly into internal and external customer satisfaction in a way that clearly benefits the company. But what about the workers? The reduced buffers certainly can contribute to more stressful work conditions. Janice Klein reports that when buffers were removed between and within work teams, American workers complained about their loss of team identity and individual freedom.[13]

The reduced buffers and the resultant tightened linkages, however, also have benefits for both workers and the firm. On the positive side, from the company's viewpoint, these practices make error more readily visible and subject to accountability. From the workers' side, customer satisfaction themes provide challenges to which they can relate, thereby reducing the seemingly arbitrary nature of managerial decision making. The emphasis on customer satisfaction tightens perceived connections among quality, job security, and employee motivation. In short, employees can see a connection between their own job security and company goals like customer satisfaction and increased market share. These connections also provide an avenue for union cooperation in quality improvement initiatives.

Impact of "Market-in" on Managerial Support
for Participation

Let us look now at the impact of market-in on management. Market-in increases managers' willingness to support participation in at least three ways. First, it increases participation's perceived utility to managers. The quality improvement methodology involves cascading customer satisfaction and other improvement goals down through the organization, assuring managers and executives that participation is controlled and directed toward important organizational outcomes (thereby also reducing management's fear of changing routines). Because market-in imposes customer requirements on the organization, it underscores the strategic importance of participation for the firm's prosperity and survival. Market-in also speeds response times and helps pinpoint quality problems, thus lessening throughput time for business processes and ensuring prompt delivery for internal and external customers. Managers are only too happy to reap the benefits associated with these activities.

A second way market-in promotes managerial support is by decreasing internal factionalism and increasing cohesion. Observers of groups have long known that people cooperate more readily with others from the same in-group, and also when they perceive a common threat or superordinate goal. De-buffering, by constantly bringing information about customer demands and competitor threats to a wide range of organization members, increases employees' self-identification as firm members instead of members of antagonistic subgroups (e.g., engineering versus production, or labor versus management). [14]

Third, market-in can enhance managerial commitment to participation through the creation of a common language of customer needs as well as methods and techniques designed to satisfy those needs. Given a common language, all employees regardless of status and department are better able to communicate with one another, and it becomes more credible for everyone to believe that all employees have valuable contributions to make. In the most fundamental sense, it is a common language that creates and sustains the existence of effective social groups and organizations. These three impacts of market-in, or de-buffering, on managerial support for participation are shown in Figure 4.1.

The belief that all employees have a valuable contribution to make is important because the market-in approach depends on management's decentralization of decision making and problem-solving activities. Without an ability to make rapid on-the-spot decisions by those involved in the work process, market-in would be an organizational nightmare. There is no time for moving decisions up to higher-level superiors.

Notwithstanding the synergy between market-in and participation, there is no doubt that the focus on using the market as a driver, if not managed in a balanced fashion, can lead to excessive pressure on workers in the name of satisfying customers. Indeed, just this theme emerged in Japan in the late 1980s, particularly in the auto industry where long working hours have been associated with an excessive emphasis on meeting customer needs. In a rare example of joint positions, both the normally acquiescent Japan Autoworkers

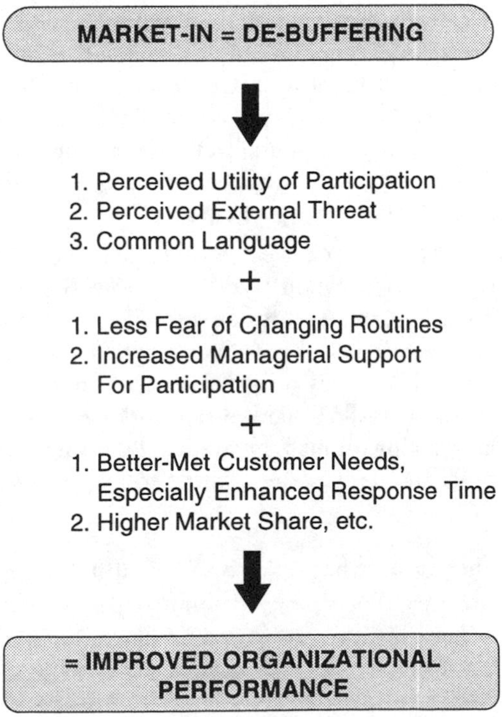

MARKET-IN = DE-BUFFERING

1. Perceived Utility of Participation
2. Perceived External Threat
3. Common Language

+

1. Less Fear of Changing Routines
2. Increased Managerial Support
   For Participation

+

1. Better-Met Customer Needs,
   Especially Enhanced Response Time
2. Higher Market Share, etc.

**= IMPROVED ORGANIZATIONAL
PERFORMANCE**

Figure 4.1 The consequences of market-in as de-buffering.

Union and the Chairman of the Japan Automobile Dealers Association, Ken-ichiro Ueno, attributed the economic problems of the Japanese domestic auto industry to the "excessive desire by manufacturers to maximize customer satisfaction." In particular, an overabundance of model and option variation greatly complicated the work process and created stressful work conditions.

Bringing It All Together

Let us return now to the weaknesses of the Western participation tradition (noted in Table 4.1), to show how a blending of participation with quality improvement addresses those weaknesses. The responses to the following items overcome the weaknesses at the system/organization level referred to in Table 4.1. In addition to offering employee rewards (described above), the blending secures managerial support by providing an organizational context and focus for participation.

- *Addressing flabbiness*—Recall that employees are typically unclear about the nature of participative activities as they relate to the work process, and they lack a systematic work improvement methodology. Linking participation to quality addresses all these issues. The modern quality movement stresses continuous improvement (Kaizen) through better-designed work processes, and it has a well-defined problem-solving methodology. Participation is tied to the achievement of a publicly identified organizational objective: quality. This umbrella theme has intrinsic appeal to employees. At the same time, it has content and concreteness as opposed to the vagueness of the term "participation."
- *Addressing absence of strategic context for group activities*—The second major problem with the participation tradition is that the work team is portrayed as context-less; the team is not embedded in the work flow and not linked to a customer. The linkage of participation with quality through a market-in approach ensures a strong internal and external customer focus. It is possible to flowchart every work process and identify the process's immediate or ultimate customer. By giving the work team the responsibility for job design, the teams become an integral part of the work flow.

In sum, what the Japanese have shown us is that, taken separately, quality and participation are weak concepts with limited potential to transform the firm. Once wedded, however, they are powerful in concept and consequences.

Conclusion

We believe that powerful interactive properties exist between a modern approach to quality and participation. This interaction arises because using quality as an umbrella theme for broad-based participation provides a plausible route to improving organizational performance. The connection of participation with organizational performance through quality can attract managerial support for participation, whereas participation alone garners little support. To pursue participation without quality has proved ineffective—a recipe for failure in today's competitive markets. The most notable examples in the United States were the failure of many quality circle programs in the early 1980s. These failures resulted from the lack of strong management support, which in turn derived from the flabbiness of the conventional participation concept and the absence of a linkage to achieving core business objectives. The linkage of participation with quality not only solves this problem, but joining the two can also operate as a significant motivating force for workers. Workers can benefit directly in terms of expanded responsibilities and skills and indirectly in union situations through negotiations to secure their fair share of organizational success.

Japanese and leading Western companies such as Motorola have demonstrated that participation, when framed as an avenue to the highly ranked corporate objectives of quality and waste reduction, becomes a credible organizational approach. This is not to say that we must precisely follow the Japanese formula or that the particular Japanese way of combining quality with participation is without its problems. To the contrary, customer satisfaction, taken to an extreme, can be coercive and counterproductive. Indeed, in response to such problems, some leaders in the Japanese quality movement recently have added to their traditional calls for customer satisfaction (CS), the new slogan CS + ES. That is to say, customer satisfaction must be combined with employee satisfaction. Such adjustments remind us that we should learn from the mistakes of the Japanese as well as their successes.

Finally, preliminary data analysis supports the view that the quality movement has become the major driving force for the participative movement in the United States. In their analysis of the 1987 national survey conducted by GAO, Lawler and associates found that quality accounted for the biggest reason that respondents (72%) gave for adopting employee involvement.[15] Moreover, in analyzing this finding, Levine and Kruse discovered that those companies reporting that improving quality was their reason for initiating employee involvement had more success with employee involvement practices than those giving other reasons.[16] Quality was the most consistent correlate of organizational success as measured by increased productivity, worker satisfaction, customer service, competitiveness, employee quality of worklife, profitability, and lower turnover and absenteeism. In short, initial data analysis supports our interpretation that linking employee participation initiatives to the quality initiative can yield strong positive results for the firm. We enhance managerial and worker acceptance by using quality to refocus participatory initiatives towards more organizational-level outcomes. In so doing, we increase the probability of bottom-line results for the firm. This, in turn, further increases managerial and worker acceptance, thereby creating a "virtuous cycle."

Notes

We are indebted to David Levine for his thoughtful comments. He is not responsible for our use of those comments.

1. See, for example, Thomas Bailey, "Discretionary Effort and the Organization of Work: Employee Participation and Work Reform Since Hawthorne," paper prepared for the Sloan Foundation, August 1992.
2. For descriptions of the new quality paradigm, see Kaoru Ishikawa, *What Is Quality Control* (Englewood Cliffs, NJ: Prentice-Hall, 1985); Joseph Juran, *Juran on Leadership for Quality* (New York: The Free Press, 1989); and Shigeru Mizuno, *Company-Wide Total Quality Control* (Tokyo: Asian Productivity Organization, 1988).
3. For an overview of the various characteristics, see Peter Dachler and Bernhard Wilpert, "Conceptual Dimensions and Boundaries of Participation in Organizations: A Critical Evaluation," *Administrative Science Quarterly*, 23 (1978): 1–39.
4. Edward Lawler III, Gerald Ledford, Jr., and Susan Mohrman, *Employee Involvement in America* (Houston, TX: American Productivity and Quality Center, 1989).
5. David Levine and Laura Tyson, "Participation, Productivity, and the Firm's Environment," in Alan Blinder, ed., *Paying for Productivity* (Washington, DC: Brookings Institution, 1990), pp. 203–204.
6. Bailey, op. cit., p. 51.
7. David Levine, "Public Policy Implications of Imperfections in the Market for Worker Participation," *Economic and Industrial Democracy*, 13 (1992): 183–206.
8. Edwin Locke and David Schweiger, "Participation in Decision-making: One More Look," in Barry Staw, ed., *Research in Organizational Behavior*, 1 (Greenwich, CT: JAI Press, 1979), pp. 265–339.
9. Robert E. Cole, *Work, Mobility & Participation* (Berkeley: University of California Press, 1979), pp. 101–113.
10. Masahiko Aoki, *Information, Incentives, and Bargaining in the Japanese Economy* (Cambridge: Cambridge University Press, 1988).
11. Richard Nelson and Sidney Winter, *An Evolutionary Theory of Economic Change* (Cambridge, MA: Belknap Press, 1982) pp. 107–11.
12. John Stinesen, "T50 Seminarium med ABB: Kompetensutveckling Nyckelord För

Ny Industriell Revolution" [T50 Seminar with ABB: Competence Development, a Key term for the New Industrial Revolution] *Nya Verkstads Forum*, 1 (February 1992): 11–12.

13. Janice Klein, "The Human Costs of Manufacturing Reform," *Harvard Business Review*, 67 (1984): 60–66.

14. Muzafer Sherif, *In Common Predicament: Social Psychology of Intergroup Cooperation and Conflict* (Boston: Houghton-Mifflin,1966).

15. Ibid.; Lawler et al., op. cit.

16. David Levine and Douglas Kruse, "Employee Involvement Efforts: Incidence, Correlates and Effects," Unpublished manuscript, University of California, Berkeley, 1990.

5

Marketing and Total Quality Management

RAYMOND KORDUPLESKI, ROLAND RUST, AND

ANTHONY ZAHORIK

Marketing: Quality's Missing Link

An organizational commitment to serve the customer, at both strategic and tactical levels, is essential for the successful performance of quality programs. In his Introduction, Cole includes it on his list of critical factors. Dr. Kano identifies customer satisfaction as one of the four basic concepts necessary to implement TQM in his survey of the history of the U.S. quality movement, and includes as one indicator of a mature quality programs a recognition of the importance of achieving customer satisfaction over concerns about the costs of quality.[1] And yet many of the failures of quality programs that Cole alludes to have been due to the failure of quality-related "fads" to improve products and services in ways that were meaningful to customers. How can this be?

Putting the customer first is a very old concept, although it is certainly not always done as well as it should be. Are there any companies that don't at least claim to be concerned about their customers' needs? Many companies now even routinely monitor their customers' satisfaction. In addition, these same companies often employ sophisticated TQM methods, regularly checking processes using control charts and other tools described by Dr. Kano. A sincere desire to satisfy customers combined with a concerted effort to improve quality should be a formula for success. And yet that success has not always been forthcoming.

The reasons are often not in the lack of will or good intentions, but in the implementation. Organizations with high quality goals don't always relate them to customer needs. Too often results of customer satisfaction studies are not properly related back to internal control measures. In this chapter we will discuss a procedure to assure that quality process measures are focused on those aspects of quality most meaningful to customers.

Losing Sight of the Customer

Quality programs almost always refer to themselves as customer-driven, market-driven, customer-oriented, or the like. Satisfying customers is essential to success; an effective organization must listen to its customers and serve them effectively. Yet if we look closely at what many quality programs are actually doing, we find much less attention being paid to the customer than we might expect.

Because all work is part of a process, the typical quality program places considerable effort on improving business processes. Improvement teams, quality circles, and quality councils are all designed to examine an organization's internal processes. When managers refer to such terms as TQM, what they usually mean is using the tools of quality to improve internal business processes, to produce Quality in Daily Work, as described by Dr. Kano.[2] When improvements are made, too often the customer benefits arising from these activities are merely incidental.

Why? To get some idea, let us take a close look at who the people in the quality movement are. There is considerable participation by quality control engineers, manufacturing people, operations managers, human resources people, and organizational behavior experts. A group notable by its absence is the function closest to the customer: marketing.

Whatever happened to marketing? Why are marketing people not more involved in quality improvement? Who is to blame?

The answers to these questions are not simple. One common problem is that the marketing function has not shown much interest in the quality movement. This is because being close to the customer has traditionally been marketing's job. Thus, marketing people tend to see quality movement people as "Johnny come latelys" intruding on their turf.

In fact, protecting turf is a major impediment to progress in the quality movement, because quality improvement by its very nature crosses functional boundaries. If marketing feels that it "is already doing it," then any intrusion in getting close to the customer on the part of the quality movement is likely to be resented. Mizuno notes that one of the primary obstacles to quality improvement is the managerial type who believes total quality "is being applied when actually it is not."[3]

Marketing's lack of participation in the quality movement is not entirely marketing's fault, however. Marketing traditionally has been focused *outside* the organization. With quality improvement programs focused on *internal* processes, the link between marketing and quality is not natural. Thus, it is easy to leave marketing out. Yet without marketing's involvement, how can the organization be sure that its internal improvements are relevant to the customer?

Marketing people typically have the primary responsibility for determining customer needs, and developing programs for meeting those needs better than competitors. Greater involvement by marketing in focusing quality improvement efforts can result in process improvements that deliver the customer benefits needed to capture market share. Marketing, and especially marketing's role as the voice of the customer in the organization, has too often been ignored in quality management, with the result that internal process improvement often has had no clear connection to customer needs.

Even in services, the emphasis of quality improvement programs has generally been on the improvement of internal business processes, through techniques such as flowcharting processes, instead of focusing on the needs and wants of the customers. One result has been that the link between customer-perceived quality (which we call true quality) and business process quality (which we call internal quality) has been underemphasized. So has the link between customer sales response and quality improvement.

It is true that almost all quality-oriented organizations do customer surveys. But too often the survey is conducted, results are tabulated, and then nobody knows what to do. No structure ties customer satisfaction to internal business processes. The customer side of quality is seldom linked effectively to process quality improvement effort. But customer satisfaction surveys, professionally managed by marketing, can provide the strategic intelligence needed to direct the forces working on process improvement so that their impact is an increase in market share.

Total quality management implies managing and controlling processes to provide total quality to the customers. Total quality means completely satisfying customers on the full range of product and service needs. Thus, we define quality in terms of customer satisfaction, and view a business process as a means to an end, rather than an end in itself. It is crucial that the business process be solidly linked to eventual customer satisfaction and market response.

Making the Link

Let us consider how this link can be established. Customers have needs, and quality may be defined as the ability of a business to meet those needs. In other words, quality management must first be customer-directed. Only then do internal business processes become relevant, and only to the extent that they affect the business' ability to meet customer needs.

A few existing methods help make quality more customer-directed. The "house of quality" approach, otherwise known as quality function deployment (QFD), may be used to relate design quality to customer needs.[4] This method shows how products or services can be created in such a way that customer needs are explicitly considered and linked to specific design decisions. QFD is very useful for designing new products or services. It is less useful in the context of existing products or services, in which the continual improvement of the *delivery* of the product or service is the focus, rather than the one-time design of a new product or service.

Any product or service may be thought of as involving four distinct aspects: the physical product, the service product, the service environment, and the service delivery. The quality perceived by the customer is formed by the perceived quality of all these aspects. Let us consider, for example, a customer shopping for a new car. The physical product is the car itself, the service product includes such things as how the sales staff is trained to interact with customers ("extended negotiations" or "no haggling" constitute one service product decision), the service environment includes, for example, the showroom, and the service delivery is the actual interaction between the dealership personnel and the customer (e.g., was the salesperson too pushy?).

Quality of the physical product is often thought to be measured by conformance to mechanical specifications. Statistical quality control is used to assure product quality. This overlooks the importance of customer perceptions. We may talk meaningfully of both internal quality (how well the product conforms to specifications) and external ("true") quality (how good the customer thinks it is). Internal quality is not much use unless it links to true (customer-perceived) quality, because ultimately the customer has all of the votes (dollars).

Thus, to make the quality improvement program link to the customer, we must accomplish the following tasks:

1. Identify and measure customer needs.
2. Link customer satisfaction measures to internal process measures.

To link the quality improvement to the shareholder we must also measure the link between perceived quality and market share, revenues, and profits.

Identifying and measuring customer needs actually involves two distinct steps. First, customer needs must be determined. This almost always requires a nonstructured, exploratory approach (focus groups, depth interviews, analysis of complaints and suggestions, MBWA, and similar techniques). Only after the most important customer needs have been identified is it appropriate to measure perceived quality on any sort of rating scale. A common error is to obtain scaled responses on perceived quality, based on items *management* thinks are important, rather than finding out directly, and in the customer's words, what the important customer needs are. This risks making changes based on extensive quantitative data about issues that are unimportant to the customer.

For example, consider the bank manager who measures customer satisfaction on those aspects the manager "knows" are important: interest rates, account fees, and special charges. Results of a customer satisfaction survey based on those aspects will likely result in minor adjustments in rates and charges. Suppose, however (as two of us actually found in research we conducted for a Southern bank), that the key drivers of customer satisfaction and customer retention are actually such "warm and fuzzy" aspects as whether the bank "listens to my needs" or "whether the bank manager knows me." The survey on satisfaction with rates and charges would turn up nothing about this. A truly effective survey would have to include the variables that the *customer* thought were important.

Making Process Improvements Meaningful

Once the levels of perceived quality are known, it is then necessary to use this information to affect management within the organization. The processes of a business exist primarily to satisfy customer needs. Therefore, the quality of the output of the process is the degree of customer satisfaction generated. To a manager or process team wishing to improve quality, the most important customer-oriented issue in quality is relating internal process measures to customer satisfaction. The idea is that the internal process measures directly involve performance that can be managed. Thus, if management can improve the internal measures, and if a statistical link exists between the internal process measures and quality as perceived by the customer, then a predictable improvement should also take place in customer-perceived (true) quality.

For example, let us consider the billing process. What is its purpose? Many managers would immediately respond with, "To get the money." Therefore, the measurement of the process would be "Did we get the money?" and such things as 30, 60, or 90 day collection indexes would be calculated. Obviously, any quality management efforts would be focused on improving those numbers.

Yet if we look at billing from a customer's perspective, it's easy to realize that the billing process exists to provide accurate, easy-to-pay bills, with no surprises. Accurate billing, easy payment, and account inquiry services are important issues in the quality of the billing process. But how many businesses measure the percentage of bills that contain surprises, or the percentage that cannot be resolved in one call? How many quality improvement initiatives really focus on customer needs?

To show how this might work, consider the following example. Suppose that customer satisfaction surveys indicate that a bank's customers are unhappy about the time they spend waiting for a drive-through window. The true quality measure in this case is the degree of customer satisfaction with waiting time. A plausible internal measure might be the actual time waited, collected from a sample of drive-through customers, using stopwatches. Each drive-through location would then have an average waiting time and an average satisfaction with waiting time. A strong relationship between the two would imply that decreasing the waiting time would positively impact satisfaction, and an emphasis on decreasing waiting time would then be an appropriate quality goal. Improving the process (decreasing waiting time) is only appropriate once the link to customer satisfaction has been established.

This link is especially useful to management if the true quality measures are obtained separately for each major managerial process (e.g., billing, sales, product, maintenance, and repair). The internal process measures, also within processes, are then linked to the appropriate true quality measure. The process-specific true quality measures may then be used in combination to provide a link to overall measures of customer satisfaction.

Ultimately, justifying a quality program must involve a connection to the bottom line. Thus, the next step must involve determining the marketing impact of quality in terms of sales and market share. We see that the customer side of quality involves understanding customer needs, measuring true quality, linking it to internal quality, and tracing the results of internal quality all the way back to customer behavior in the marketplace, in the form of sales and market share. The next section shows how to link internal process measures to customer satisfaction/service quality measures. The following section then addresses how to link improvements all the way to revenues and market share.

Making Quality Measures Managerially Meaningful

A common scenario is repeated all too often at corporations throughout the world. The company collects measures of service quality and/or customer satisfaction, to see where it stands with the customers. The results are tabulated and then scrutinized carefully by management. But those results are not used systematically and logically to make changes. Consequently, the customer surveys have little direct impact on management. For all practical purposes, the customer satisfaction/quality information might as well not have been collected.

What has happened? The questions seem irrelevant to management because no link to managerial processes or managerial responsibilities is present. Consider the question "How friendly are the Ace Bank personnel?" This might seem useful because it will tell us something about friendliness, which presumably is important to customers. But there is no link to any particular managerial process—no way for anyone to *take ownership* of the results. Who should become more friendly? Is it the tellers, the managers, the drive-through personnel? To be useful, the question must be asked so that managers of a specific process can take responsibility.

What is missing? The information from the customer, while potentially valuable, is wasted because it is not linked to the processes that are being managed. The purpose of collecting the quality measures in the first place is to improve management. With that in mind, it is clear that the customer survey information must be structured around the design of the organization itself. In other words, the information obtained must directly relate to specific business processes.

If questions are to be asked in such a way that they correlate with specific business processes, what should those questions be? It is essential that they refer to *customer* issues, selected by the customers themselves, in their own words, and not to internal process measures.

At some point, however, internal process measures must be tied to customer needs. This provides a method of measuring whether the process is meeting those needs; these internal measures must be related statistically to the customer needs measures.

An overview of a plan for linking quality measures and implementing quality improvement is shown in Figure 5.1. This schema depicts the hierarchy of quality measures collected by the General Business Systems Division of AT&T. In addition to its widespread implementation at AT&T, this approach has been implemented by several companies internationally.[5] This approach was also used by AT&T Universal Card in its Baldrige Award-winning quality program. We will examine each part of the diagram in detail, to explain how the measures are collected and used.

Business Processes

To make the quality measures relevant to management, these measures are grouped by business process. In the case shown, the business processes used are Product, Sales, Installation, Repair, and Billing. The processes selected will vary by company, but every process allow a particular business unit and manager to take ownership over the results. For example, there is presumably a manager in charge of the billing process who has the authority to make quality improvements.

We see from the diagram that overall quality is made up of the combined quality of the various business processes. In fact, if we collect an overall quality measure from each customer, as well as an overall quality measure for each of the business processes, then the business process overall quality measures can be used to predict the customer overall quality measure. In our example we see that 30% of the variation in overall quality is explained by Product, 30% by

	Business Process	**Customer Need**	**Internal Metric**
Overall Quality	Product (30%)	Reliability (40%)	% Repair Call
		Easy to Use (20%)	% Calls for Help
		Features/Functions (40%)	Function Performance Test
	Sales (30%)	Knowledge (30%)	Supervisor Observations
		Response (25%)	% Proposal Made on Time
		Follow-up (10%)	% Follow-up Made
	Installation (10%)	Delivery Interval (30%)	Average Order Interval
		Does Not Break (25%)	% Repair Reports
		Installed When Promised (10%)	% Installed on Due Date
	Repair (15%)	No Repeat Trouble (30%)	% Repeat Reports
		Fixed Fast (25%)	Average Speed of Repair
		Kept Informed (10%)	% Customers Informed
	Billing (15%)	Accuracy, No Surprises (45%)	% Billing Inquiries
		Resolve on First Call (35%)	% Resolved First Call
		Easy to Understand (10%)	% Billing Inquiries

Figure 5.1. Strategic marketing information used to focus business processes.

Sales, 10% by Installation, 15% by Repair, and 15% by Billing. This gives some preliminary idea of where the best opportunity may be for quality improvement. We see, for example, that service aspects contribute 70% of the variation.

Customer Needs

While organizing the measures by business process may be helpful to management, we still must be careful to determine the most important customer needs, *in the customer's words.* Thus, for example, under Billing we see that the most important customer needs in Billing are "accuracy, no surprises," "resolve on first call," and "easy to understand." All these items can be monitored. For example, the question "Was your bill easy to understand?" is perfectly meaningful to a customer, and it can be included on a service quality questionnaire.

Figure 5.1 shows the most important customer needs identified for each of the five business processes. Again, we may evaluate the relative importance of each need with respect to the impact it has on the related business-process overall perceived quality measure.

Identification of customer needs is best accomplished as a preliminary research step, using exploratory techniques. Some useful methods for identifying customer needs are focus group interviews, discussions with front-line employees, analysis of complaints, and the critical incident technique.

Internal Metrics

Customer needs are generally not expressed in managerially meaningful language. To make customer needs relevant, there must be a link between customer needs and processes that can be directly managed. Thus, we attempt to construct, for each customer need, an internal metric associated as closely as possible with that customer need. If we are successful, there should be a strong statistical relationship between the internal metric and the quality score for the corresponding customer need.

As an example, consider the customer need "accuracy, no surprises," under Billing. An internal metric that seems to associate with this is "percent billing inquiries," the percentage of billed customers who make an inquiry about their bill. The idea is that if the bill is wrong, the customer is more likely to inquire. If the number of inquiries goes down, that probably is a sign that fewer customers are finding mistakes. Note that we *do not assume* that this link is actually there. Rather we directly ask about billing accuracy, and monitor percent billing inquiries separately. Assuming we can find a strong statistical link between the two, only then are we justified to use percent billing inquiries as a market-driven quality measure.

Internal measures are of great managerial usefulness because:

1. They link very closely with processes which can be specifically managed.
2. They are usually collected more continuously than customer measures, which means that there is opportunity for more immediate feedback in the quality improvement process.

In many organizations internal process measures have existed for far longer than true quality measures such as customer satisfaction. Companies with more of a production orientation tend to have many internal measures (and perhaps not so many customer measures). In our experience, companies that start collecting quality/customer satisfaction measures, and then correlate them with internal measures, are sometimes in for a shock.

For example, consider the travel agency that desired to improve the quality of its telephone operations. To address this, they set up a service specification stating that the phone should be answered in two rings or less. They then measured the proportion of the time in which this occurred. Several years later they began a customer satisfaction measurement program and measured the satisfaction with telephone service. The expectation was that agents who answered the phone quicker would have more satisfied customers.

Much to the company's surprise, there was a *negative* relationship between the internal and external measures. Further investigation revealed that agents who answered the phone quickly did so by quickly and abruptly getting rid of customers on other lines. Those customers became unhappy with the service they received. Improving the speed of answering was actually *counterproductive* to improving quality. Number of rings was the wrong internal measure to collect.

In this case, assuming that the customer satisfaction measures have been collected appropriately, the challenge is to find new internal measures that do a better job of predicting changes in customer perceptions of quality. Changing the internal measures to be more customer-relevant can be traumatic to many managers who are used to the old measures, and it can present a formidable political problem.

An Implementation Story

The development of appropriate internal measures is not without problems. Consider a test program at AT&T's long distance repair center in Columbus, Ohio, which was used to develop and implement some of the "internally taken, externally focused" customer measures shown in Figure 5.1. The center had a history of average customer satisfaction ratings, as measured by the percent of customers choosing "good" or "excellent" responses to the question "Overall how satisfied were you with the repair service? Would you say it was poor, fair, good or excellent?" In particular, before the test began, an average of 85% percent of customers said they were satisfied with the overall repair experience, with 55% rating the service as good and 30% rating it as excellent.

Besides the question about the overall service, the customer questionnaire also contained questions about specific processes and their dimensions—for example, "Did you have to report the trouble again?" and "Did the technician keep you informed of the status of the repair?" These questions were asked to help the repair center diagnose the specific drivers of customer satisfaction and dissatisfaction with repairs. While looking for statistical relationships among responses, the data could also be used to derive the relative importance weights of the individual service components to overall service.

Before the test began, the repair center team was given the list of customer needs and their importance weights. The team was instructed to develop internal measures of process results that could be taken on a daily basis that would match as closely as possible the list of customer needs. After statistically determining that the internal measures did indeed track closely with customer satisfaction, the measures were to be used by the team for a day-by-day estimate of how well they were doing on the things that mattered to the customers.

The managers and staff were hesitant to participate at first. They felt they were already subject to too many measurements and didn't want to be held accountable for even more performance indicators. They also believed they were already providing good customer service and could not afford to drive the satisfaction scores into the high 90s. For example, statistical analysis of the data had indicated that customers liked to be regularly kept informed of the status of a repair. Customers who had answered yes to the question "Were you kept informed of the status of the repair progress?" were also much more likely to answer the overall satisfaction question with a good or excellent rating than customers who were not kept informed. It seemed natural to suggest that measures be kept on the repair center's ability to keep customers informed. But when a repair technician was asked if he called all customers on a regular hourly basis to keep them informed he responded that the repair center couldn't afford to do it: there just wasn't enough time or personnel. Keeping track of how often information calls were made to customers seemed to him to be a complete waste of time and effort. Besides, he said, "Most customers would be annoyed with the frequent calls"—another illustration of what Dr. Kano describes as the use of "intuition" over "data." He did occasionally call customers back with the status of their repairs, but only when they were disturbed with the repair progress and they specifically asked to be kept informed. In other words, AT&T was apparently calling only those customers who were already dissatisfied and trying to placate them.

As the study got underway, the center's managers asked to be relieved of many of the measurements that were currently being reported on a regular basis to upper management. They realized that the study's approach to developing measures was the correct one, and that it was producing measures more relevant to customer concerns than many current operational measures in use, such as phone answering speed, the amount of time spent talking, and the number of problems handled per technician per day.

After the new measures were established, it quickly became apparent that the results would be worth the effort. Within three months the overall satisfaction level improved from 85% to 100%. In addition, the percent of customers who rated the service as excellent went from 30% to 70%. The members of the test center team were excited. Using the continually monitored internally-taken, externally-focused customer measures, the test center could predict the levels of customer satisfaction with service components. For example, the internal records now indicated whether the repair status and follow-up calls were being made, and based on that knowledge the center team could predict improvements or drops in customer satisfaction levels.

The team was recognized at the first AT&T Quality conference. They were established as a role model for others to follow. Their story was written up and circulated to other similar centers in the company.

Quality and Market Share

In the previous section we saw how to link customer needs fulfillment to internal business processes and measures. That is one part of the marketing side of quality improvement. The other part is the outcome in terms of measurable consumer behavior: specifically, the impact of quality on sales and market share and, ultimately, profits. Research linking quality to behavioral outcomes has proliferated in recent years.[6] Some of it has demonstrated the link from quality to customer attitudes and behavioral intentions, while other research has measured the impact of quality on customer retention[7] or on the financial performance of companies.[8]

In fact, many quality programs are pulled before they have had time to achieve their intended results because managers fail to understand the market dynamics and time lags involved in building market share from quality improvements. Investments in quality must be treated like other investments: Money must be spent where it will have the greatest impact on sales and market share, and must be given sufficient time to produce results. If the growth in sales is large enough compared to the money spent to achieve it, then the investment is worthwhile.

This remark suggests that quality improvements are not all equally valid uses of funds. To make knowledgeable investments in quality improvements, managers should understand how great an impact the changes are likely to have on customer satisfaction, and how long it will be before the effects are realized. From this information it is possible to estimate the likely "return on quality" from various expenditures and to allocate resources to the most productive ones.[9]

How Market Share Results from Quality

Figure 5.2 shows how market share can result from quality. We see two primary pathways: the retention of existing customers and the attraction of new ones. Existing customers may be presented with high or low quality. This influences two important behaviors. A satisfied customer (one who perceives quality at or above expectations) is more likely to be retained as a customer and also more likely to engage in positive word of mouth. Potential new customers may then be swayed by this positive word of mouth and be attracted to the

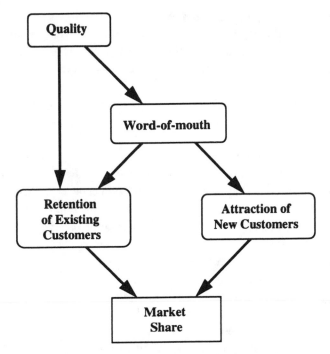

Figure 5.2.   How market share results from quality.

product or service. Thus, quality has both an offensive and defensive effect: offensive through word of mouth, and defensive through customer retention (as well as word of mouth from other customers).

We specifically exclude advertising from our immediate consideration. For example, Ford used its "Quality Is Job One" slogan for years before sales picked up. It was not until quality actually started to improve noticeably that Ford's market share rebounded strongly. The advertising alone was fruitless without the impact of customer retention and positive word of mouth.

Time Lags in Market Share Effects

One reason for the rejection of quality initiatives described by Cole[10] was the short-term focus of managers and their demands that quality programs pay instant dividends. This expectation is generally unrealistic even for dramatic changes in product quality.

From Figure 5.2, we can make some predictions about how market share (among current choices) will react to improvements in quality. First we can see that existing customers may be retained in higher numbers. In product markets, however, this is subject to the effect of the purchase cycle. Customers, even if they have been exposed to high quality, are unlikely to purchase again until the end of the purchase cycle. For example, consider a customer who purchases a mainframe computer. It may be five or more years before satisfaction with this purchase affects the next purchase. Thus, we can see that improvements in quality may have a lagged effect on market share. A similar mechanism may occur in service markets. For example, a vacation traveler may not take the next trip for a year, and the effect of this year's service will not be felt until then.

Lag effects may also result from word of mouth. Customers do not immediately tell all their friends and acquaintances about their experiences with a product or service. Instead, the extent of word of mouth gradually tapers off over time. Consider a potential customer who is contemplating a purchase. That customer may receive many pieces of information based on word of mouth. It may take several positive reports for that customer to change a negative quality perception (or vice versa). Thus, an improvement in quality should not be expected to have its greatest impact immediately. That impact will occur only after the positive reports have had enough opportunity to filter in.

To get some sense of the time lag in market share following an improvement in perceived quality, we present an example from one division of AT&T. Figure 5.3 shows the market share effects at various lag lengths. Because the purchase cycle is quite long, it is most likely that these lags represent word-of-mouth lag effects. In other words, it takes a few months in this industry for the good news (or bad news) about quality to diffuse. We see that, according to our data, the lag is about four to six months. A quality improvement today would have its greatest impact on market share about four to six months later. Of course, in another industry with a different purchase cycle and different patterns of word of mouth, a very different lag structure might be encountered. For example, Federal Express calls itself a 48-hour business, because if they don't meet their customers' needs on any given day, they will begin to lose market share in about 48 hours. That's how fast the purchase cycle is in that market!

The Customer Defines Quality

Market success results from customer decisions. Thus, the customer is the ultimate judge of quality. The customer side of quality involves the needs, satisfaction, and buying behavior of customers. These are precisely the issues that have been less adequately addressed by the quality movement so far. Of course, it is not customer needs, customer satisfaction, and buying behavior *in isolation* that are important to the quality improvement process. One must *link* these factors to the management process. *Without totally satisfying customers by*

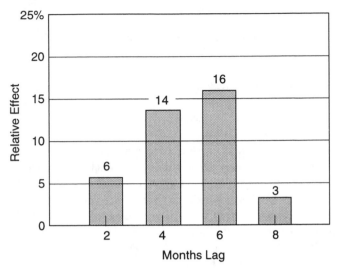

Figure 5.3.   Time lags in the effect of quality on market share.

identifying customer needs, expressed in the customers' own words, linking customer satisfaction and customer-perceived quality to internal managerial processes, and measuring the impact of quality improvement on the marketplace, there can be no true Total Quality Management.

Marketing, business' most customer-oriented function, is primarily *externally* focused. This focus is at odds with quality improvement, which, unfortunately, is in many firms primarily *internally* focused. Thus, the challenge for quality programs is to incorporate the marketing side of quality, which requires making customer needs and perceptions meaningful internally. Similarly, the challenge for marketing is to ensure that the information it collects about the customer may be used strategically to improve quality. In other words, the key is finding ways to link external measures of customer needs fulfillment and purchase behavior to internal quality measures. Ideally, the internal measure should reflect the quality of the internal process that drives the external measure of customer satisfaction. The problem involves modeling statistical relationships, but the true challenge is not the statistics (which often may be kept simple), but the invention of appropriate internal measures and rewards that correspond strongly to the external customer measures.

There is no Total Quality Management until *both* customer needs and marketing impact are measured, and both are linked to internal business processes. Only by understanding this critical relationship can the firm expect to deliver quality as customers define it.

Notes

1. Noriaki Kano, "A Perspective on Quality Activities in American Firms," Chapter 11 of this volume.
2. Kano, op. cit.
3. Shigeru Mizuno, *Company-Wide Total Quality Control* (Hong Kong: Nordica International, Ltd., 1992), p. 27.
4. See "The House of Quality" by John Hauser and Don Clausing, in the May-June 1988 *Harvard Business Review*.
5. See, for example, "Driving Your Business with Customer Satisfaction Measurements," by Rodger Gallagher, Telecom Corporation of New Zealand Ltd., 1992.
6. See "Modeling the Impact of Service Quality on Profitability: A Review," by Anthony Zahorik and Roland Rust, in *Advances in Services Marketing and Management*, edited by Swartz, Bowen, and Brown. Greenwich, CT: JAI Press, 1992.
7. See "Zero Defections: Quality Comes to Services," by Frederick R. Reichheld and W. Earl Sasser, in the September-October 1990 *Harvard Business Review*.
8. See *The PIMS Principles* by Robert Buzzell and Bradley Gale. NY: The Free Press, 1987.
9. See *Return on Quality* by Roland Rust, Anthony Zahorik and Timothy Keiningham. Chicago: Probus Publishing, 1994.
10. Robert E. Cole, "Introduction," Chapter 1 of this volume.

6

Downsizing, Quality, and Performance

KIM CAMERON

In this chapter, I discuss the nature of organizational downsizing and its frequent adverse impact on quality. Although it is widely practiced, downsizing stands as a major threat to the success of the quality movement unless it is approached in a way that reinforces quality values and principles. Cole's list of reasons for spectacular failures in the American quality movement in the introductory chapter does not include downsizing, but that is only because downsizing is not generally viewed as a quality initiative. Downsizing often precedes or accompanies quality initiatives in organizations, however, and its consequences are most often inhibitors to successful TQM. Moreover, based on the reported plans of companies in the United States, the pervasiveness of downsizing is not likely to diminish during the current decade.[1] In fact, the number of U.S. firms engaging in downsizing has been escalating each year since the mid 1980s. Without merging these two activities—downsizing and quality—neither will be as successful as it could and should be.

The Prevalence of Downsizing

It is not news that organizational downsizing has become the norm rather than an exception experienced by only a few companies in trouble. Almost every practicing manager who reads this chapter will likely have encountered downsizing firsthand in some part of his or her organization. It is rare to go a week without reading about one more firm's massive layoff or downsizing effort. Almost no companies, especially those of medium and large size, have avoided downsizing in the last decade. In fact, a recent survey by the American Management Association found that between a third and a half of medium- and large-sized forms in the United States had downsized *every year* since 1988.[2]

It is not only for-profit companies that have caught the downsizing fever, Reductions are commonplace in sectors ranging from the federal government to trade unions. A law was recently passed, for example, mandating a reduction of over 30% of military personnel in the United States by 1995. This legislation will eliminate the jobs of over a million people, and it motivated a recent Jim Berry cartoon in which two military officers are shown studying a personnel chart with a downward trend line labeled "Operation Downsize." One commented to the other, "Peace is hell."

Unfortunately, downsizing and quality improvement are often antithetical. Cost considerations replace quality considerations as the priority, and paring down overhead takes precedence over customer satisfaction and employee empowerment, responsibility, and loyalty.

This frequently negative relationship between quality and downsizing exists because most firms are still typified by a seat-of-the-pants approach to downsizing. Strategies are guided by anecdotal experiences from colleagues who have downsized previously, habitual responses developed after having downsized multiple times, or mere "gut feel" for doing what seems right at the time. A set of validated guidelines or principles have not been widely adopted. Thus, downsizing is probably the most pervasive yet unsuccessful phenomenon in the business world. Its impact on quality and performance has been lamentable. One columnist recently concluded, "Downsizing, as commonly practiced, is a dud."[3]

Two empirical studies of multiple organizations are summarized and integrated in this chapter—one focusing mainly on downsizing using quality as a predictor, and the other focusing mainly on quality using downsizing as a predictor—in order to identify the ways in which downsizing and quality improvement can be mutually reinforcing. These two data sets are described briefly so that the bases for the conclusions drawn at the end of the chapter are clear.

Data Sources

In the first study, 30 organizations associated with the automotive industry were investigated over a five year period, 1987–1991. Each of these organizations engaged in downsizing during the study period, several more than once. The smallest of these organizations employed approximately 100 employees, the largest about 6000. The CEO of each firm was interviewed every six to nine months over the five years, and four rounds of questionnaires were collected from a sample of employees in each company. Survey items assessed downsizing practices, organization and work design characteristics, managerial behaviors, and quality processes. In gathering data, my colleagues and I were interested in determining the stategies these firms used to downsize, the impact downsizing had on each firm's performance, and the "best practices" that characterized the most successful firms.[4]

In the other study, focused on quality, surveys were collected each year for three years in 68 businesses in the automotive industry. Respondents completing the survey were 935 upper mid-level managers—126 in 1990, 338 in 1991, and 431 in 1992. The survey assessed the quality processes, practices, and culture of each of these 68 businesses that were independent from the firms in the first study. The study had three main objectives: to determine the level of advancement in each orgainzation's quality culture; to access the differences in organizational processes and practices between businesses with high quality outcomes and those with lower levels of outcomes; and to identify the main factors that predicted improvement in quality performance over the study period.[5]

The quality survey consisted of 120 items assessing the seven dimensions constituting the Malcolm Baldrige National Quality Award plus several other dimensions such as structure, use of quality tools, organizational priorities, approach to downsizing, and culture.

Common Outcomes of Downsizing

Admittedly, downsizing announcements usually lead to positive reactions from Wall Street. Table 6.1, for example, shows the change in several well-known firms' stock prices the day after a major downsizing announcement was made. Almost universally favorable reactions occurred because of the promise of cost

TABLE 6.1.   Effects of Downsizing on Stock Market Value

Company	Announced Cut	Percent of First Day Stock Change
IBM	60,000	up 7.7
Sears	50,000	up 3.6
Xerox	10,000	up 7.0
US West	9,000	up 4.6
McDonnell Douglas	8,700	up 7.9
RJR Nabisco	6,000	up 4.0
DuPont	4,500	up 3.4

Source: U.S. News and World Report, 12/20/93.

savings, reduced expenses, and increased competitiveness. Stockholders and analysts have continued to assume that downsizing produces desirable financial results.

Dysfunctional Results

Sometimes beneficial results do occur, but too often they do not. One recent survey found, for example, that two-thirds of companies that downsize end up doing it again a year later.[6] A study by Mitchell & Company, a consulting firm, found that stock prices of firms that downsized during the 1980s actually lagged the industry average at the beginning of the 1990s.[7] A survey by Right Associates, an outplacement firm, found that 74% of senior managers in downsized companies said that morale, trust, and productivity suffered after downsizing.[8] The Society for Human Resource Management reported that half of the 1468 firms it surveyed indicated that productivity deteriorated after downsizing.[9] Table 6.2 shows the results of a Wyatt survey that found a majority of organizations that downsized failed to achieved desired results. Only 9% reported an improvement in quality.[10]

In a review of literature on the results of layoffs, turnover, and job rotation policies, Bob Cole pointed out numerous problems associated with job loss from

TABLE 6.2.   Effects of Downsizing on Desired Outcomes

Desired Outcome	Percent of Firms That Achieved Desired Results
Reduced expenses	46
Increased profits	32
Improved cash flow	24
Increased productivity	22
Increased ROI	21
Increased competitive advantage	19
Reduced bureaucracy	17
Improved decision making	14
Increased customer satisfaction	14
Increased sales	13
Increased market share	12
Improved product quality	9
Technological advances	9
Increased innovation	7
Avoidance of a takeover	6

Source: Wall Street Journal, 6/6/91.

traditional downsizing. Among them were (1) loss of personal relationships between employees and customers; (2) destruction of employee and customer trust and loyalty; (3) disruption of smooth, predictable routines in the firm; (4) increases in formalization (reliance on rules), standardization, and rigidity; (5) loss of cross-unit and cross-level knowledge that comes from longevity and interactions over time; (6) loss of knowledge of how to respond to nonroutine aberrations faced by the firm; (7) decrease in documentation and therefore less sharing of information about changes; (8) loss of employee productivity; and (9) loss of a common organizational culture.[11] A 1993 *Time* magazine article accused many U.S. organizations of "dumbsizing" instead of downsizing because of the deleterious actions taken in pursuit of cost savings.[12] The point is, downsizing has become a strategy of choice for a great many organizations, yet its results are not always in harmony with quality principles or positively correlated with performance improvements.

In previously published work, my colleagues and I reported a series of attributes that we have discovered in most organizations that engage in downsizing or that face declining marketshare or revenues.[13] We have labeled these attributes "the dirty dozen," and they are summarized in Table 6.3.

The Dirty Dozen

In brief, we discovered that when most organizations engage in downsizing or experience the need to downsize, the threat-rigidity response tends to occur. That is, organizations become rigid, hunker down, and become turf-protective. They react first with conservative, across-the-board directives. Communication channels become constricted, and it is generally only good news that is passed upward. The emergence of organized, vocal, special-interest groups increases politics and conflict among organization members, and employee morale suffers. A "mean mood" overtakes the organization. Slack resouces (such as contingency accounts, reserves, or new project funds) are eliminated, but this sacrifices flexibility and the ability to adapt to future changes. Savings are used to meet operating expenses. An escalation of centralized decision making occurs where top managers increase their control over a decreasing resource pool, and mistakes become both more visible and less affordable. Lower level employees become increasingly fearful of making important (or risky) decisions without the approval or sign-off of upper management. This centralization leads to scapegoating of top leaders, however, as the frustrations and anxieties of organization members mount. The credibility of the top leaders suffers because of their implied failure to avoid the painful circumstances the organization is experiencing. A short-term orientation predominates so that long-term planning as well as innovation—inherently costly and risky—are abandoned.

TABLE 6.3. Negative Attributes Associated with Downsizing (The "Dirty Dozen")

Attribute	Explanation
Centralization	Decision making is pulled toward the top of the organization. Less power is shared.
Short-term, crisis mentality	Long-term planning is neglected. The focus is on immediacy.
Loss of innovativeness	Trial-and-error learning is curtailed. Less tolerance for risk and failure associated with creative activity.
Resistance to change	Conservatism and the threat-rigidity response lead to "hunkering down" and a protectionist stance.
Decreasing morale	Infighting and a "mean mood" permeate the organization.
Politicized special	Special interest groups organize and become more vocal. The climate becomes politicized.
Nonprioritized cutbacks	Across-the-board cutbacks are used to ameliorate conflict. Priorities are not obvious.
Loss of trust	Leaders lose the confidence of subordinates, and distrust among organization members increases.
Increasing conflict	Fewer resources result in internal competition and fighting for a smaller pie.
Restricted communication	Only good news is passed upward. Information is not widely shared because of fear and distrust.
Lack of teamwork	Individualism and disconnectedness make teamwork difficult. Individuals are not inclined to form teams.
Lack of leadership	Leadership anemia occurs as leaders are scapegoated, priorities are unclear, and a siege mentality prevails.

The point is, we found that downsizing produces these factors in almost all organizations—few avoid them. They are obviously attributes that are antithetical to principles of total quality management, and, thus, are damaging to quality improvements. A myopic focus on internal dynamics drives out a focus on satisfying customers; cutting costs replaces preventing errors as a key objective. However, some organizations do avoid the dirty dozen, and it is those few that are especially noteworthy. In other words, some firms downsize in ways that enhance customer focus and improve quality. I will describe them below.

First, however, it is important to be clear about what we mean by downsizing. The popular press usually equates downsizing with layoffs, but the term is used in a much broader sense here.

What Is Downsizing?

The term downsizing, of course, is less and less in fashion. Beginning in the late 1980s, rightsizing, then resizing, then restructuring, then re-engineering were substituted. I have kept track, in fact, of the terms being attributed for downsizing in the organizations I have studied over the past six or seven years. Table 6.4 lists several of the ones encountered so far.

In most cases these alternatives are used to avoid the negative connotations associated with downsizing. Regardless of the word or phrase used, however, what these terms have in common is a set of activities, generally undertaken on the part of the management of an organization, designed to improve organizational efficiency, productivity, and/or competitiveness. They each represent a strategy implemented by managers that affects the size of the organization's workforce, costs, and work processes. Here I use *downsizing* as the encompassing concept.

On the surface, downsizing can be interpreted as merely a reduction in organizational size. But when this is the case, downsizing is confused with the concept of *decline*, which also can be interpreted as a reduction in organizational size. Thus, four major attributes of downsizing help define it and identify the commonalities among all these similar concepts—*intent, personnel, efficiency,* and *work processes.*

TABLE 6.4.   Alternate Labels for Downsizing

Building-down	Rebuilding
Compressing	Redeploying
Consolidating	Redesigning
Contracting	Redirecting
Declining	Reduction-in-force
De-hiring	Re-engineering
Demassing	Renewing
De-recruiting	Reorganizing
Dismantling	Reshaping
Downshifting	Resizing
Functionalizing	Restructuring
Leaning-up	Retrenching
Racheting-down	Revitalizing
Rationalizing	Rightsizing
Reallocating	Slimming
Reassigning	Slivering
Rebalancing	Streamlining

Intent

Downsizing is not something that happens *to* an organization, but it is something that organization members undertake purposively. This implies, first of all, that downsizing involves an intentional set of activities.

Personnel

Second, downsizing usually involves reductions in personnel, although it is not limited solely to headcount reductions. A variety of personnel reduction strategies, such as transfers, outplacement, retirement incentives, buy-out packages, layoffs, and attrition, are associated with downsizing. Some instances might occur in which new products, sources of revenue, or additional work are added without a commensurate number of employees. In this case, because fewer workers are employed per unit if output compared to some pervious level of employment, technically the workforce has been reduced.

Efficiency

The third characteristic of downsizing focuses on improving the efficiency of the organization. The main intent of downsizing is to reduce waste. This usually occurs as a reaction to a loss, a decline, or a threat, but it may also happen proactively (in anticipation) in order to contain costs, enhance revenue, or bolster competitiveness.

Processes

Finally, downsizing affects work processes, wittingly or unwittingly. When the workforce shrinks, for example, fewer employees are left to do the same amount of work, and this has an impact on what work gets done and how. Moreover, when downsizing includes restructuring and eliminating work (e.g., discontinuing functions, abolishing hierarchical levels, merging units, redesigning tasks), this also leads to a redesign of the retained processes.

This way of defining downsizing focuses on the *organization* as the unit of analysis, not the individual or the industry. Intent, personnel, efficiency, and processes all refer to what the organization does as a unit. At the individual level of analysis, quite a lot is known about the effects of downsizing on the psychological reaction of individuals to layoffs and job loss. Impacts on financial well-being, physical and emotional health, personal attitudes, family relationships, and other personal factors have been investigated widely.[14] Similarly, industry-level downsizing or restructuring is also a well-researched topic, including studies of merging companies, segmenting markets, divesting unrelated businesses, forming multinational economic alignments, consolidating industry structures, and managing national employment trends.[15] On the other hand, the relationships between downsizing and quality at the organizational level of analysis have hardly been investigated. Little empirical work has appeared to date on the association between downsizing and total quality management (TQM) objectives.

This chapter focuses on organizational-level downsizing, or the intentional set of activities implemented to improve organizational costs, efficiency, and performance. Unfortunately, the intended positive benefits from downsizing have often been disappointing, and the relationship of downsizing with quality and customer focus have all but been ignored. In fact, in many organizations interest in achieving quality objectives is postponed or shelved entirely when downsizing becomes the required priority. To see how downsizing and quality can be mutually reinforcing, however, it is necessary to review the ways in which firms institute downsizing strategies.

General Strategies for Downsizing

One of the key findings from the five-year study of downsizing was the emergence of three different types of strategies used by organizations to downsize. Only one of these strategies is compatible with principles of TQM, and it is by far the least frequently used alternative. Table 6.5 summarizes the characteristics of these three strategies. I have labeled them: (1) *workforce reduction strategies*, (2) *organization redesign strategies*, (3) *systemic strategies*.

Workforce Reduction

Every organization in my study employed workforce reduction strategies between 1987 and 1991. These strategies focus mainly on eliminating headcount or reducing the number of employees in the workforce. They include early retirements, transfers and outplacement, buy-out packages, golden parachutes, attrition, job banks, and layoffs or firings. Such actions were ususally executed immediately via top-down directives, and they were almost always implemented across-the-board since the objective was to reduce headcount numbers quickly.

The disadvantages of workforce reduction strategies are illustrated by comparing them to a scenario of throwing a grenade into a crowded room, closing the door, and expecting the explosion to eliminate a certain percentage of the workforce. It is difficult to predict exactly who will be eliminated and who will remain. It is hopeless to predict which employees will take advantage of an early retirement offer or buy-out package, for example. It is also impossible to deter-

TABLE 6.5.   Three Types of Downsizing Strategies

| | Downsizing Strategies | | |
	Workforce Reduction	Work Redesign	Systemic
Focus	Reduce headcount	Redesign jobs, levels, units	Change the culture
Eliminate	People	Work	Standard operating procedures
Implementation time	Quick	Moderate	Extended
Payoff target	Short-term payoff	Moderate-term payoff	Long-term payoff
Inhibits	Long-term adaptability	Quick payback	Short-term savings
Examples	Attrition	Combine functions	Involve everyone
	Layoffs	Merge units	Simplify everything
	Early retirement	Redesign jobs	Bottom-up change
	Buy-out packages	Eliminate layers	Target hidden costs

mine what relevant knowledge, what institutional memory, and what critical skills will be lost to the organization when employees leave.

The main advantage of these strategies, in addition to providing an immediate shrinkage, are that they capture the attention of members of the organization to the serious condition that may exist, they motivate cost savings in day-to-day work, and they create readiness in the organization for further change. Quick-hit, across-the-board cuts get attention. In terms of Kano's "Quality Sweating Theory" discussed in the concluding chapter of this volume, workforce reduction can create the needed "crisis consciousness."

On the other hand, the harm caused by workforce reduction strategies may offset the positive effects of unfreezing the organization. Because downsizing is defined as a temporary program to be completed and abandoned under this strategy, it contradicts some cardinal principles of TQM, namely: continuous and long-term improvement, involving and empowering everyone, investing in human resources, and improving processes. When implemented in the absence of other strategies, "grenade-type" approaches to downsizing were rarely positive and generally negative in their consequences.

Organizational Redesign

The second type of downsizing strategy—organization redesign—aims at cutting out work in addition to or in place of workers. A little less than half of the organizations investigated in my study implemented a redesign strategy at least once during the study. These strategies include eliminating functions, hierarchical levels, divisions, or products; consolidating and merging units; and reducing work hours. These strategies are difficult to implement quickly because some restructuring of the organization is required. They are by and large, medium-term strategies in that they require some advanced analysis of the areas that should be consolidated or redesigned, followed by an elimination or a repositioning of subunits within the organization to reduce required tasks.

Unlike workforce reduction strategies, redesign strategies help avoid the problem of eliminating workers while maintaining the same amount of work for the organization to perform. Instead of piling more work on fewer employees, thereby risking overload and burnout, organization redesign strategies help assure that changes are targeted at the magnitude of work and organizational arrangements. The downsized organization can achieve a greater degree of efficiency because of its simplified structure.

These strategies are more compatible with TQM principles than headcount reduction strategies since they focus on work reduction as a priority over human resource reduction. They adopt a longer time horizon in terms of desired impact, and they have a less adverse effect on employee commitment, morale, and loyalty. On the other hand, workforce reduction strategies ignore continuous redesign of work processes, dissemination of an overriding philosophy of never-ending improvement, and holding everyone in the organization responsible for advancement—all key attributes of a TQM philosophy. Relationships with customers and knowledge of their preferences may still be destroyed, and downsizing is treated as a finite program with a beginning and an end. The ultimate target of change is organizational efficiency, not developing human resources and better serving customers.

Systemic Strategies

The third type of downsizing strategy, implemented by less than a third of the organizations in the study, is fundamentally different from the other two. It focuses on changing the organization's systems, culture, and the attitudes and values of employees, not just the size of the workforce, the configuration of the structure, or the magnitude of the work. It is systemic—that is, focused on *systems*—in two ways. It focuses on internal systems (e.g., values, communication, production, and human resource systems) and on external systems (e.g., the production chain including upstream suppliers and downstream customers). This type of strategy involves redefining downsizing as a way of life, as an ongoing process, as a basis for continuous improvement, rather than as a program or target. Downsizing is equated with simplification of all aspects of the organization, including suppliers, inventories, design processes, production methods, marketing and sales support, and so on. Costs all along the customer chain, especially invisible and unmeasured costs, are the main targets. Examples of downsizing targets include reducing wait time, response time, rework, paper, incompatibilities in data and information systems, number of suppliers, rules and regulations, unused training, excessive audits, and so on.

Instead of being the first target for elimination, employees are defined as resouces to help generate and implement downsizing ideas in other areas. All employees are held accountable for reducing costs and finding improvements. A continuous improvement ethic is applied to the task of downsizing, and cost savings throughout the entire system of interorganizational relationships are pursued as a never-ending objective. Downsizing is not an activity that reaches an end point; instead, it continues indefinitely as a general philosophy for doing business. Organization revitalization is the objective. Serving customers, meeting their needs, and exceeding their expectations remain a core goal of downsizing activity, not just size reduction. Systemic strategies are obviously the most compatible with principles of TQM.

Because this third type of strategy requires a long-term perspective, it may not cause the immediate improvement in bottom-line numbers that workforce reduction strategies sometimes generate. Along with redesign strategies, systemic strategies often require some up-front investment in employee training, system diagnosis, and team formation. On the other hand, they avoid the need to continually implement grenade-type strategies each time cost savings are needed. One major auto company in the study, for example, has announced seventeen major downsizing actions in the last 30 years, each time a top-down, workforce reduction strategy that produced only temporary changes. Downsizing had to be repeated over and over because it was never treated as a way of life in the firm.

Implementing workforce reduction strategies may be necessary, of course, when a severe economic hardship is encountered. But the short-term payoffs are usually negated by long-term costs. The violation of the implicit employment contract between the organization and its employees leads to a loss of loyalty and commitment among the workforce and a deterioration in willingness to go the extra mile in behalf of customers. An attitude of "me-first" becomes dominant among employees. The dirty dozen flourish. The objective of systemic strategies, on the other hand, is to change systems in order to help avoid, over the long term, the need to implement continual, repetitive workforce reduction strategies.

These three downsizing strategies are not mutually exclusive, of course. Most organizations implemented several alternatives in a single type of strategy (e.g., layoffs, early retirements, buy-outs—all workforce reduction strategies). That is, they relied on one overall strategy type (usually workforce reduction) but used multiple examples of it. On the other hand, several firms implemented all three types of strategies, and the effects on quality when all three were applied were dramatically different than when workforce reduction strategies or organizational redesign strategies were used alone.

Effects of Downsizing on Quality and Performance

Not surprisingly, an increase in the dirty dozen attributes (see Table 6.3), which are likely to result from workforce reduction and organization redesign strategies implemented alone, is associated with a decrease in total quality in organizations. This is because the 12 negative attributes are directly contrary to principles of TQM. They inhibit participation, teamwork, empowerment, suggestions for improvement, innovation, and a focus on customers, among other things. The organization's focus on creating customer satisfaction is replaced by a focus on self-protection and survival. As Cole pointed out in the introductory chapter, "[traditional] cost cutting solutions ignore customer needs and penalize loyal employees." When the dirty dozen increase, in other words, quality decreases.

Unfortunately, most organizations in my study experienced an increase in the dirty dozen after they engaged in downsizing. A few, however, avoided the dirty dozen and, in addition, improved their effectiveness and performance. I was interested in discovering what accounted for this positive aberration.[16]

Research Results

Measures of organizational performance were obtained from the ratings of 2001 managers across 30 downsizing firms regarding the extent to which their organization's performance had improved as a result of downsizing. Respondents rated the relative effectiveness of their firm compared to (1) the expectations of key customers, (2) its best domestic and best global competitors, (3) the organization's own goals, and (4) its previous two years' performance. The presence of the dirty dozen attributes also were assessed, and data on productivity and costs were obtained from company records. These various measures of organizational performance were each analyzed separately using statistical procedures. In addition, the five highest performing firms were compared against the five lowest in order to uncover the factors that accounted for performance differences.

The results of these various statistical procedures are summarized in Table 6.6 Factors that significantly predict more than one desired outcome are included in the table. These factors indicate that of the most powerful predictors

TABLE 6.6. The Most Powerful Predictors of Positive Organizational Outcomes in Downsizing Firms—Improvement, Effective Performance, and Avoidance of the Dirty Dozen

---

Factors That Enhance Positive Outcomes When Downsizing

FACTORS RELATED TO HOW DOWNSIZING IS IMPLEMENTED

- Systematic analysis of tasks, processes and personnel (e.g., skills, time use, training) is conducted in advance of downsizing.
- Downsizing is implemented gradually and incrementally.
- Employees increase the amount of involvement and effort in their work.
- Positive goals and targets are established for downsizing results.

FACTORS RELATED TO QUALITY PROCESSES

- An advanced quality culture exists.
- Excellence is achieved in creative quality.
- Excellence is achieved in processes that detect quality errors.
- Hourly and salaried teamwork increases.
- Communication and participation increase among employees.
- Employees increase their involvement in planning and implementing downsizing.
- Close coordination occurs with customers and suppliers in downsizing.

Factors That Inhibit Positive Outcomes When Downsizing

FACTORS RELATED TO HOW DOWNSIZING IS IMPLEMENTED

- Downsizing occurs via headcount reduction strategies, i.e., attrition, layoffs, early retirements, and outsourcing.
- A top-down mandate serves as the motivation for downsizing.
- No work reduction occurs, just worker reductions.
- Reward and appraisal systems are introduced that are inconsistent with downsizing goals.

FACTORS RELATED TO QUALITY PROCESSES

- A less advanced quality culture exists.
- No improvements are occurring in product and service quality.

---

of the three major outcomes—improvement in firm performance, effectiveness that exceeded customer expectations and competitors' achievements, and avoidance of the dirty dozen—the presence of TQM processes dominate the list. Of the 11 factors positively associated with firm success, 7 are TQM processes. Of the significant factors that inhibit firm success, 2 of 6 indicate an absence of TQM processes.

Specifically, increases in employee teamwork, communication, participation, and close coordination with and involvement of customers and suppliers all are associated with positive firm performance when downsizing. Each is a key feature of TQM. Other predictors of success focus on the way downsizing was implemented, but the TQM factors are the most numerous and account for the most variance. A lack of quality improvement is a significant predictor of poor firm performance, although workforce reduction strategies dominate the list of negative predictors.

The most important predictor of positive organizational performance in the study, however, is the *quality culture* of the organizations. When firms had an "advanced quality culture," downsizing tended to be successful. When they had a "less advanced quality culture," downsizing tended to be less successful. To understand this important result, it is nescessary to explain what is meant by advanced and less advanced quality culture.

Quality Culture

A great deal of attention has been paid lately to the concept of organizational culture.[17] It refers to the underlying values, assumptions, beliefs, and meaning that characterize an organization. These underlying factors, in turn, are manifest through the organization's symbols, rituals, structures, and practices. The culture of an organization provides the context in which all activities are performed, so it is not surprising that organizational performance is influenced substantially by the type of culture developed. Significant differences have been found, for example, in firms from the same industry in Denmark and Holland because of the differences in national culture.[18] Various dimensions of culture have been identified in organizations, ranging from national culture to decision-making culture.

My own study of 68 organizations in the automotive industry (the second study described above) found that firms differ in terms of their values, assumptions, beliefs, and meaning (i.e., their culture) regarding quality. That is, different organizations have developed different quality cultures.

Quality culture refers to the general orientation or definition of quality adopted by an organization. Aside from the tools, techniques, or procedures used by members of an organization, different organizations tend to differ in the way they think about quality, approach quality, and define its main objective. Three different culture types were identified, which, not surprisingly, have developed chronologically over time as organizations have become more sophisticated in understanding and pursuing quality. A detailed explanation of these three types is available elsewhere,[19] so I will provide only a brief description here. No organization has a single, exclusive quality culture, but almost all are dominated by one culture type more than others.

The three types of quality culture range from a less advanced to a more advanced stage. A majority of organizations in my study operate in the stage of quality culture labeled *error detection*. In producing a product or service, these organizations try to avoid mistakes and reduce waste (e.g., rework, repair, scrap). They produce an outcome or deliver a service and then check to make certain that it was done correctly. In other words, they "inspect in" quality. In their relationships with customers, they try to avoid annoying or dissatisfying them by responding to complaints in a timely and accurate manner. They focus on what customers need or require, and ask customers after the product or service has been delivered how satisfied they are with it. By and large, this is a reactive or defensive approach to quality. It assures that the organization meets basic requirements, but errors are identified after the fact.

In a second, more advanced quality culture—*error prevention*—the organization shifts its emphasis toward avoiding mistakes by producing a product or service right the first time. Errors are prevented by focusing on *how* the task is accomplished (the process) and by holding all team members accountable for quality, not just inspectors or checkers. Finding out why mistakes occurred is more important than finding the mistake itself. Regarding relationships with customers, the emphasis moves from mere customer requirements and specifications to the preferences and expectations of customers. Nice-to-have criteria supplement need-to-have criteria. The organization strives to exceed basic expectations and to help customers reach a high level of satisfaction with the product or service, not just non-annoyance. This may happen by training customers before a product or service is delivered so that they know what to expect, and by gathering customer and noncustomer preferences and expectations before the product or service is produced. That way, customization can occur.

A third and still more advanced culture type couples innovation with continuous improvement. I have labeled it *perpetual creative quality*. This type of culture focuses on improvement rather than mere prevention of errors. The organization's standard changes from hitting a target to improving performance. Its objective is to achieve levels of quality in products and services that are not only unexpected but also unrequested. The organization solves problems for customers and provides benefits to them that they don't expect. Things gone right supplement, and sometimes replace, things gone wrong as the focus of measurement. New standards are created for customers because the organization surprises and delights them. Innovations (large, discontinuous improvements) are combined with unremitting small wins (minute, incremental improvements), so that customer loyalty and trust are strengthened.

Each type of quality culture is more advanced than its predecessor because each adds to the general approach of the former type. Error detection and inspection, for example, are not ignored or necessarily abandoned, they are just supplemented and made less necessary by an emphasis on error prevention and process improvement. Similarly, perpetual creative quality adds to the former two cultures by combining improvement and innovation in the quality objective. Several authors, including those in this volume, have argued that the world's best firms are typified by this third type of quality culture.[20]

Most organizations in my study of 68 firms are still dominated by an error detection culture. Figure 6.1 provides an illustration of the modal quality culture profile emerging from those organizations. These profiles were produced by having respondents rate the extent to which various scenarios written on a survey were similar to their own organization. Each scenario described attributes of a different type of quality culture.

The importance of quality culture in the context of downsizing is that successful downsizing is more likely when a more advanced quality culture is

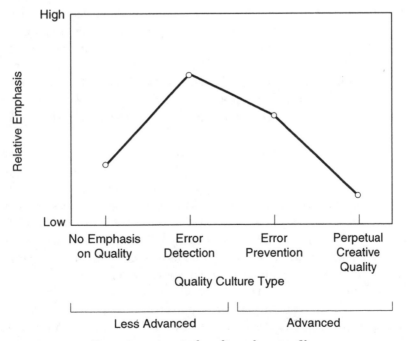

Figure 6.1. A typical quality culture profile.

present in firms. As Table 6.6 points out, advanced quality cultures and excellence in achieving creative quality are major predictors of positive organizational outcomes when downsizing occurs. Conversely, a less advanced quality culture (i.e., no quality activity or an emphasis on error detection) serves as a major inhibitor to successful downsizing.

This relationship is also important as it relates to the downsizing strategies implemented by firms. The more advanced the quality culture, the more likely the firm is to approach downsizing using systemic strategies. In less advanced quality cultures, workforce reduction strategies are more likely. This result may not be surprising *post hoc* because systemic strategies are compatible with and include values of TQM, whereas workforce reduction strategies do not. In other words, an association exists between downsizing being defined as a way of life and as a prerequisite to successful quality achievement (systemic strategies) and an advanced quality culture. This is illustrated in Table 6.7 which reports that firms with an advanced quality culture are characterized to a significantly greater degree by systemic strategies when they downsize.

Conclusions Regarding Downsizing and TQM

The findings from these two studies, and our discussion of the nature of downsizing, lead to three main conclusions. One is that most organizations downsize in a way that both contradicts principles of TQM and inhibits positive organizational performance. The most common workforce reduction strategies in downsizing are neither consistent with TQM nor lead to desirable outcomes. As previouly pointed out, most organizations are not benefited by downsizing, hence they must continue to repeat it over and over. A major reason is the absence of TQM principles incorporated into the downsizing strategy employed.

A second conclusion is that quality outcomes and enhanced organizational performance are associated with a certain type of downsizing strategy—systemic downsizing—that is most congruent with TQM principles. Most organizations face the need to downsize, and when systemic strategies are implemented when doing so, positive outcomes tend to occur. The data from two empirical studies indicate that improvements in firm performance over time, attaining higher effectiveness than customers expect and than competitors achieve, and avoiding the dirty dozen all are enhanced when downsizing is conducted in harmony with TQM principles.

A third conclusion is that downsizing's success is enhanced when an advanced quality culture has been developed in the organization. An advanced

TABLE 6.7. The Relationship Between Advanced Quality Cultures and a Systemic Downsizing Strategy

Dominant Culture Type	Proxies for Systemic Downsizing (Mean Scores)	
	Constantly Reducing Costs[a]	Continious Downsizing[b]
No emphasis on quality	2.9	3.9
Error detection culture	3.6	4.2
Error prevention culture	3.9	4.5
Perpetual creative quality culture	4.0	4.3

Using analysis of variance, the significance of the difference between a less advanced and a more advanced quality culture is

$$T = -10.033 \quad d.f. = 2016 \quad P < .0000$$

[a] Respondents rated the following surey item: "We are continually reducing our costs and resource requirements without sacrificing quality. That is, we have adopted a continuous downsizing mentality in pursuing quality."

[b] Respondents rated the following survey item: "Continuous downsizing (i.e., doing more with less) is viewed as a prerequisite to long-term success in quality."

quality culture means that the organization has adopted an "error prevention" or a "perpetual creative quality" perspective. In such organizations, quality means preventing mistakes, searching for root causes of problems, surprising and delighting customers through innovation, anticipating customer expectations and acting in advance of requests, continuously improving all aspects of performance, involving customers in product and service design, using improvement as the standard of performance instead of defect rates, involving every employee in quality improvement teams and activities, and so on. When the values and assumptions that underlie these kinds of quality processes become part of the culture of the organization, they help guide approaches to downsizing as well. The pursuit of quality and continuous improvement become as typical of downsizing as they are of product and service delivery.

In sum, after seven years' research on downsizing and quality, I have come to believe that successful downsizing implies a successful quality program and a successful quality program implies successful downsizing. It is rare to have one without the other. Achieving high quality involves constantly reducing costs, redundancies, and inefficiencies. Successful downsizing means changing the culture so that continuous improvement becomes a way of life. The following ten prescriptions, in fact, have emerged from these parallel streams on downsizing and quality, and they are offered as an illustration of how both concepts can and should be compatible with one another.

1. Both downsizing and quality must be a way of life, not a program or a target.

2. Both downsizing and quality must be the responsibility of every employee, not a single department's or top management's.

3. Both downsizing and quality require maximum communication and information flows to everyone in the organization.

4. Both downsizing and quality must focus on every aspect of the organization, not just obvious or easily measured factors.

5. Both downsizing and quality must treat people as human resources, not as human costs or liabilities.

6. Both downsizing and quality must involve employees in identifying what needs to change and in implementing the changes.

7. Both downsizing and quality require active, aggressive, accessible leaders who lead by vision and example.

8. Both downsizing and quality must have as a foundation continuous training and development of employees, beginning before major changes take place.

9. Both downsizing and quality require a measurement system that assesses more than just numbers of employees, defects, or productivity, but also assesses factors such as time use, process efficiency, knowledge and learning, and so on.

10. Both downsizing and quality require appraisal, reward, and development systems that reinforce the primary objectives of customer satisfaction, continuous improvement, and employee involvement, not just profitability and productivity outcomes.

Consistent with Dr. Kano's arguments in the concluding chapter, Japanese firms seem more inclined than U.S. firms to approach challenges of cost containment and efficiency enhancement by coupling principles of advanced quality culture and downsizing. The above ten prescriptions, in other words, are more likely to characterize Japanese firms today than American firms. One potential reason is that downsizing continues to connote headcount reduction and restructuring in the United States but seems not to carry that same implication in Japan. An important message in this chapter, therefore, is not that the term downsizing should be abandoned, replaced, or narrowed (although terms such as revitalization or renewal may be more descriptive of a systemic approach to downsizing). Rather, the message is that downsizing should be thought of as inclusive of, not contradictory to, TQM principles in its implementation. It should be coupled with continuous improvement, employee involvement, and customer focus in its definition. Bob Cole pointed out that, unfortunately, "downsizing is the right term for how most American firms do it, and continuous improvement is the right term for how most Japanese firms do it."[21] This should change so that systemic downsizing—downsizing systems more than headcount—becomes the strategy of choice.

One implication is that if principles of TQM are joined with a systemic approach to downsizing, the root cause of the need to downsize is addressed, not just its symptoms. Instead of being merely a cost reduction or redesign strategy, downsizing will focus on changing the organization's culture, producing not only leaner processes, reduced waste, faster response time, and more satisfied employees, but organizational learning, continuous improvement, and shared responsibility as well. In turn, the organization then can produce higher levels of customer service, satisfaction, and loyalty, all of which will cultivate new sources of revenue and an increased need for jobs. In the end, downsizing will change from dumbsizing to continuous improvement.

Notes

1. These results are part of a survey reported in A. Bennett, "Downsizing Doesn't Necessarily Bring an Upswing in Corporate Profitability," Wall Street Journal, June 6, 1991, B1, B4.
2. See Ronald Henkoff, "Getting Beyond Downsizing," Fortune, January 10, 1994, 58–64.
3. This conclusion was reached by Henkoff, op.cit.
4. See Kim S. Cameron, "The Downsizing of an Army Organization: An Investigation of Downsizing Strategies, Processes, and Outcomes" (Washington, DC: Army Research Institute, 1993); Kim S. Cameron, Sarah J. Freeman, and Aneil J. Mishra, "Downsizing and Redesigning Organizations," in George P. Huber, and William H. Glick, (eds) Organizational Change and Redesign (New York: Oxford University Press, 1993), pp. 19–65; and Kim S. Cameron, Sarah J. Freeman, and Aneil J. Mishra, "Best Practices in White-collar Downsizing: Managing Contradictions," Academy of Management Executive, 5 (1991): 57–73.
5. More statistical and theoretical detail is found in a paper I presented at the Academy of Management Meetings in Dallas, Texas, in 1994: "An empirical investigation of quality culture, practices, and outcomes."
6. This finding was reported in Henkoff, op.cit.
7. From an article by Steven Pearlstein, "Corporate Cutbacks Yet to Pay Off," The Washington Post, January 4, 1994, B6.
8. Reported in an article by Roanld Henkoff, "Cost Cutting: How to Do It Right," Fortune, April 9, 1990, 17–19.

9. From the article by A. Bennett, op.cit.

10. This result was reported in Bennett, op.cit., p. B1.

11. See Robert E. Cole, "Learning from Learning Theory: Implications for Quality Improvements of Turnover, Use of Contingent Workes, and Job Rotation Policies," *Quality Management Journal*, 1 (1993): 9–25.

12. See Bernard Baumohl, "When Downsizing Becomes Dumbsizing," *Time*, March 15, 1993, p. 55.

13. These findings came from studies of more than 300 organizations, reported in Kim S. Cameron, Myung U. Kim, and David A. Whetten, "Organizational Effects of Decline and Turbulence," *Administrative Science Quarterly*, 32 (1987): 222–240; and in Kim S. Cameron, David A. Whetten, and Myung U. Kim, "Organizational Dysfunctions of Decline," *Academy of Management Journal*, 30 (1987): 126–138.

14. For a comprehensive review, see Steven W. J. Kozlowski, Georgia T. Chao, Eleanor M. Smith, and Jennifer Hedlund, "Organizational Downsizing: Strategies, Interventions, and Research Implications," *International Review of Industiral and Organizational Psychology* (New York: Wiley, 1993). Also see Joel Brockner, "The Effects of Work Layoff on Survivors," in B. M. Staw, and L. L. Cummings, (eds.), *Research in Organizational Behavior*, Vol. 10 (Greenwich, CT: JAI Press, 1988).

15. For a well-known representative study, see Michael Porter, *The Competitive Advantage of Nations* (New York: Free Press, 1990).

16. See Kim S. Cameron, Sarah J. Freeman, and Aneil K. Mishra, 1993, op.cit.

17. For an excellent review of the literature on organizational culture and climate, see Daniel R. Denison, "What Is the Difference Between Organizational Culture and Organizational Climate? A Native's Point of View on a Decade of Paradigm Wars," University of Michigan working paper. Also see Daniel R. Denison, *Corporate Culture and Organizational Effectiveness* (New York: Wiley, 1990); Gerte Hofstede, *Culture and Organizations: Software of the Mind* (New York: McGraw-Hill, 1991); Jo Ann Martin, *Cultures in Organizations: Three Perspectives* (New York: Oxford University Press, 1992); and Harrison Trice and Janice Beyer *Thw Culture of Work Organizations* (Englewood Cliffs, NJ: Prentice-Hall, 1992).

18. These findings are from G. Hofstede, B. Neuijen, D. Ohayv, and G. Sanders, "Measuring Organizational Cultures: A Qualitative and Quantitative Study Across Twenty Cases," *Administrative Science Quarterly*, 35 (1990): 286–316.

19. More detail and empirical analyses are contained in Kim. S. Cameron, "An Empirical Investigation of Quality Culture, Practices, and Outcomes," Working paper, School of Business Administration, University of Michigan. A version was also presented at the Academy of Management Meetings, Dallas, Texas, in 1994.

20. For a fairly comprehensive discussion on quality programs and initiatives throughout the world, see Richard T. Green, *Global Quality: A Synthesis of the World's Best Management Methods* (Homewood, IL: Business One Irwin, 1993).

21. Personal conversation with Bob Cole, February 1994.

7

Total Quality Management in a Small, High-Technology Company

MICHAEL J. PRICE AND E. EVA CHEN

If you work in a small, high-technology company you are probably not involved in Total Quality Management (TQM). The managements of most of these companies have avoided TQM because they believe it is too bureaucratic, cumbersome, complex, and expensive. They fear that TQM may stifle creativity and initiative and reduce the ability of the organization to react quickly. Not only are these perceptions incorrect, but if a small, high-technology company wants to obtain long-term viability, it must adopt TQM.

All companies are facing increasing competitive pressures. Many large companies have recognized the important contribution TQM can make in dealing with these pressures; however, the TQM systems implemented by these companies are not well suited to small companies unless certain changes are made. The TQM system can be tailored to adapt to the needs of small companies in a practical, applied manner.

Building on the "house of TQM" described by Dr. Kano in the concluding chapter (Figure 11.1), we will present the *motivation* for adopting TQM in a small, high-technology company followed by a description of the *tools* to be used (TQM concepts, techniques, and vehicles). We will also discuss methods for managing the changes inherent in adopting TQM, accompanied by real implementation experiences (both good and bad). Specific tools are furnished that have been used to good effect in several companies.

Why Is TQM Important to Small, High-Technology Companies?

The small, high-technology company is faced with the challenge of obtaining long-term, sustainable success—that is, becoming a viable business. A company's early success is often based on technological innovation or positioning within a rapidly growing market. As the company grows, it is faced with challenges that can only be met if it develops additional strengths. The implementation of TQM creates a much stronger focus on customer needs and expectations, more effective and efficient business processes, and the execution skills to deliver low-cost, high-quality products and services. These strengths combined with the company's technological capabilities will assist in creating viability.

For a small, high-technology company, two critical success factors are rapid time to market and product differentiation. TQM sets the foundation for both.

Rapid product development is enabled when decision making is delegated to empowered project teams and TQM provides the framework to make this happen. The reduction of cycle time, especially in the new product development process, can be accomplished through the use of TQM and is one of the more visible, valuable, and tractable problems to be addressed (see step 2 in chapter 8). Empowerment and cycle time reduction are both described in more detail later in this chapter.

Product differentiation is accomplished by listening to customers to identify those product characteristics that are the basis for customer delight. This goes beyond merely satisfying the customer. TQM provides an excellent framework for the identification of quality characteristics and their implementation in products and services.

What Is Total Quality Management?

TQM is a management system, not a series of programs. Many of the tools promoted as part of TQM can be successfully applied within any organization, but the full benefits cannot be obtained without changing the attitudes and priorities of day-to-day operations. For TQM to be successful, it must be adopted throughout the organization and it requires a long-term commitment from the top down.[1,2]

TQM is a general philosophy of management. It can be tailored for a particular environment and there are as many ways to implement TQM as there are companies adopting it.[3,4] However, they share one common objective: Everyone in the organization is always striving to provide products and services that consistently meet or exceed their customers' expectations. Well-defined processes are used to achieve the continuous improvement of these products and services.

TQM is a system that prioritizes customer satisfaction before profit. Customer satisfaction produces long-term, sustainable profits, but a profit priority creates a short-term focus at the expense of long-term health. TQM is a system that comprises a set of integrated philosophies, tools, and processes used to accomplish business objectives by creating delighted customers and happy employees.

There are four key elements forming the foundation of TQM: people, continuous improvement, process, and the customer. The chart in Figure 7.1 shows an example of an implementation plan for each of these four elements. Implementation begins at the center and moves outward.

People.   The goal is to empower people so that optimal business results can be accomplished through teamwork. The path to this goal starts with training that focuses on *communication skills, interactive skills,* and *effective meeting skills.* Such training permits people to participate effectively in group activities, allowing them to be actively involved in the continuous improvement of products and processes. Further training leads to improved *teamwork* that forms the basis for *empowering* employees.

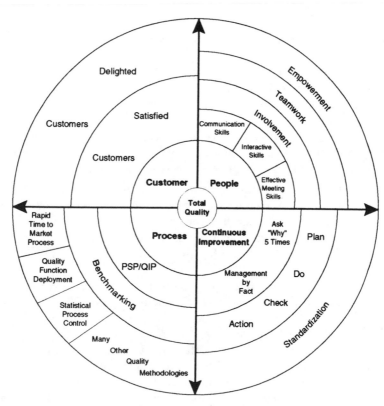

Figure 7.1.   TQM plan.

Continuous Improvement.   Employees are taught to gather data so that intelligent decisions can be made by *asking "why" five times* to get to the root causes of problems. Continuous improvement embodies the fundamental principle of Quality: the PDCA (Plan, Do, Check, Action) cycle,[5] shown in Figure 7.2, also known as the Deming cycle. The iteration of the cycle is the never-ending pursuit of excellence. *Standardization* is the process of adopting successful practices as the standard mode of operation through the use of documentation and training.

Process.   The *Problem Solving Process* (PSP) in Figure 7.3 and the *Quality Improvement Process* (QIP) in Figure 7.4 provide people with basic tools and a common language for continuous improvement.[6]

A team uses the PSP as a guide as it analyzes a problem, chooses solutions, develops an action plan, and evaluates implementation results. The evaluation may cause the team to start at Step 1 again to further refine the solution or to address problems disclosed by solving the original problem.

The use of the QIP helps focus attention on the customer and customer requirements. The QIP defines a step-by-step procedure for reducing customer requirements to a specification and the specification to a defined work process. As in the PSP, the concept of PDCA is central: the final result is evaluated and the QIP is repeated in the pursuit of continuous improvement.

The *Benchmarking Process* encourages people to identify "best-of-class" role models and strive to adopt similar methods. The use of benchmarking makes TQM truly strategic by trying to match the performance of the best companies.

Many other tools are available as part of TQM that are used to achieve productivity and quality improvements. These advanced tools tend to be more specialized and people are selectively trained in their use.

Customer.   The primary focus of TQM is the customer and customer satisfaction. Dr. Kano proposed five customer perceptions of quality (which he calls quality elements) that correlate to customer satisfaction.[7] Of the five, three are of particular importance: *expected quality, satisfying quality,* and *delightful quality.* The other two are indifferent quality and reversed quality.

Expected quality refers to those features or characteristics that customers expect and therefore do not explicitly request. When these features are present customers are not dissatisfied, but when they are absent customers are very dissatisfied.

Satisfying quality describes those features or characteristics that customers specifically request. When they are present customers are satisfied; when they are absent customers are dissatisfied. Satisfying quality satisfies customers and meets, but does not exceed, customers' expectations.

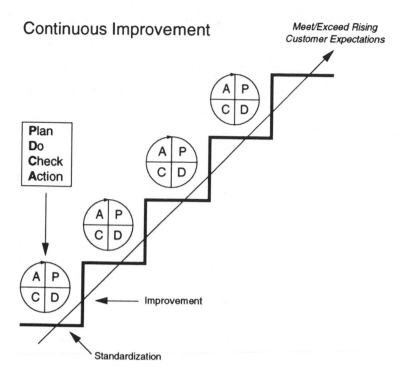

Figure 7.2. Continuous improvement through the PDCA cycle.

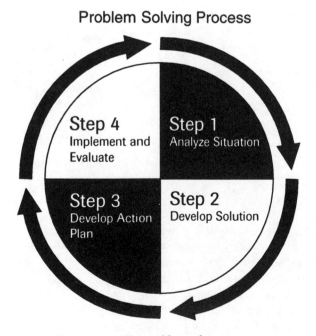

Figure 7.3. The problem-solving process.

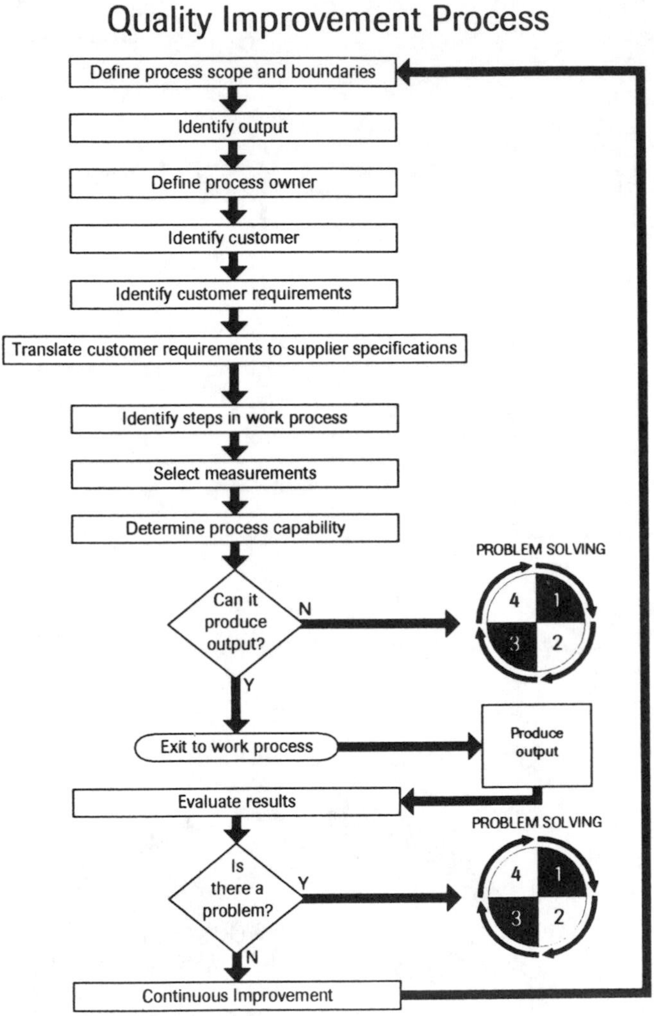

Quality Improvement Process

Figure 7.4.   The quality improvement process.

Delightful quality refers to those features or characteristics that customers do not request because they do not know of their possible existence. When these features are present customers are very pleased; and when they are absent customers are not dissatisfied. Delightful quality exceeds customers' expectations and delights them.

Expected quality must be fulfilled to prevent customer dissatisfaction. Satisfying quality has to be delivered to meet customers' expectations and therefore satisfy them. Delightful quality will exceed customers' expectations and delight them. Customer delight is the key to product and service differentiation.

The Small, High-Technology Company

A small company is one that is in between startup and maturity. "Maturity" is used to describe a company that has developed the skills and systems needed for long-term viability. The phase between startup and maturity is a company's adolescent period. The company is striving to build on its early successes and to create organizational systems capable of supporting growth. A company may mature without necessarily becoming large.

High technology companies are those in which product contributions are made through the development and application of new technology. In these companies, the product development activity receives considerable attention and is often viewed as the primary contributor to the company's success. This is usually a valid point of view for a startup company, but the primacy of product development is gradually reduced in the transition to maturity. This transition is one of the complicating factors when adopting TQM in a small, high-technology company.

Quality characteristics of the three phases of company growth are described in Table 7.1. Characteristics of the startup phase are shown to provide some continuity and comparison.

The Transition from a Small to a Mature Company

Many changes occur during the transition from a small to a mature company. For example, during this period the original company founders may give up control to more experienced managers. The forces that motivate such changes also affect how the quality system should be adopted.

Small companies rely on individual contributors to produce results. There are few written policies or procedures to follow. As a result, many activities can be performed by only one particular individual. The knowledge of how to perform the task resides in the mind of that individual and is lost should the individual leave; there is no organizational memory or experience. This fact forces small companies to be very people oriented to make sure that key knowledge is properly preserved.

As the company grows, departments are created to take ownership of particular functions. These departments hire new employees and need to train them in their job function. At this point, the knowledge kept in the minds of individuals needs to be made explicit so that it can be passed on to others. The

TABLE 7.1.   Quality Characteristics of Companies

Type of Company	Organization	Primary Business Focus	Quality Systems	Primary Quality Focus
Startup	Many functions not yet established	Producing initial products	Lower priority than shipping product and building functions	Focus on shipping product
Small	Functions established but minimally staffed	Producing follow-on products and expanding market share	Early implementation and adoption	Establishing processes and metrics; training
Mature	Functions established, staffed, and experienced	Protecting share and expanding into new markets	Established and well tested in most areas	Continuous improvement; PDCA

company's interest lies in capturing this knowledge for the organization through the establishment of processes and procedures. Teamwork begins to supplant individual contributions.

Table 7.2 shows some important transitions. These transitions are difficult, especially since they involve cultural changes at all levels of the organization. The company's managers must implement these changes in a manner consistent with short-term business goals. This usually means that changes must be introduced gradually, thus allowing the organization to adopt a new culture with minimum disruption.

TABLE 7.2.   Transitions from Small to Mature Company

Small Company	Mature Company
One person performing multiple functions	Several people supporting one function
Quality system has more people focus	Quality system has more process focus
Individual contributions dominate	Teamwork dominates
Standardization through individuals	Standardization through process and organization

Picking the Proper Balance in Cultural Change

During the change caused by the gradual adoption of TQM and the transition to maturity, the small company will be faced with picking a balance between the old and new cultures. These balances occur in all aspects of company culture, but particularly in management style, individual contribution, and business trade-offs.

Management Style

- *Control versus empowerment*—Empowerment implies a loss of control. Managers must give up some authority to be able to empower employees. At the beginning, employees may lack the training necessary to be fully empowered and the managers will exercise considerable control. As the employees become more capable, their level of empowerment can increase and the managers will gradually lose some control. Striking the proper balance throughout the transition period is essential. Too much empowerment given too soon may lead to poor business results and require overruling employee decisions. Too little empowerment prevents TQM from working.

- *Evolution versus revolution*—Small companies, and especially startup companies, generally favor revolutionary ideas. They look for the large reward and are willing to assume large risks. TQM is built on evolutionary principles with the PDCA cycle a central tool. The adoption of TQM does not require a company to abandon its revolutionary tendencies. TQM is the vehicle to establish, maintain, and improve processes incrementally to enhance the company's ability to execute its plans. This reduces the risks inherent in developing revolutionary ideas.

- *Flexibility versus discipline*—Managers like discipline because it contributes to predictability and repeatability, but teams should be encouraged to cut corners and be creative in the pursuit of their goals. If empowerment is to work, a certain freedom to make decisions is needed. Empowerment implies flexibility, but TQM also promotes standardization as a powerful technique with which to build on success. The challenge is to develop "repeatable flexibility"—flexibility within a boundary. Processes or procedures that have been proven to have significant impact should be documented and promoted. These will form the boundaries for activities. The employee is empowered to apply them or to improve them as appropriate. Successful new or improved procedures can be adopted. Those procedures that are trivial or have little impact should not be formalized, permitting individuals to be creative.

Individual Contribution

- *Leader-manager versus doers*—Small companies need doers, people who can get the job done, but these people are often not the right types to lead TQM. TQM leaders must have an appreciation for process, continuous improvement, and customer satisfaction. There is often an expectation that one type of skill precludes the other. This is not necessarily true, but often occurs in a small company with a small number of different people to draw on. Small companies often can't afford to have both and must use people with some balance of skills.

- *Superstars versus solid contributors*—Small companies, and especially those starting up, often rely on the skills of superstar individuals for their early success. As the company grows, it is not possible to rely on these superstars and the company requires solid contributors to do the basic, routine tasks required. The increasing importance of teamwork also reduces the role of the superstar. These superstars are often the founders of the company who enjoy certain prerogatives. It is important to engage the company's superstar contributors in the promotion and implementation of TQM from the earliest moment. Their endorsement and participation will encrease the ease of adopting TQM; their antagonism can prevent TQM from being successful.

Business Trade-offs

- *Rapid time to market versus product perfection*—Quality becomes a driving force in the company when TQM is adopted. This is often interpreted as meaning that the company will not ship any product until it is perfect. On the other hand, business realities prevent the unending polishing that accompanies a search for perfection. Customers cannot be satisfied if the product never ships. When the management of the company makes trade-off decisions that result in less than perfect products, the credibility of TQM and the quality commitment are perceived to be at risk. The employees need to be educated to appreciate the bases for the decisions made. The most important aspect of this training is creating an appreciation for the customer requirement for timely product releases. Once informed, employees are more likely to understand the situation and actively participate in decisions.

- *Rapid time to market versus changing customer requirements*—The focus on customer satisfaction is often interpreted as meaning that the company should respond to every request resulting in "creeping features" among other problems. TQM provides tools, such as Quality Function Deployment, to better understand customer requirements and define products.

Customer satisfaction often means producing a solution to a problem quickly even if incomplete. A complete understanding of the customer requirements must include knowledge of the delivery time desired by the customer as well as the product's feature content. TQM provides tools that can assist in choosing the proper balance of time and functionality.

- *Short-term survival versus long-term growth*—Quality processes often require long-term investments in training and development. When business pressures focus the company's attention on the short term, quality activities are often sacrificed as the company falls back on its old ways. The investments in quality processes must be fully compatible with the company's short- as well as long-term objectives. TQM can also focus on short-term activities and adds considerable value through its focus on management by fact, teamwork, and the PDCA cycle. These can help the company place its attention on the root causes rather than the symptoms of problems.

- *Technology driven versus customer driven*—Small companies are often driven by technology instead of customers. High-technology companies do not want to lose the technological advantages on which the success of their companies have been built. On the other hand, as the number of customers served by the company increases, it will need to learn how to invest in customer satisfaction as well. TQM can facilitate the transition to more of a customer focus. TQM can also improve the processes the company uses to take new technologies to the market, reducing the time required, improving the quality, lowering the cost, and improving the likelihood that the products will be well accepted by the customers.

Resistance to Change

Within most companies, regardless of size, there is a tension between long-term interests in establishing processes and the immediate desire to get the work done. This tension is especially acute in small companies in which there is typically more need to react quickly. Resistance to establishing processes in small companies results from several factors.

1. Many activities for which a process could be defined are executed by one person. That person often resists documenting their understanding of process, declaring the effort to be a waste of time.

2. Change is rapid, causing procedures to become obsolete quickly. This creates the attitude that establishing procedures is a waste of time and should be postponed until more stability is achieved.

3. The small company is often engaged in activities for which there is little or no previous corporate experience since it is a young organization.

There is a resultant lack of confidence on defining a process for an activity not fully understood.

4. There are usually several individuals who possess unique knowledge about how to perform tasks. If a process is established that captures some of the knowledge of these individuals, they become less indispensable. Since TQM emphasizes the creation of processes as a primary vehicle for continuous improvement, many individuals see TQM as job threatening.

Counteracting this resistance to TQM, and to change in general, is the first step in the implementation process. The employees need to be convinced that TQM solves problems they have and actually improves their job satisfaction.

Motivating Employees to Accept TQM

Several techniques can be used to motivate employees to accept TQM. Such motivation can create a significant "pull" for TQM techniques, greatly increasing the chances for overall success. Some positive impacts of TQM that provide motivation for employees are:

Reduction of firefighting by focusing on process and root causes rather than symptoms.

Ability to solve long-standing problems that have not received the attention of management.

Future avoidance of problems already encountered through the use of standardization.

Improvement of personal skills and capabilities.

Improvement of team skills and capabilities, which results in much more effective meetings and project management.

Introduction of the notion of the internal customer—this helps to break down departmental barriers.

Empowerment of the individual.

Integrating the Quality Drive

When employees are trained in the use of TQM tools, they are eager to try them out. In these trials, considerable energy may be expended on low-priority items. This poisons the attitudes toward TQM since these trials distract the employees from their normal work, have poor ROI, and often fail due to lack of any real interest in the result.

A better method is to teach TQM tools as part of the regular job assignment. The particular tools chosen for training should be directly applicable to the tasks the employees are currently engaged in. This maximizes the chances of success by increasing interest in the result and reducing distractions from normal assignments. A job-focused approach to TQM can also create a demand for training from the employees as they identify additional opportunities on their own.

Integrated TQM training also increases the likelihood that TQM will produce positive business results quickly. Focus should be placed on time-to-market, cycle time reduction, quality, and cost since these will produce tangible and valuable results.

Building Quality from the Grass Roots

One of the cornerstones of TQM is the empowerment of employees. Empowerment puts decision making into the hands of these closest to the work. Teams are often given ownership by company management but are not provided with the proper training, direction (overall framework), or authority to become truly empowered. Empowered groups can truly assume ownership only when they are given the proper authority, responsibility, accountability, and support.

Small, high-technology companies rely heavily on new product development for continued success. The product development activity often receives more focus and it is here that TQM can be put to immediate use. One important concept that can be applied is the core team. The core team includes members from each of the functional departments that have a role to play in the development of a product. (see Figure 7.5).

Core teams are formed at the beginning of the project and their composition is determined by specific project objectives. The purpose of the core team is to place, under one team leader, all the people necessary for the development of a new product and to empower them to make decisions needed to complete that project. A core team is different from the traditional, cross-functional project team because it *is* empowered. The core team also provides a vehicle for the implementation of concurrent engineering, design for manufacturability, and other rapid time-to-market concepts.

Much of the success of total quality as applied to product development depends on the abilities of core teams and for this reason considerable attention needs to be paid to making them work well. Core team leaders are chosen who are capable of leading and motivating the team as well as anticipating problems it will face. Proper training is provided and team building exercises are conducted. The empowerment of the team is emphasized on every occasion. The

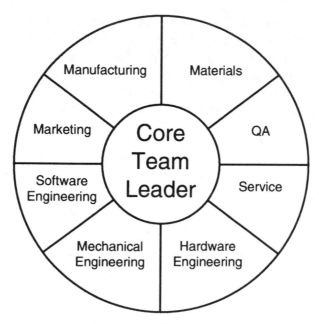

Figure 7.5.   The core team.

team is encouraged to make its own decisions and to eliminate obstacles in whatever manner they choose.

At the end of the project, the core team conducts a review in which the team's successes and failures are analyzed. The most common result of this analysis is a checklist that serves as a reminder for future core teams of project deliverables and steps necessary for avoiding problems. The members of the core team join other teams and carry their experiences with them.

A common mistake is to establish core teams and give them autonomy too quickly. It takes time and experience for a core team to learn to be productive. The core team leader must learn how to best lead a cross-functioned team. The team members need to learn the skills necessary to be properly empowered. During this time, the management of the company should provide facilitation to help the core teams be successful. The core team approach is no panacea but can be an important aspect of a company's TQM system.

Growing into TQM

TQM should be adopted gradually and not wholesale. The company should identify a few important initial projects and demonstrate success before taking additional steps. The first applications should be chosen to provide tangible benefits for the business.

The reduction of cycle time, regardless of what process or where in the organization, can generate immediate benefits. Repeated processes exist in every department and there is considerable value in asking "How can this activity be done more quickly?" In many instances, the employees will suggest immediate improvements they have always known about but didn't mention for lack of a forum.

The benefits of a TQM focus on cycle time reduction are that it

Produces tangible, quantifiable improvements.

Generates improvements that "matter"—reduces expenses and increases capacity.

Engages the employees in successful TQM programs in their daily work.

Encourages the employees to become interested in improving company performance.

Improves employees' job satisfaction.

Once enthusiasm for TQM inspired improvements has been created, additional training can be conducted. Eventually, core teams can be formed to carry the program forward and provide a focus for employee empowerment. The results of successes are advertised, further developing a desire for TQM produced benefits. This process is shown in Figure 7.6.

Companies must make sure that teams evaluate their performance by focusing on the PDCA cycle; documenting successes and standardizing processes with large impacts; creating checklists to capture successful procedures and avoid repeating problems; providing the core teams with assistance to ensure success; and moving people from one core team to another to facilitate dissemination of experiences.

Once teams begin to see successes in the application of TQM tools to their daily work, they will be ready for more sophisticated tools and procedures. A properly designed training program offers new tools just at the time when employees are ready to apply them. Often, motivated teams will be proactive in requesting training tools for which they perceive a need.

The Prevention of Bureaucratization

As companies mature, there is a natural inclination for organizations to specialize functionally, which creates a resistance to change. This resistance reduces flexibility, hampers programs of continuous improvement, and stifles empower-

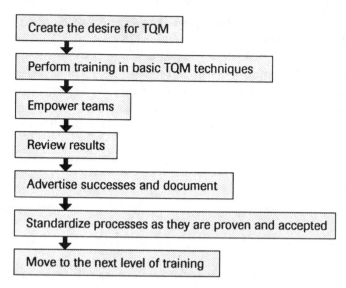

Figure 7.6.   Growing into TQM.

ment. One consequence is the establishment of entrenched procedures. These specialized organizations form a constituency for maintaining the status quo. TQM can assist in fighting this specialization by emphasizing PDCA and empowerment.

Several guidelines can assist in avoiding organizational ossification.

- Don't create processes and procedures only as a management tool. Make sure that the processes established and documented are intended to facilitate rather than control activities. The purpose should be to capture successful methods so that they can be repeated and provide a basis for continuous improvement. The procedure established solely to give management control or to force visibility is a poor substitute for participatory management.

- Don't emphasize checks and balances too heavily in procedures. Reviews are needed to ensure the early detection of errors, but the focus should be on creating processes that produce zero defects. Design procedures so that the competent team can act quickly. If the process is designed with the assumption that things will always go wrong, the competent team wastes considerable time in reviews that find no problems. Design procedures that permit rapid progress when things go well and focus attention on the tools and training needed to ensure that all teams have the skills needed to perform their functions well.

- Empower cross-functional teams. These teams create a powerful resistance to organizational barriers. Team members will fight obstacles that hinder progress and make it difficult for functional organizations to establish islands of control. These teams also have a customer focus that crosses functional responsibilities and creates loyalties outside reporting structures.

- Keep procedures simple and allow them to grow as needed. Let the users of the procedures expand them as they gain experience. Resist the creation of complex processes until simple ones have been tried. Use checklists and flowcharts instead of lengthy prose to communicate procedures. Keep documents short.

- Establish processes only where substantial benefits will result. Don't invest significant efforts to establish processes for activities with little impact on the company's success. Also, don't tackle the largest problems until successes have been accomplished with simple problems. Choose problems whose scope matches the organizations' skills in process creation.

- Review and update processes regularly. Conduct periodic reviews of processes to identify opportunities for improvement. A good point to review processes is at the end of a project in which the processes were used. The review will benefit from the users' recent experience with the processes and the discussion can focus on specific examples.

The Importance of People

Small companies have less organizational "memory" than large ones. This is because the experiences of the company are possessed by individuals. There is little time to extract, from individuals, knowledge of interest to the company. As the company grows, there is an increasing need to share the skills of individuals by cross-training and documentation. Eventually, processes and procedures will be established, thus permitting continuous improvement.

Meanwhile, individuals are the "process." As the company becomes more "process focused" rather than "people focused," the preservation of employee job satisfaction should be a company priority. Measurement of job satisfaction can provide important information to company management. It can offer insights into how well the quality transformation is proceeding, predict trends in productivity, and identify potential trouble spots. When used as part of a PDCA cycle in people management, it can supply a quantitative indication of progress.

The chart in Figure 7.7 can be used by employees to communicate their level of job satisfaction in five areas: salary, accomplishment and rewards, learning and challenge, career advancement, and enjoyment. It provides a quick, visual indication of the level of job satisfaction. In this example, the chart shows an individual who is well paid and has had several accomplish-

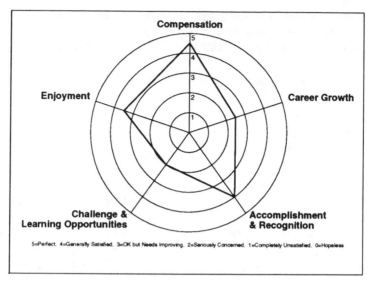

Figure 7.7.   Job satisfaction.

ments, but is unhappy about the level of challenge and how well the work is contributing to career goals. This indicates a potential problem.

Employees often find it easier to fill out this chart than to talk to their supervisor. Hence, it can be a good "ice-breaker." It also focuses the attention of the employees on several aspects of their own satisfaction that may help to clarify concerns they have about the company and their work

Adopting Processes from Other Companies—
An Example

As companies begin the adoption of TQM, they borrow tools, procedures, and ideas from other companies. Even though these may have been used successfully elsewhere, they should be viewed as only a starting point. Companies who have been using TQM for a long time will have fully developed procedures that may be too cumbersome or foreign to be adopted without change by a company just beginning TQM implementaion. A good example of such a procedure is the product development process.

The product life cycle encompasses the entire lifetime of a product from the earliest conception to end of life. This is one of the most important processes in a high-technology company and, has consequently received much attention. A typical Product Life Cycle (PLC) procedure appears in Figure 7.8.

Transition from one phase to the next occurs following successful completion of a phase review.

Concept Phase 0	Definition Phase 1	Design Phase 2	Verification Phase 3	Ramp Phase 4	Production Phase 5	End-of-life Phase 6
• Product Proposal • Preliminary Feasibility Study	• Product Specification • Completed Feasibility Study • Core Team Assignments • Development Plans • Master Schedule • Business Plan • Critical Issues Report • Capabilities Analysis • Product Requirements Summary • Preliminary Product Design Document	• Product Architecture Document • Design Document • DVT Plan • Field Test Plan • Prototype Units • DVT Results • Working Unit Approval • Compliance Test Results • SCDs Complete • Supplier Selection Complete • Alpha Test Plan • Alpha Test Complete	• Beta Test Plan • Pilot Run Completed • Launch Plan Initiated • Life/Strife Tests • Beta Test Complete • Product Release • Service Training Completed • Finalize Production Schedule • Product Announcement • Release to Customer Ship	• Completion of Internal Release & docs • Supplier Processes Operational • UMC Review • Customer Satisfaction Targets met • Yield Targets Achieved • Final Signoff	• Product Promotion • Customer Satisfaction Metrics Measured • Product Line Planning • Value Engineering • EOL Proposal	• Transition Plan • MRP Coordination • Financial Summary • Product Life Review

Figure 7.8. The product life cycle process.

The documentation for such a PLC usually consists of a binder that includes checklists, glossaries, policies, flowcharts, standards, generic agenda for review meetings, approval forms, and so on. These binders often contain 100 or more pages. A large company may need such a procedure to coordinate all aspects of a complex project but, for a small company, this level of detail and control is usually unnecessary and counterproductive. Most team members are inclined to "get on with it" rather than read, much less absorb, the contents of an elaborate PLC procedure; this is a positive attitude.

The purpose of a PLC procedure is to facilitate the rapid development of products that delight customers. This is a complex issue and cannot be properly discussed here,[8] but a simple approach can be used to generate results quickly: Start with a simple structure and use the PDCA cycle.

The small company already has experience at producing products. This experience can be captured in a few basic documents that can be extremely valuable to new project teams. These documents together are used as the initial PLC procedure. The following three such documents have been proven to be highly valuable.

1. *Lists of deliverables required at various milestones.* An example is a list of all the documents needed to release a product to manufacturing. The list is used by a new project team as a reminder of the tasks to be performed, as a project planning tool, and as a checklist for completion.

2. *Template schedules for generic activities.* Many activities are similar from one project to another. A generic schedule can be created showing the tasks to be performed and the average time these tasks have required. These templates represent the experience of the organization. They are a model for how the company has performed in the past and provide planning insights as well as performance targets.

3. *Summaries of errors to be avoided.* Errors are always made during product development. Often these are errors of omission or oversight. Awareness of these errors helps new project teams profit from past experiences.

These documents are intended to help the core team complete their project quickly. They are used as guidelines and the team is encouraged to adapt them to each specific situation. Most teams adopt schedules and checklists thankfully and augment them throughout the project. These updated documents are often incorporated into the PLC as part of the review and PDCA activity at the end of each project. The core team is also expected to delete items from the PLC documentation when they are incorrect, obsolete, unimportant, or useless. The company may eventually have a PLC procedure as complex and thorough as that in Figure 7.8, but it will be focused on those aspects of product development that have been shown to be important to the success of projects, leaving everything else to the discretion of the team.

Management reviews, normally part of a PLC, slow the project team down and serve to reduce the level of empowerment. Management should take the time to meet informally with team members to become aware of status rather than require formal periodic reviews that disrupt schedules, slow progress, and, if the team is competent, add no value. If a team is unsuccessful, the root causes are usually lack of training, insufficient resources, or confusion about objectives. These cannot be addressed by bureaucratic procedures.

Some Errors Made in Adopting TQM

There are several errors commonly made when adopting TQM.

- Company-wide training in TQM was conducted before the need or desire for TQM was created. Employees were unable to apply their knowledge on programs that mattered and forgot the details by the time they encountered a real need.

- Many early projects were not pertinent to the daily work of the employees, causing them to view the activity as unnecessary.
- TQM was perceived as "large company bureaucracy" and early implementation wasn't directed at dispelling this concern.
- Insufficient training was conducted on the importance of PDCA and the standardization of simple processes and procedures.
- Too much emphasis was placed on the need to establish processes and document procedures. This resulted in burdensome documents that were perceived as stifling initiative and impeding rapid action.
- Complex processes were established that required long learning curves, negating much of the intended improvements.
- Experiences were not captured as part of a PDCA cycle and documented for future use. This resulted in errors being repeated and no standardization of successes.

These errors can be avoided if the TQM implementation plan follows the guidelines described here. And the most important reminder: Stay focused on results. Don't establish quality processes for the sake of TQM alone.

Additional Challenges

There are many other challenges facing the small company as it implements TQM. Some of these are:

- Senior management must give up micro-management of the organization. In the startup phase, the senior managers typically exercise control of all aspects of the company's operations. As the company grows, this tendency to micro-manage must be overcome so that empowerment can occur. This is one of the hardest transitions to make.
- Product development and manufacturing teams are the easiest to empower since they have clearly defined goals, quantifiable results, and are usually engaged in producing something tangible with repeated processes. Other teams in the company also need to be empowered to make TQM work. This is harder when the teams produce intangibles or do not follow the same process each time. Despite these difficulties, TQM does offer many benefits.
- TQM training creates a heightened awareness of customer satisfaction in the organization. Frequently, because of a lack of resources, some of the newly discovered customer satisfaction issues cannot be resolved quickly. This may lead to employee frustration and skepticism about management's commitment to TQM.

- During initial implementation of TQM the primary focus is on establishing processes instead of improving them. Since it is easier to quantify and measure results when improving processes than creating them, it is more difficult to motivate employees during these early activities.
- Training is most economical when conducted with a class size of 10 or more. Small companies may find it difficult to keep daily operations going when a sizable percentage of the employees is in a training class. It is also a challenge to conduct effective training when there are external demands on the employees.

Conclusion

Total Quality Management is an essential component of establishing long-term viability for small, high-technology companies. The experiences of large companies with TQM have demonstrated its effectiveness in improving quality, customer satisfaction, and competitiveness. These benefits can be obtained by small companies without sacrificing the innovation, rapid response capability, and individual contribution on which their success depends.

We have presented methods for adopting TQM that are tailored for the needs of small, high-technology companies. Of particular importance is understanding that small companies undergo considerable changes as they mature and that the adoption of TQM must be integrated with these changes.

Many small companies have realized significant benefits from adopting TQM. We hope that more managers of small, high-technology companies will be encouraged to investigate TQM further. By itself, TQM cannot guarantee the long-term viablity of a company; yet, without it, the small, high-technology company is faced with a daunting and, perhaps, insurmountable competitive environment.

Notes

1. Karou Ishikawa, *What Is Total Quality Control? The Japanese Way* (Englewood Cliffs, NJ: Prentice-Hall, 1985).
2. J. M. Juran, *Juran on Leadership for Quality, An Executive Handbook* (New York: The Freeman Press, 1989).
3. Bob King, *Hoshin Planning, The Developmental Approach* (Methuen, MA: GOAL/ QPC, 1989).
4. NIST, *Malcolm Baldrige National Quality Award 1993 Award Criteria* (Gaithersburg, MD: National Institute of Standards and Technology).

5. Masaaki Imai, *KAIZEN, The Key to Japan's Competitve Success* (New York: Random House, 1986).
6. Xerox, *Leadership Through Quality, Quality Improvement Process Workbook* (Stamford, CT: Xerox Corp., 1986).
7. Noriaki Kano, Nobuhiku Seraku and Shinichi Tsuji, *Attractive Quality and Must-be Quality* (Methuen, MA: GOAL/QPC. 1991)
8. Preston G. Smith and Donald G. Reinertsen, *Developing Products in Half the Time* (New York: Van Nostrand Reinhold, 1991).

8

"Working on the Work" to Make Enterprisewide Quality Improvement

PHILLIP E. WILSON

"Working on the work" is an approach to enterprisewide quality improvement that I developed for use when top management does not support a quality program. It aims at quickly achieving business results by using quality concepts and tools to solve visible, significant, and tractable problems in the most important workflows of the business. Strategic extension of the process along these key workflows lays a foundation for quality improvement at the enterprise level.

"Working on the work" differs from conventional quality programs. Unlike many top-down programs, achieving measurable results for the business takes precedence over quality education, training, and promotion ("hoopla"). While skeptics find it easy to attack training programs and "hoopla," it is hard for them to resist an approach that tackles difficult, important business problems and delivers results.

Unlike "just-do-it" approaches, "working on the work" stresses strategic integration of improvement projects. Effective integration of discrete projects requires leaders of quality improvement to understand thoroughly the key workflows in their business. They must use this understanding to link and leverage successful projects as they proceed from project to project. In this way, they systematically move toward enterprisewide quality improvement.

In this chapter, I will first explain the origin of "working on the work" as a quality improvement approach. Second, I will briefly characterize the problem "working on the work" aims at solving. Third, I will describe the elements of "working on the work" as a process for quality improvement. Fourth, I will summarize benefits of this approach. Finally, I will explain four pitfalls—"watch-outs"—I have encountered and offer maxims I keep in mind as I work on the work and engage others in my efforts.

Origin: The Practices of Quality Are Important;
Their Names Aren't

I coined the term "working on the work" to capture the essence of the approach I developed to pursue quality improvement in tough situations. I learned from personal experience in various work environments that people can help use quality practices to improve workflows without knowing it. This possibility is especially important in environments where people resist the idea of a quality program. Success with quality practices opens minds to learning the names as well as the uses of quality concepts and tools. My learning started at home.

My father, who had no formal knowledge of quality practices, introduced them to me. He was born and reared on a farm and owned one almost until the day he died. He maintained fire roads and firebreaks to qualify for government reforestation programs. That meant work. When I was old enough to drive a tractor, wield an axe or shovel, or handle a chain saw, he drafted me to help.

He approached the work as a purposeful owner and manager and a committed conservationist. As a teenage conscript, I approached it from the point of view of a hired laborer who wanted nothing more than to get assigned tasks done and go home. The difference created tension and brought out contrasts in our approaches to work. I remember a few examples.

1. When my father stopped to ponder barely visible ruts in the road, for example, I impatiently urged him to work on "real" problems where the road was deeply eroded, washed out or blocked by a fallen tree. Once I recall muttering, "If it ain't broke, don't fix it." He calmly replied, *"If it ain't broke, that's the best time to make it better."* Continuous improvement and preventive maintenance, I learned later.

2. Once, our tractor was mired in mud. I got behind it, ready to use brute force to solve the problem. My father looked at the wheel, rut, and resources at hand. He took a chain off the tractor, wrapped one end around the axle and the other around a short log, and placed the log across the rut in front of the wheel. He slowly accelerated the engine, tested the rigging, then gradually increased power to the axle. The tractor lifted itself out of the rut on the log. Diagnose the problem you face and plan your solution before you act. Later, I learned formal methods of problem-solving and *Plan, Do, Check, Act (PDCA)*.

3. We found the farm's entrance gate lying on the ground. I fixed it while my father examined tire tracks around it. I thought we had finished the work, but my father drove to a house where two boys lived. Two off-road motorcycles sat in the yard. My father talked with the parents, then the boys: "I need your help keeping my fire roads open and safe," he said. "If the ruts get deep, you won't be able to ride your motorcycles there, and I'll lose reforestation subsidies. Here's a key to the gate, and here's my

phone number. Call collect if there's a tree across the road, a place where the creek has washed out the road, or a rut needs fixing so you can ride safely." Dad knew his business, understood "employee" involvement, and believed in partnership with suppliers, customers, and other stakeholders. *"Make people a part of the answer, not a part of the problem,"* he said.

My father never formally learned quality concepts or tools. But he knew a lot about quality practices. I have now learned names for practices he knew in his bones. As a laborer in limestone quarries and mills, an engineering co-op student in a foundry, a teacher and administrator in a great research university, an executive in a multibillion-dollar manufacturing firm, an executive in an entrepreneurial high tech startup company, and a consultant, I confronted frustrations he no doubt felt while working with me. I developed "working on the work" as an approach to implementing quality practices when more conventional programs are a problem, not a remedy.

The Problem

Your company faces no crisis that forces comprehensive quality improvement and awakens top management from complacency. Or, your company has failed in one or more false starts at implementing a quality program, and the environment is poisoned for new attempts. Or, it is a small startup company where people believe "TQM" smacks of bureaucracy that stifles adaptability, flexibility, agility, and creativity. Or, it is a company whose culture fosters a "Superman" approach to leadership, management, and problem solving or thrives on succeeding by dint of "brute force and great people" instead of effective and efficient workflows. Or, it is a company of highly educated and motivated knowledge workers who believe everything they do is "quality" work and resent the "not-invented-here" aspect of quality programs.

Yet you are confident quality practices can help you achieve better results. You see advantages to your company in implementing them. You know quality concepts, which Dr. Noriaki Kano describes in Chapter 11 as one of the pillars of "The House of TQM." These concepts come from Juran, Deming, Feigenbaum, Ishikawa, Imai, Crosby or other teachers. You've been exposed to quality improvement tools and practices (the "Techniques" and "Vehicles" pillars of "The House of TQM") from simple problem-solving processes to Taguchi methods, multiple regression analysis, failure mode and effects analysis, design of experiments, policy deployment, or quality function deployment. You see that they might be effectively applied to improve business results in your company. You are missing the "Motivational Approach" required in "The House of

TQM." Without it, you cannot get people in your business to do the "sweating work" of quality improvement.

Under these circumstances how can you bring about change and move your company toward implementing quality practices?

"Working on the Work": A Pragmatic Remedy

"Working on the work" means improving work that delivers value to customers and carefully picking the work to improve first. Companies do work to satisfy customers. Customers pay the bills and choose whose bills they will pay. If a supplier consistently works faster, better, or cheaper than its competitors, it wins the customer's business. If it doesn't, eventually, it falls behind. Effective and efficient work delivers value. The better the right work is done, the greater the value delivered.

Quality concepts, tools, and practices are powerful means for improving the way work gets done, including the work of choosing the right work for a businesss to do. Improving work, especially mission-critical work at the core of the enterprise, delivers business results—both short-term bottom-line results and long-term competitive advantage. Improvement in results justifies quality practices. Quality practices don't justify themselves.

If we forget that quality practices are means to get business results, not ends in themselves, we are confusing means with ends. We may produce a conceptually perfect program and a lot of hoopla, but few results. If we don't produce results, we lose the commitment of managers and rank-and-file employees alike. They are accountable for results—including customer satisfaction, timely delivery, financial performance, product or service quality, and continuous improvement. They will welcome the help of quality efforts in improving these results clearly and immediately.

Many factors have caused quality programs to fail. Behind many of these lies the mistake of having pursued quality practices for their own sake, rather than as means to achieve business results. "The bellowing of top management about quality, without any follow-through," as Dr. Robert Cole puts it in his Introduction, exemplifies top management's promoting quality practices for their own sake.

Top managers often talk about quality as a goal for others, but do not apply quality practices in their own work. They urge employees to learn quality concepts and tools, yet they do not apply the tools to problems in workflows for which they are themselves responsible. These top managers have jumped on the quality bandwagon, but have not understood their own work and how quality practices can most profitably be used to improve that work.

The failure of "bellowing" without doing, along with many other failures Dr. Cole cites, may taint the environment for openly promoting quality practices. Then what can be done to reap the benefits of quality practices for the business?

The Remedy

"Working on the work" provides a five-step approach to implementing quality practices:

1. Develop a thorough understanding of the key, mission-critical workflows in your business; they are the "pattern in the carpet" as you implement the next four steps.

2. Select visible, significant, and tractable problems in the key workflows.

3. Define and agree on the work and teamwork required to solve these problems and create improved workflows.

4. Demonstrate the power of quality improvement tools as you proceed from one successful improvement project to the next.

5. Move strategically from one to another visible, significant, and tractable problem.

Step 1: The "Pattern in the Carpet"

I use the phrase "pattern in the carpet"[1] as shorthand for the set of mission-critical workflows an enterprise uses to define, create, and deliver value to customers. To implement enterprisewide quality improvement by "working on the work," you have to understand these workflows. They guide your efforts, and implementing quality practices throughout them is your goal.

You don't have a top-down quality program to guide you, but you must know the work your company does that creates value for your customers. In the absence of leadership of quality improvement from the top, as the leader of quality improvement work, you must set priorities, integrate discrete projects, and achieve completeness in implementing quality practices throughout the enterprise.

To do so, you must understand the mission-critical workflows to select projects that matter most to the business, to link and leverage successes as you proceed, and to ensure that you bring enterprisewide scope to "working on the work" by ultimately applying quality practices to the mission-critical workflows themselves. If you don't understand how your business works—its "pattern in the carpet"—success and completeness will come only by luck.

Each business has unique mission-critical workflows that define the way it creates value for customers. Dr. Armand V. Feigenbaum, while consulting at a company where I worked, made a useful generalization about three workflows that underlie operations of virtually all companies:

1. *Business planning and development,* which is the distinctive work of top management.

2. *New product planning, development, and introduction,* often the work of cross-functional teams led by middle management.

3. *Delivery of product and services,* typically the work of the company's "rank and file."

These three workflows provide a generic framework for discerning the "pattern in the carpet" unique to your business. They can help you select and link problems attacked in "working on the work." They help identify problems that are mission-critical and therefore important for the success of the company. They help define relationships between discrete activities and functions so that successive projects can be strategically selected to link with each other and thus leverage early success in subsequent projects and ultimately complete enterprisewide improvement.

Finally, they define "enterprisewide": Quality practices are implemented throughout the enterprise when these three workflows and the teamwork they require are defined in detail and agreed on, their efficiency and effectiveness are measured, and they are continuously improving.

Prior to Dr. Feigenbaum's work in the company where I met him, we had faltered in a traditional approach to implementing a TQM program. We had launched a campaign, including a motivating slogan and extensive training. We focused on teaching quality improvement tools and techniques to all employees. Both quality circles and individual improvement initiatives were encouraged at all levels throughout the company. Yet our efforts stalled. We had not defined and agreed on the key workflows and teamwork required for us to succeed with our customers in our business approach. Dr. Feigenbaum's involvement helped us get over these pitfalls.

To lead enterprisewide quality improvement by "working on the work," you must know the mission-critical workflows—the "pattern in the carpet"—of your business. You use the "pattern in the carpet" to select problems to attack that are visible and significant because they are in business processes that directly affect the delivery of value to customers.

As projects are completed, you use the "pattern in the carpet" to select new projects that are linked by the workflows. Linkage creates momentum and exploits leverage. It leverages one success on another by taking advantage of the supplier-customer relationships inherent in workflows, capitalizing on the learning and experience of participants or beneficiaries of prior improvements in a workflow, and using the "context" to reinforce improvements in adjacent segments of the flow. Keeping the "pattern in the carpet" in mind helps you strengthen the cumulative effect of your improvement projects by linking discrete successes and thus serves to the make up for the absence of top-down promotion of quality practices.

The Next Four Steps

Approaching enterprisewise quality improvements by "working on the work" means systematically laying the foundation for effectiveness, efficiency, and continuous improvement of mission-critical workflows. It means selecting each project strategically, attacking it effectively, delivering business results, and moving on to the next problem strategically to leverage prior success.

The next four steps define a cycle that is repeated. The endpoint may be tacit installation of total quality management without the acronym "TQM" and without having used overt programs and hoopla, or it may be successfully winning support of top management so that a more standard programmatic approach to enterprisewide implementation of quality practices may be used to complete organizational transformation. Or, the end may be the journey of continuous improvement. In any case, the cycle expands over time to exert a greater and greater influence over quality results for the entire enterprise.

Step 2: Select Visible, Significant, and Tractable Problems in Mission-Critical Workflows

It is tempting to begin working on the first problem that presents itself, or to attack a problem that falls in an area where management or the environment welcomes quality practices. Often these problems occur in workflows that support mission-critical workflows—such as human resources, finance, or facilities—but are not directly in a mission-critical workflow. If the problems you attack are not directly and apparently in a key workflow, they may be significant and tractable, but they are not sufficiently visible. Linkages to mission-critical workflows will "pull" improvement in supporting flows. Financial, human resources, and information systems will have to be improved to enable improvement in the key workflows. They should be improved as required, not as primary projects themselves.

Early on, it is critical to achieve visible results in improving mission-critical workflows. Results in these areas show that the approach clearly benefits the business and makes key managers successful. They then become allies. Furthermore, your work, like all work of the company, should focus on achieving the most important business results first. Achieving visible results is more important than touting quality practices.

"Significant" means that the problems you choose to solve should be in a mission-critical workflow and be prominent in that flow. By solving these problems, your work will have a measurable effect on revenue, customer satisfaction, cost, product or service quality, or delivery performance.

For example: Like many others, your company may experience extremely high order rates at the end of each quarter and the fiscal year. These spikes may result in high error rates on orders, in purchasing or manufacturing scheduling and shipping, and on invoices. The wrong products or services may be delivered to the customer, or the invoice may be wrong, which leads to slow payments, customer dissatisfaction, and costly rework. Delays may mean that revenue may not be recognized in the quarter or year desired. This problem in order-entry management, which I have seen in the "delivery" workflows of three very different businesses, is visible and significant.

Improvements in order entry are measurable and quantifiable, and they benefit a wide variety of stakeholders in the business—customers who want what they ordered, when and where they expected it, under the terms and conditions they agreed to pay; the sales force that receives commissions on revenue that gets booked on time; the manager and employees of the order entry function who periodically feel "under the gun"; and top mangement and shareholders who benefit from improved quarterly and annual results.

The question then becomes "Is the problem 'tractable'?" Can you use quality concepts and tools to solve it? Is working on this part of the firm's work a "doable" proposition?

The order-entry problem is tractable when the root causes are in information flows that can be improved dramatically by defining steps in the workflow and applying technology effectively. Where the problem is driven by a combination of customers' budget cycles and firmly entrenched sales commission plans, the problem is visible and significant, but not tractable to quality improvement methods. Pick your battles!

If the resources and tools at your disposal are not sufficient to solve the problem, attack another problem. Tilting at windmills made a great story about Don Quixote, but it doesn't make a good quality story. Quality practitioners, like Don Quixote, are too often seen as impractical idealists. Don't run the risk of evoking this perception early in your implementation process. "Working on the work" is not about an impossible dream; it is aimed at demonstrating that business results can be immediately and directly affected by using quality concepts and tools to improve the mission-critical work of the company.

Step 3: Define and Agree on the Work and Teamwork Required to Solve Those Problems and Create Improved Workflows

Once a visible, significant, tractable problem in a mission-critical workflow has been selected, how do you "work on the work"? Many workflow improvement processes exist. (A good example is presented in Figure 7.4.) In general, they proceed along the following lines.

First, ask, "Why are we doing this work?" Understand and agree on the purpose and value of the work. The answer may be that it shouldn't be done because no customer would be willing to pay you to do it.

Then, if the work is necessary, define the way the work is currently being done. What is the existing workflow? Many effective methods are available to help with this part of the work—sophisticated CASE (Computer Aided System Engineering) programs, storyboarding with card stock or Post-its, or hand-drawn workflow diagrams.

Whatever methods are used to define a workflow, I have found that one critical result is "to make the invisible visible" to participants and stakeholders in the flow. Often, specific steps in a workflow, particularly those dealing with intangible ideas or data, are not obvious even to those who implement or manage the flow itself. Making each and every step in a workflow visible both gets knowledge of the flow into the open and objectifies the steps, which opens them to analysis without provoking defensive reactions from the steps' "owners."

Storyboarding has an advantage over CASE tools in the early stages of workflow analysis and definition. Visible and tangible cards or Post-its, placed on a wall in clear view, facilitate group interaction and collaboration. Group engagement helps create agreement about the way work is currently done, about problems in the workflow, about the way it should be done in an improved state, and about the action steps to get from the current to the improved flow.

Third, as you lead the project, use all the quality concepts and tools at your disposal to review the definition of the current flow step-by-step; to identify non-value-added steps, repetitive steps, bottlenecks, and other opportunities to improve the flow and eliminate waste—wasted time, scrap and rework, or non-value-added work of any sort. Can a step be automated or eliminated? Can it be performed faster, better, cheaper? What are the critical process and results indicators to quantify and measure this step?

At this stage the opportunity for training in quality practices is high. Individuals learn best and are most receptive to learning when they are ac-tively engaged with real problems in real work. Participants in tough projects inevitably experience educable moments as they reach the limits of their current knowledge and struggle to understand, document, and improve the workflow.

As the leader of the project, you must both sense these educable moments and bring to bear effective training, just in time. Depending on the work group's receptiveness, dwelling on the names of the tools taught in the training or the fact that they are quality tools may or may not be useful. In any case, after the tools have succeeded, participants should definitely be made conscious of what they have learned. They can then apply their new skills again on their own, and they will develop a common language and "tool set" for improvement work.

Fourth, define the new, improved flow, make it equally visible, and plan the work to implement the improved flow.

Customer input helps. The customer or customers of each step, as well as the end customers, must be identified and consulted. Get customers to participate in the process. Use surveys or other means. It is helpful to keep asking questions: "Who are our customers? Are they willing to pay us to do this? Why or why not?" If customers would not willingly pay the cost of any step, then it should be eliminated.

It is also important to ask the question "What are we not doing that customers want or expect?" In the business planning and development workflow, for example, information about sales won is usually readily available. However, data about sales lost may not be collected. Information about sales lost provides key input to product development, marketing, delivery flow improvement, or sales training. It may be as valuable as data about wins.

When the work group has defined and ageed on the way they want to do the work, the actions they will take to implement the improved workflow, the measures they will track to monitor their processes and results, then implement the transition plan.

Step 4: Demonstrate the Power of Quality Improvement Tools

This step promotes the quality improvement effort. It aims:

1. To leverage success in one area as a means to win access to subsequent areas where visible, significant, and tractable problems exist.
2. To measure and display business results achieved by having successfully applied quality concepts and tools to improve mission-critical work.
3. To clearly link the results achieved with one or more of the mission-critical workflows in the company.

It differs from the hoopla associated with many quality programs in that its purpose is not to publicize TQM for its own sake or to inspire broad employee enthusiasm for TQM. Rather, it functions to help insinuate "working on the work" into other parts of the "pattern in the carpet."

Managers in key workflows inevitably face visible, significant problems. Their problems often are not tractable to their solutions. These managers are likely to be open to help from those who have shown they can improve business performance. They may be less open to those who tout TQM or quality practices as a solution to all problems.

The thrust of promotion in "working on the work" is not to market quality practices used in successful projects, but to communicate business results achieved. At a later stage, when successes are numerous and visible, it may be appropriate to begin explicitly stressing the role of quality practices in achieving results. But don't risk provoking early resistance by stressing TQM or quality practices until results are clear and definitive.

Finally, top management recognition helps, and, ultimately, to achieve enterprisewide improvement, top management must work on their work. While you can pursue an improvement campaign indefinitely using the "guerrilla" tactics of "working on the work," recognition and support from top management can be earned. If they are made aware of the visible, significant business results your efforts have achieved, they will work for you—or at least not against you. They may never be ready to sign up to lead a TQM program; they may, however, become supportive of the work you are doing.

In a small computer manufacturing firm, the vice president of hardware engineering faced rising costs and schedule slippages in design and development work because his engineers were frequently called on to solve problems with products in production. The designs had not appeared to be flawed, but manufacturing processes were not capable of consistently producing quality computers.

The vice president was biased against quality practices in new product planning, development, and introduction. He had experienced rigid, cumbersome, and time-consuming processes that were not practical in his rapidly changing, unstructured environment. He was not sure what to do about his problem, but he was open to help from a quality advisor who had achieved results in another workflow.

The quality advisor facilitated a cross-functional work group, led by the vice president of engineering, which defined and agreed on a product development process for hardware. The process included a flow of critical checkpoints, success factors, participants, reviews, and approvals required to move a product with great success from concept to production. Because it was captured in a one-page responsibility matrix showing each step in the process, it was accepted not only as a reliable way to prevent hardware production problems, but also as simple, fast, and practical. It was similar to the one described by Price and Chen in Chapter 7 (Figure 7.8).

To demonstrate the power of quality concepts and tools in improving workflows:

1. Measure and display business results you achieve.

2. Explain how quality concepts and tools achieve results; teach, don't preach.

3. Link your work to key workflows in your company—the "pattern in the carpet."

4. Seek every opportunity to earn the support of top management.

Step 5: Move Strategically to the Next Visible, Significant, Tractable Problem

In standard quality programs, top management is responsible for ensuring that improvement work leads to a coherent and complete management system in which mission-critical workflows are defined and agreed on, key indicators are adopted, and continuous improvement is achieved.

In "working on the work" the leader of quality management must discern and keep in mind the "pattern in the carpet." Whether in parallel or in sequence, discrete improvement projects must fall into a complete and coherent system for managing and continuously improving the performance of the enterprise as a whole.

The "pattern in the carpet"—the mission-critical workflows of your business—provides the generic framework for deciding where to extend the improvement effort and how to join discrete projects into a coherent whole. These key workflows must be defined and agreed on completely and in their unique detail in your business. Process and results indicators must be identified and adopted, and teamwork required among participants within and across functional boundaries openly defined and agreed on. Until this end is reached, enterprisewide improvement and continuous improvement are not achieved.

Depending on resources available, projects should be engaged in a sequence that follows one or more workflow, or in parallel to improve more than one flow simultaneously. Progress overall will be accelerated if improvement work proceeds in all three key workflows in parallel.

The leader of quality improvement has to define "enterprisewide" to create a "doable proposition" for the quality effort. In a large company, work might focus on mission-critical workflows in a division, group, or function of manageable size. In a small company "enterprisewide" may be the company as a whole.

As work proceeds, choices of problems to attack should be linked to prior problems that have been successfully solved. In a key workflow, immediately adjacent steps are prime candidates for extending improvement work. Successes can and should be leveraged by drawing on the learning and commitment of customers, suppliers, colleagues, and peers who participated in or benefited from previous work.

Remenber that top managers have their own problems. Demonstrate that you can help them succeed, and they will open doors for you to work on their work. They are responsible for "the pattern in the carpet." When you work on projects at their level, the level of the mission-critical workflows themselves, you are approaching the goal of enterprisewide quality improvement.

A high-tech start-up company, where I worked and Dr. Kano consulted, risked failure because of inadequate business planning and development. Top management took for granted a business approach that had worked in another firm years before. They failed to see that their industry and markets had matured and that strong competitors had firmly established themselves.

The terms of competition had changed. Large investments in hardware and software had dramatically raised customers' switching costs. The approach that worked five years before was no longer competitive. No matter how efficiently people in the company worked, they could not win until the business approach itself changed, and the business was restructured appropriately.

At the very foundation of business planning and development there must be a clear definition of the company's business approach—its purpose, mission, and values; its markets, customers, and products or services; and the measurable grounds on which it will compete and attempt to sustain advantage. People in the company may do things right on their own, but they need adequate guidance to do the right things. They need to know what the company is trying to achieve and how it plans to achieve it to minimize the role of luck, and maximize the effectiveness of managment and leadership.

If the business approach is not clear, business success and success in implementing quality improvement will be coincidental or fortuitous, not necessarily the result of effective management and leadership. Ultimately, top management must execute its responsibility for defining a business approach that is achievable, potentially successful, and measurable. Quality concepts and tools help.

In summary, moving into new projects along mission-critical workflows has four distinct advantages:

1. Linked successful projects in a flow build critical mass and momentum in the improvement of that flow. Customers and suppliers in the flow reinforce the knowledge and behavior you are building into the improved flow.

2. Adjacent segments where successes have been achieved sustain the effects of improvement work in each other. If improvement work has been done by engaging stakeholders in the process, then customers and

suppliers will have already committed themselves to approaches and solutions you have used and may use again to improve their segments of the workflow.

3. It is likely that improvements in a particular segment of a workflow will have exposed bottlenecks or problems in adjacent segments. This opens the door for your help.

4. It positions the quality leader to seize the first opportunity to work on the work of top management—that is, to attack a problem that spans one of the mission-critical workflows as a whole, rather than one of its parts.

"Working on the work," as an approach to enterprisewide quality improvement, will overcome the deficiencies of "project-by-project" improvement, noted by Dr. Juran, only when it addresses the company's "fundamental quality problems." Fundamental quality problems are tackled by improving the mission-critical workflows themselves, not just their parts. Most important, the business planning and development workflow must include improvement targets that are derived from customer data and linked to customer value. "Quality planning" is thus effectively achieved, even if not called by that name. "Quality control" and "quality improvement" are effectively reached by the cumulative successes of "working on the work" projects, if they are linked and leveraged along the mission-critical workflows of the business.[2]

Benefits

Pursuing quality improvement by "working on the work" positions the quality leader as a business person, who delivers business results and provides technical expertise in business process improvement, problem solving, and change management. This contrasts sharply with stereotypes of the quality advocate as impractical idealist, blind disciple of Juran, Deming, Crosby or any other quality "guru," or thoughtless proselyte of Japanese-style management.

From this pragmatic, business-oriented position four important benefits flow:

1. "Working on the work" delivers business results immediately.

2. The power of quality concepts, tools, and practices to achieve business results is showcased for the entire organization. To skeptics, quality may move from the realm of dogmatic idealism to responsive pragmatism.

3. Success on discrete projects or a series of projects keeps the quality "ball" rolling. It creates momentum and prepares for moving to a more

standard approach if circumstances change and become conducive to a quality program led from the top.

4. The leader of quality improvement—whether a quality professional or functional manager—can experience personal satisfaction, show demonstrable results for the business (even where TQM programs have failed in the past), and make effective allies.

The critical factor in deriving these benefits from "working on the work" is quickly and steadily achieving business results on visible and significant problems in mission-critical workflows. Successes in areas that are not visible, relatively insignificant for business results, or outside key workflows do not provide the same benefits. Failures are, of course, always a risk, but can be avoided by selecting tractable problems.

Watch Outs

Many things can cause failure on specific projects. I will not try to enumerate all of them here. Instead, I will point out four pitfalls in "working on the work":

1. *Don't forget to "work on the work."* While working on the work, don't fall into the trap of emphasizing the virtues of quality concepts and tools, rather than getting results for the business. Managers and employees whom you are helping to improve their workflows probably don't care much about the "machinery" you use to help them. The more urgent their need for results, the less they will attend to the means you use to get them. After you deliver results, take time to teach them quality techniques and help them understand quality tools. First, give them bread, then teach them to make it themselves. But never stop working on the work; never lose your focus on delivering visible results that matter to the business.

Maxim 1: Deliver results; don't dogmatize and don't proselytize.

2. *Don't thoughtlessly gore sacred cows of the culture.* In the United States, especially in knowledge industries, people jealously guard a sense of their own ability to innovate, make decisions, and produce quality work. Freedom and creavity are "sacred cows," along with a variety of related values—flexibility, adaptability, informality, speed, agility, simplicity, individualism.

These "sacred cows" are frequently cited as reasons for not entertaining quality practices. For many "quality" has come to suggest constraint, rigid processes, and stifling bureaucracy, or a process, rather than results, orientation. Don't attack "sacred cows" head-on. Rather, select your problems carefully—visible, significant, tractable ones—and solve them quickly and effectively. Deliver results.

However, in spite of their persistent demands for freedom, people also often feel that they don't have adequate information about the work they should do to make the business successful. They want the freedom to do their work creatively and effectively; and they welcome guidance about what work to do to serve the ends of the company best. The trick is to provide guidance, as effectively applied quality practices do, without turning it into unwarranted constraint on their capabilities. They want to keep it simple.

Maxim 2: Preserve the freedom to be creative; give the guidance to be productive.

3. *Don't lose sight of the "pattern in the carpet."* You have to weave the various problems you attack and the solutions you help implement into an enterprisewide solution. You can't so it if you lose sight of the set of mission-critical workflows that define the way your company creates and delivers value to customers. You'll choose less visible problems to attack, and you'll fail to deliver significant results. You need guidance yourself to be productive in your work. The trick is to maintain the balance between your enterprisewide goal and the specific tasks at hand that must collectively get you to your goal.

Maxim 3: Keep the "pattern in the carpet" well in mind, but always work on the work at hand.

4. *Don't forget that top management support is better than not having it.* Ultimately you must engage top management in "working on the work" or you won't fully implement enterprisewide quality practices. The distinctive contribution of top management comes in business planning and development. They define and agree on the business approach of the company. They establish the systems, processes, and structures to pursue that approach. They allocate resources and settle competing demands. If top management does not work on its work, quality improvement will always be constrained. They do not have to embrace or promote TQM by name or for its own sake, but they do have to engage their work, just as others must work on their work. The mission-critical workflows themselves must be defined, agreed on, and measured, and this requires top-management involvement.

Maxim 4: Engage top management when they're ready to work on their visible, significant, tractable problems.

Demonstrate business results. Pick your battles. Engage top management in working on their work when the time is right. When their problems are visible, significant, and tractable, and they appear to be stuck, there lies your opportunity to work on their work. And that completes work on the "pattern in the carpet."

Conclusion

We may dream of working in an organization—Motorola, Florida Power and Light, Xerox, Milliken, Federal Express, or Solectron—where the CEO aggressively promotes and leads a TQM program.

But the reality is, most of us don't. We work in organizations where the culture, past failures of quality programs, or top management does not support quality improvement and the implementation of quality practices.

Some of us, in fact, relish the challenge of leading improvement, using concepts and tools we know and respect, in an environment where we move to key opportunities, build relationships, and deliver results without the framework of a top-down program directing us. We want our own freedom to be creative. Showing people that they don't know that they don't know about the power of quality practices to help them be more successful is not a problem, it is just part of the work.

"Working on the work" addresses the needs of those of us who are on our own—without a sanctioned program to support our efforts—and provides an approach that can achieve immediate results while extending itself to encompass the entire enterprise over time.

My father showed me that people don't have to know quality tools by name or realize that you are applying quality tools to achive quality improvement. This does not mean that you shouldn't teach people the tools they can use to continuously improve their work. When they are receptive, you can and should teach them that the tools they used to improve their work are quality tools. Thus, they derive the added benefits of being skilled to strike out on their own more easily and of developing a common language for improvement work. However, the essential factor is to serve the ends of the business, not to create new disciples of quality practices.

Notes

1. I borrow this metaphor from the art of Oriental rugs. It refers to the images master rug weavers carry in their heads to guide the knotting of the various colors of yarn into the beautiful pile that distinguishes the whole and defines its type.
2. J. M. Juran, *Juran on Leadership for Quality:* An Executive Handbook (New York: The Free Press, 1989), pp. 10–11, 23–24.

9

Quality Improvement as Survival Strategy at Southern Pacific

JAMES M. CARMAN

Can Continuous Quality Improvement (CQI) be used to turn around a company in serious trouble and fighting for survival? The quality folklore would answer no: CQI takes years to change behavior and culture; it is expensive and requires a big, front-end investment; don't look to break even on quality spending for at least six years; it pays off for bureaucratized companies but not for those that already have a culture of employee empowerment or companies near death. To emphasize these points but not to change meaning, this chapter uses the term "continuous quality improvement" instead of "total quality management." As emphasized in the next chapter on the Alcoa experience, a total quality program requires a change in culture that is based on a clearly defined vision, mission, and set of values. Changing culture and values requires learning and time. Starting a TQM program is the easy part; implementing it, changing culture and values, and holding the gains is far more difficult.

Southern Pacific Lines knows and respects this folklore. However, it is out to prove that the folklore is overly pessimistic. In 1990, the company gave itself five years to prove CQI could be used as a turnaround strategy. If it fails, the company is likely to fail too. Now, three years into this turnaround strategy, it looks like Southern Pacific (SP) just may make it.

This story is worth telling even before the final chapter has been written for two very important reasons. First, it shows how to do the right things in implementing a CQI program, particularly when on a tighter time schedule than is usually thought to be prudent and operating in a hostile environment created by the economy, the industry, and the firm's own internal climate. Second, and perhaps more significant, we can see in SP's experience a potential melding of what would normally be thought of as conflicting value systems of business management: a belief that capital is the most important scarce resource and generating returns to capital in the short run is the key to a successful turnaround, versus a belief that human initiative is an equally important scarce resource for revitalization of a firm.

Moreover, Southern Pacific's CQI initiative is a good example of how to apply several of the key elements for success suggested in earlier chapters:

- A sustained top management leadership for the quality initiative.
- A relentless focus on the customer, both in setting strategic objectives and in building organizational routines that strongly link all units and levels of the firm as well as firm suppliers.
- A breaking down of organizational barriers between departments and levels in a company with strong unions so that cross-functional management starts to become normal operating procedure.
- A unique approach to providing the information required to "manage by facts."

The Situation

The Southern Pacific was a, if not the, leading western U.S. railroad from the driving of the golden spike in 1869 that completed the first intercontinental rail line into the 1960s, when it was still ranked as one of the country's best Class I railroads. It has broader coverage of Pacific ports, Gulf ports, and Mexican border crossing than its three main rivals with 25% fewer track miles than the average of the three. In the 1970s it tried to maintain growth by diversification. These efforts distracted the firm from responding to the new competition of deregulation in 1980. In that year it began merger talks with the Atchison Topeka and Santa Fe that were not completed until December 1983. However, the federal government ruled that the merged company would have to divest one of the two railroads. The holding company then sold, and pocketed most of the profits from, some of the diversified subsidiaries including SPRINT. Southern Pacific Transportation Company ended up spending five years in trust when, in late 1988, it was purchased by Philip F. Anschutz. It then became a privately held company that had had little leadership, trust, or direction for almost two decades. In addition, the new company was not one but a collection of divisions and subsidiary railroads. The Denver and Rio Grande Western Railroad, joined to the system as a part of the Anschutz purchase, was one-ninth the size of SP, fiercely independent, and had no shared culture with it.

What were the strategic alternatives for turning around this heterogeneous mixture of people and fixed assets? One was to sell off the assets, but it was not clear that the railroad was salable as a going business. *Downsizing of the core business of a service company is not really a strategy for survival.* Keep in mind that there were significant constraints on the company's decision making.

No time.   The company was losing money. Its physical assets were decaying and out of date. They and the cash wouldn't hold out very long—perhaps five years.

No money.   It was difficult to find lenders to a company that had been dying for twenty years and had no viable avenue for recovery. Whatever strategy selected had to be one that didn't require a great deal of investment and would conform to the covenants of existing debt instruments.

Customer hostility.   Industrywide, the railroad business was flat and not competing well against the defection to truck transport. Many old customers had switched to the Santa Fe, thinking it was going to be the survivor of the merger. But perhaps most disheartening was that the customers who remained, and many did so because they had no alternative, were not just dissatisfied—they were hostile. They would do anything to avoid doing business with Southern Pacific Lines. Thus, productivity improvements alone would not solve the problem. Customer service had to be substantially improved.

Marginal physical facilities.   Interestingly, SP had done some investment during the trust period. Indeed, they had plowed back more into their system than any of their competitors. Much of this was due to the lure of the intermodal container business as waves of imports arrived from the Far East. SP built a very modern container transfer terminal in Long Beach and upgraded its mainline track to a very high level. However, they didn't run many container trains over this track. The steamship companies designed and build their own rail cars for hauling containers. They then hired SP and the other western railroads to haul their trains east.

Unions.   Problems of dealing with organized labor in this company were far more complex than they were in, say, General Motors. More craft unions contract with more subsidiaries in more dispersed locations than in the automobile industry or other industries where CQI has been introduced.

Nonintegrated railroads.   The company had multiple cultures that developed because the management in some of the operating companies (and even some SP divisions) were unable to get along with one another; they simply protected their own fiefdoms and went their separate ways. The problems created by geographic dispersion alone were particularly significant. The system has eastern gateways in Chicago, St. Louis, Memphis, and New Orleans and two main lines west through the central and southern routes. An SP manager in Portland, Oregon, had little in common and little interest in the problems of a Cottonbelt manager in Houston.

Weak processes.   Inadequate or antiquated processes and procedures were still haunting the company in 1992. There were two reasons for this. First, in tightening down the company as much as possible during the trust period, decision making had become extremely bureaucratized, even by regulated railroad standards. Employees were in a turf- and job-protecting mode. Decisions simply could not get made in a time period relevant to the problem. There were barriers to arriving at decisions and inappropriate processes for getting them made in a useful time frame. Second, the entire operation ran in a firefighting mode. Since little was done as it should be, everyone was focused on expediting whatever was creating the most heat on any given day. It became apparent in 1991 that when management scraped away the expediters, no systems were underneath for operating an in-control transportation system.

On top of these problems, morale was low and management was thin. Although the culture needed to be changed, the company had to work with what it had. And the culture couldn't be changed unless management could change the behavior of the workforce, from top executives down to craft union workers. The combination of these constraints limited the alternatives that Southern Pacific's new owner could reasonably consider.

Quality Improvement as the Turnaround Strategy

Even as Anschutz was examining his alternatives, he was making a few changes in management. In 1989, he brought in Don Orris and Peter M. Ruotsi from American President Lines to head marketing activities. Ruotsi had been with Xerox, a Baldrige Award winner, and knew something of their successes with CQI. The newcomers experimented with CQI problem-solving techniques. One test employed CQI methods to improve rail-switching systems for chemical cars in Houston.[1] While it was not unanimous among top management, the results of these tests and the continued lack of customer confidence led Anschutz, in 1990, to the conclusion that the quality improvement approach to a culture change was the *only viable strategy* that could turn the company around. However, this was a QI program that had to be successful more rapidly than any CQI program on record, in an environment as hostile as any in recorded CQI history, and with less investment than the quality gurus ordinarily recommended.

CQI in a Hurry

When Kent Sterett, now Vice President for Quality, Strategic Planning and Procurement, describes implementation of the CQI strategy, the words "parallel" and "cascading" keep reappearing in his descriptions. These terms are keys to understanding how they achieved so much in such a short period.

However, when owner Anschutz looks back, he speaks of a more linear first three phases for introducing the quality improvement strategy that he hoped would turn SP around. In his mind, the first phase was to hire Sterett, provide clear leadership for, direction to, and commitment from top management, and begin articulating the mission, the quality strategy, and the presence of leadership down through the company. Kent Sterett had been head of the quality department of Florida Power and Light, an early CQI success story, and had been a judge in the Baldrige competition. In 1990 he was in charge of quality at Union Pacific. Thus, he knew a great deal about quality management in several different environments, including other service companies and other railroads. Sterett was allowed to hire some other key staff in the quality department. That was something of a departure from what was going on elsewhere in the company, but it was an investment justified in terms of the severe time constraints.

Anschutz's phase two was Sterett's first three months on the job, November 1990 through January 1991. Sterett didn't hesitate to begin a pilot project using a fact-driven, process-focused, interdisciplinary team to see if they could get the important main line serving the West Coast between Portland and Long Beach back to the point where they could again compete against trucks (over which they had a price advantage). It was a very successful pilot project.

Doing things on the cheap, doing them in parallel, and cascading were hallmarks of the activities during this period. These activities concerned:

- Demonstrating top management leadership, commitment, and involvement.
- Gathering and disseminating information.
- Benchmarking.
- Developing action plans.
- Involving the unions.
- Involving the managers in process improvement.

While normally the first three activities would be done one at a time, in this case they were performed simultaneously. The Interstate Commerce Commission still requires annual reports from all railroads, so there was more operating detail readily available than might be true in most industries. These data showed that SP was near the top in its spending. Yet it got less in return for this spending than any other major railroad. This information along with discussions among the top management not only created the required involvement and commitment but also led to an action plan for the year. The CEO, COO, and the Vice Presidents became the Quality Council.[2] There are now regional steering committees and every regional manager must appoint a "quality facilitator" who can support team activities even when a line supervisor is unsupportive.

There is an important point here. While employees were encouraged to identify problems for team attention, the problem focus came from the top. Management targeted just four main areas. In three areas—service improvement, revenue expansion, and productivity improvement—corporate headquarters provided more structure and direction on which problems to attack than is typical. Remember, this was a company where it seemed as if practically nothing worked. If all employees had been inoculated instantly with QI, anarchy would probably have resulted from trying to tackle too much at once. Hence, focus became an important feature of this strategy.

The fourth area was union involvement. Neither in this industry nor in this company had union leaders ever been involved in management meetings. Fifty union officers were brought to San Francisco, shown the data documenting the dismal economic and operating performance, told of the new strategy, and involved in its critique. They were asked to go back to their locals, discuss the plan, and participate in the CQI program for change. They were then invited to attend the company's annual management meeting of 200 managers from throughout the system. Thus, the union leaders knew about the strategy before middle and lower managers. They also learned in this briefing that the productivity of executive and professional workers was just as poor by industry standards as the productivity of SP's unionized workers.

Union participation in the CQI program has never reached 100%. Of 13 craft unions with whom the railroad bargains, one was told by its international not to participate, and another dropped out in 1992. Subsequently, some members of these unions have been impressed by the program and have begun to participate while another union has backed away. In any case, most union leaders recognized a new environment and have behaved as believers since that meeting in January 1991. Others are skeptics, but are willing to give the company a chance because they see no viable alternative.

Another characteristic of the company's workforce that is both a limitation and an advantage is that it is older in age than is typical for U.S. industry. Not only is the average length of employment longer, but some employees are third-generation SP workers. These are employees with a strong tie to the industry and SP; they represent a potential source of commitment if managers can just mobilize them.

Building on the Foundation

Built on the foundation of the first two phases, Phase Three began in January 1991 following the management meeting. While there have been midcourse corrections, the CQI program has grown ever since. The parallel and cascading activities in this phase concern involving employees and improving corporate processes. The elements of these activities are: more leadership and communication, training, QI teams, benchmarking and key performance indicators (KPI), annual quality-based business plans, accountability, and incentives. Note that there are no gimmicks here, just proven CQI techniques in a hurry. Here is a closer look at each of these Phase Three activities.

Leadership

Any CQI initiative requires continued communication and role modeling by top management. This leadership can take many forms, few of which are unique. However, none are unusually expensive. Following the management meeting in January 1991, there was a series of town meetings in all locations designed to tell workers about the quality-driven approach to doing business, without relying on that message being delivered by first-level supervisors. A corporate officer led every meeting, and each meeting had a consistent message. This program of about 125 regional meetings every six months will continue for the foreseeable future. It is important for inoculation that CQI not be seen as a passing fashion. Corporate officers also have "walked the talk" out on the track and in the yards with the employees. These officers demonstrate and speak of the importance of team play, and team recognition gets great visibility. The quality department has made extensive use of internally produced videos to get information into the hands of a widely dispersed workforce.

Training

When Kent Sterett came to SP as Vice President for Quality, there was a Labor Relation Director but no HRD staff. He was able to participate in the hiring of a Vice President for Human Resources and to have his help in the quality training process. About two-thirds of the 23,000 employees in this company have now had some formal quality training, most of it delivered by internal staff. In addition, an annual employee survey has been made one of the important inputs into the annual process for deciding which opportunities will be pursued.[3] Consultants have been used sparingly and with specific short-term assignments. Over 100 SP employees have served as instructors in this training.

In 1993, Sterett's responsibilities were increased, so now all training, the strategic planning function, and procurement report to him. Also in 1993, with all training materials prepared and training activities leveling off, most of the quality department training staff have been sent into the field to increase the number of facilitators (SP calls them consultants) working with teams. With this group added to the Quality Facilitators who report to the operations manager in each region, there are now about twenty consultants in the field working with teams. Since each consultant can facilitate more than one team at a time, this represents a significant change in approach and support resources being given to the field.[4] Sterett and the senior managers in operations determine which teams are going to be given support resources based on who needs the help most in order to achieve the well-defined annual goals.

Quality Improvement Teams (QIT)

The operating units have formed quality improvement teams of all types. At the maximum there were almost 900 teams, with about 25% cross-functional. With increased focus, that number has been reduced. The company has its own teleconferencing capability for use by teams in different locations. Before 1993, teams didn't get much other logistic or clerical support. They were expected to write their own reports and draw their own graphs. Word processors are not made available even if someone on the teams knows how to use one. These teams had completed 252 projects as of November 1992. This number and growth rate in projects are far greater than in any organization the author has encountered. Indeed, in 1993 and the 1994 plan leveled-out the number of teams but kept the focus on the processes where the greatest gains can be achieved.

Key Performance Indicators (KPI)

Remember that in January 1991 management had only a start on information base. Managers of each operating unit were asked to identify the criteria (i.e., data) on which they would like to be evaluated given the four areas for improvement top management had identified in that year.[5] By March, measures on these criteria had been identified. The quality department then set out to find benchmarks (external measures) and KPIs (internal measures) for each of the evaluation criteria. By the early 1992 management meeting, over 100 of these measures were in place and managers knew exactly how they were being evaluated. For example, it took just three months to agree on the first customer satisfaction questionnaire and get it into the field. Minor improvements have been made subsequently, but that instrument is the basis of marketing and some operating KPIs. Chartings of KPIs and goals are now widely distributed throughout the organization, so it is clear that customer perceptions are paramount. Since 1992, the KPIs have been refined and improved some, but they still remain the primary performance measures.

Integrated Planning

For the 1993 budgeting process, the CQI priorities were made the basis of each unit's budget plan. To separate them from traditional bureaucratic budgets, management labels these unit submissions as "business plans." It is clear that QI is the backbone of each unit's yearly operating plan. Each unit manager must demonstrate in the business plan an understanding of how the planning process integrates strategy, quality, finance, marketing, and operations. The plan is driven by short-term survival, medium-term competitiveness, and long-term cash flow. Goals are stated in terms of each unit's KPIs, but the links between these KPI goals and operating margins are quite explicit.

Accountability

Beginning with Phase Three, accountability for KPI performance and incentive compensation was extended to all nonunion workers, about 15% of the total workforce. Bonuses are to be paid on an individual basis rather than a team basis (except for QIT awards). While this system might suggest that fear (negative incentives) still exist, there are at least three mitigating factors. One is that top management has been very supportive and has used positive incentives to reward success by managers who have worked actively to improve processes. The one thing that is not tolerated is resistance to the strategy of culture change through the use of quality improvement techniques.

The second mitigating factor is that SP has been operating under a salary freeze since 1989. The incentive compensation scheme has been announced and kicks in when a specific level of cash flow is reached. This should be 1994.[6] For managers below the very top, incentives are based on KPI achievement. For example, a manager's goal might be a 25% reduction in lost-time injuries. A bonus would be paid for meeting or beating that KPI goal. For the seven top executives in the company, these KPI goals have been monetized and rolled up so that bonuses are based only on total cash flow for all of SP Lines. In other words, the reward and measurement systems, as well as strategic planning system, are tied directly and obviously to the CQI program.

The third mitigating factor is that the Quality Council acknowledges that team failures can lead to individual failure to meet goals, that goals may be unrealistic, and that KPI measures are subject to measurement error. For example, the field sales representatives have a fairly standard incentive compensation plan, but they do not take the heat if an operating problem creates a new case of customer dissatisfaction.

SP executives don't claim that the incentive program leads to perfect results, but they do expect to see the measures going in the right direction.

Measures haven't been a source of complaint. Sterett puts it this way: "It is difficult for a manager to say that he can't be average, and most KPI performance isn't at industry average yet."

Some Examples

Each unit's business plan develops action plans for improving KPI performance. For 1993 and 1994 these had to be focused on less than nine specific objectives. Examples are "to continuously: improve ability to meet or exceed customer requirements; grow revenues; improve revenue collections; reduce the cost of non-conformance; strengthen operations' effectiveness; improve asset utilization; improve safety." Each of these objectives is detailed more specifically. For example, under "continuously improve ability to meet or exceed customer service requirements," the subobjectives are: "improve knowledge of our customers; improve market knowledge; increase customer responsiveness; improve scheduled service reliability; provide commercially acceptable cars."

An action plan is developed for the year for each of these subobjectives and each specific action is assigned to one or more specific managers. KPI performance goals have also been established for each subobjective. Thus, individual business units know what their goals are; they form the teams required to solve the problems blocking the achievement of goals.

Here is an example of how the processes has worked. Two subobjectives previously mentioned had to do with increasing reliability and having cars in good running order. At one point, a group of carmen, a union position, expressed concern because a company that interchanged with SP was releasing cars back to SP that were not in good running order. These cars would get out on a main line and break down, thus reducing the reliability of scheduled service. These carmen asked to form a team to work on the problem. (Note that the team was actually asking to work on a supplier's quality problem.) One manager, who had to deal with this supplier, thought these craftsmen should not be allowed to take on such a project. Their supervisor and the regional facilitator disagreed. The team was allowed to proceed. They followed the steps learned in their training, successfully worked with the supplier to ensure that cars were in good running order when they were released back to SP, and succeeded in significantly improving KPIs for these two subobjectives in their region. In recognition, they were flown to San Francisco to present their report (that they had prepared on their own) before the senior management team. They were away from their jobs for only one day, the tangible awards they received were of little value, but the intangible awards were very great.[7] The team is now the envy of their yard.

Another example of CQI in practice at SP is in the area of pricing and revenue collections. There are few businesses where pricing is as complex as in the transport industry and few businesses in the transport industry where pricing is as complex as in the railroads. The industry grew up with ICC rate setting. A main argument for deregulation was that price administration had become impossible under the regulated tariff system. Thus, deregulation and competition generally led to very undisciplined pricing practices throughout the industry. Another complexity for railroads is the large number of interconnections with other lines where the revenues from an order must be split among the carriers. One approach to simplifying the rate structure was to negotiate contract rates with regular customers. However, contract business was often lost before the negotiated rate could get approved by all the parties involved within the railroad.

Several SP teams had addressed this problem working under the objective "to continuously improve revenue collections." Today in the area of contract approval, 67% of SP business is conducted under contract rates, and because of the work of a QI team, it takes just five days to get a contract negotiated and approved—down from more than two weeks.

The pricing and billing problem involves both marketing and accounting; many teams are thus cross-functional, and cross-training was one implemented recommendation. Teams have been formed to reduce the complexity of the pricing structure, to lower the number of errors in billing, to increase the number of invoices for forwarded freight that can be priced by computer (in 1991, no invoices were rated by computer for traffic received from other railroads), and to increase the percentage of bills that are not contested by customers.

This is another case where SP invited customer CQI teams to work jointly with SP teams. Because contesting invoiced amounts is costly for both buyers and sellers, in 1992 about a half dozen joint SP/customer teams were working on invoice problems at any given time. As a result of these CQI efforts, the number of uncontested bills rose from 77.5% in 1991 to over 90% by the end of 1992.[8]

The Customer Service Department

Also benefiting from CQI is the Customer Service Department, which has played a pivotal role in SP's turnaround. One may have trouble just visualizing a customer service department in a service company with such low levels of reliability. This function was centralized under a new vice president in Denver, Dennis Jacobson, who had managed the Customer Service function at Union Pacific. Jacobson believes that gaining perspective on the problem was the key to his success—he had to define the problems before he could solve them. "The noise in a low performance company will mask an understanding of the real problems unless some systematic data analysis is undertaken," he observes.

His staff, now about 100, was organized around commodity teams. They were given CQI training that taught them to define the problem, get the data they needed to address it, implement a solution, and continue to monitor performance. It's interesting to note that many people who have received CQI training have commented that what they were taught was simply a logical approach to problem solving. Perhaps they had learned this earlier in their lives but had fallen into ad hoc approaches to doing their jobs. This reintroduction to logical, systematic, data-based problem solving has helped improve their productivity. The result is that complex process and organizational changes that were required at SP have been accomplished more smoothly than without the CQI approach and training.

The only CQI cross-commodity team established within the Customer Service Department was one to develop a system for logging complaints and analyzing what caused the complaint. In other words, the process—training $\longrightarrow$ data $\longrightarrow$ solve problem—required a computer systems development step that was carried out along with training and manual data collection and analysis.[9] A server system attached to a local area network now almost transparently downloads all the necessary information required to trace a problem shipment, provides it to the Customer Service representative, and compiles a scorecard of delivery, recovery, and performance.

These efforts have paid off. In the customer satisfaction survey for the eighteen months between June 1991 and December 1992, customers rating SP on "problem resolution" as 4 or 5, on a 5-point scale, went from 38% to 50%. The Customer Service Department also is responsible for the Electronic Data Interchange program among shippers and carriers that permits computers in different companies to exchange information about shipments. Southern Pacific is now returning to a position of leadership in this service.

By early 1992, customers had been convinced SP was interested and responsive to solving problems. By mid-1992, the emphasis could be shifted from *responsiveness* to *reliability*. There are two facets of this program. One is to work with customers in providing rather precise delivery promises that can be kept. The other is to supply operating managers with weekly and monthly scorecards on how they are doing in terms of meeting delivery promises and minimizing complaints. The score is a published ranking of the performance of various parts of the system. While this stack ranking definitely points to problems of particular managers, a *teamwork* approach is offered to those managers for improving the *processes* that are causing the low rankings.

Another tricky job for the Customer Service Department and for all marketing was the management of customer expectations. They wanted perceptions of quality to improve; they also wanted expectations to go up—but at a rate that SP could meet. Don Orris, Senior Vice President for Distribution Services, believes they probably did oversell the abilities of the "New SP" in 1991 even though they tried not to promise too much. The revitalized Customer Service Department coupled with centralization of the Transportation Control Center may provide the ability for marketing to better balance expectations and performance. It is a concept management had recognized, and they speak of it as something that can and should be managed.

Lessons Learned

Southern Pacific's experience offers some valuable insights into how a beleaguered company can successfully apply CQI and see results within a relatively short time—and on a modest budget. Briefly, here are the lessons learned.

- *With knowledgeable leadership, a parallel implementation of CQI can be successful.* It is not necessary for large numbers of employees to be trained up front or for all the data to be in ideal form to begin implementation of a CQI program. Training, communication, data collection and dissemination, and team formation can all take place in parallel as long as the message regarding strategy and objectives is clear from the CEO and all of top management.

- A *strong and clear leadership statement of mission and strategy is essential.* This message must make clear that quality *is* the strategy. President and COO Michael Mohan made the point this way: "Without this strong focus, we would have ended up just another limited buyout focused on cash flow and nothing else." The amount of resources available for implementation needs to be clear. At SP, capital budget priorities are communicated downward so that people know how their investment needs rank in the total capital rationing process. In addition, the annual planning process was modified so it became an integral part of the quality improvement process. Sterett says that the focus showed clearly to everyone the link between CQI and quick bottom-line returns.

- *There needs to be a strong emphasis on team building.* At SP, it was made clear at the outset that the company would survive only if diverse groups of people could build themselves into a team—both within and across departments, operating units, and regions. Little tolerance was granted to managers unwilling to accept the new approach. Managers who resisted were invited to leave. While the CQI program encourages grassroots teams, team projects must relate to KPIs for identified, focused objectives as articulated by top management and each budget unit's business plan. This is a more subtle process to implement.

- *Develop data for key performance indicators as early as possible.* One thing stressed in CQI training and stated explicitly as a basic principle of the SP quality improvement process is that problem identification and analysis should be based on data. Thus, quality improvement teams deserve to have the data they need to attack problems. The organization must be tooled up to collect and disseminate the data needed by teams. SP had the advantage of a wealth of industry benchmark data that could serve to identify areas requiring improvement. Where needed data didn't exist, which happened with customer surveys and employee surveys, these data were collected very early in the process. In 1993, SP invested heavily in electronic technology to collect information on car loadings and car location. In the area of Automatic Equipment Identification technology and use of the information generated, SP is now among industry leaders. The lesson is: Don't skimp on the management information needs of a CQI program.

- *Involve unions.* Mohan said it this way: "Heavy unionization is no excuse not to implement CQI. It is a main reason for moving ahead with the program. Nothing melts down walls better than communications." SP took the communications task very seriously—both to internal and external customers. The invitation to union leaders to attend the "annual leadership conference" (the new name of the annual management meeting), the town hall meetings at all work sites attended by a vice president or above, and extensive use of videos produced in-house as well as the usual house organs have been characteristics of the SP CQI program. The workers understand.

- *Communicating to employees and establishing accountability can solve the middle management problem.* Anschutz has said that he thought they had been subject to the same problem experienced by most CQI programs, that is, failure to get middle management buy-in. He feels more attention should have been given in 1991 and 1992 to communicating with this group. Mohan, on the other hand, feels Anschutz may be too hard on himself about this problem. Communication to employees and establishing performance accountability at all levels were explicit subobjectives of the program for 1992. These plus flattening the organization structure have made believers of the vast majority of middle managers.

- *Don't skimp on training.* Despite the parallel approach, notice that information and training were always given high priority. SP had been training employees in quality improvement at a rate of 600 per month. This is not just a single course. There is a menu of courses with a plan for who needs to have taken which courses. Almost all this training has been done in-house.

- A *quality program can be cost effective.* By hiring a knowledgeable quality professional like Sterett and a small group of other quality specialists, the cost of this quality program has been very modest for its scope and diffusion rate. They didn't try to reinvent the wheel. They made only modest use of expensive consultants and borrowed from others where possible. Changing culture doesn't require bringing in a large number of outsiders. The benefits of this program—the possibility of turning SP into a long-term, extremely profitable railroad—are so great and will reap returns so far into the future that short-term costs and returns understate the real payoffs of this program. Nonetheless, on a short-term basis, the cost savings and revenue gains have already provided a handsome rate of return on the investment in quality. For two of the objectives for which action plans were developed, the annual cost of nonconformance (e.g., rework and overtime) was $500 millions dollars and the cost of personal injuries was $113 million dollars. QIT cost savings in these two areas have exceeded the direct cost of the quality department. A $1 million solution presented by first-level union employees has become an expected feature at the monthly officer meeting.

Comparison to the American Quality
Foundation Findings

How does Southern Pacific's experience with CQI compare with the experiences reported by Ernst and Young Consulting in the third installment of their International Quality Study for the American Quality Foundation? In it, comparisons are made between "high-performance," "medium-performance," and "low-performance" organizations on the relative importance and payoffs from the various CQI program elements. Southern Pacific is a low-performance organization by their classification. Does SP confirm or refute the findings of the American Quality Foundation study? The lessons learned, as noted above, agree with the findings for low-performance organizations concerning the importance of: communicating clearly to all employees that quality is the core of the company's strategy, building teams, rewarding and holding managers accountable for quality-based performance measures, and training.

However, the Southern Pacific experience differs from the findings of the American Quality Foundation study with regard to the importance of benchmarking. The study suggests that looking to industry benchmarks causes lower performers to take their eyes off the things they need to do most to improve. There may be a way to reconcile this difference, but Southern Pacific believes external benchmarks are essential and have, in fact, increased the velocity of improvement. *The target for any particular performance indicator has no credibility unless it is based on what the competition is doing.*

The reconciliation of these two positions can probably be found in the fact that Southern Pacific does not expect their managers to become "world class" over night. The SP accountability performance indicators provide statistics on the 1991 baseline, the target for the current year, a benchmark based on best practice, and the unit's current performance. Targets for the current year are provided in activities that most differentiate SP performance from that of its more successful competitors. Managers are then asked to develop a plan to close the gap. If the manager does not feel it is possible to reach the average of all western railroads, the target is set on the next worst performing railroad. Some managers who have been isolated in their jobs are taken to visit companies where performance is at a higher level as a way of establishing a shared vision of what is possible and how it can be accomplished. In other words, managers are not expected to be "world-class" immediately. They are only asked to be average or tied for last after a year or so. However, even to achieve this requires that the manager be shown "world-class" performance firsthand. Competitive success is therefore measured against the competition, not by what had previously gone on in a low performing company.

Any benchmarking program requires careful attention to the problems of information management. It is common for companies undertaking a quality improvement program to have trouble in developing the internal and external measures required to hold employees accountable for quality-based performance and then collecting and disseminating data on these measures to large numbers of employees. Financial accounting data covers only a small corner of the data requirements. It is necessary to set up a management information group, with at least a "dashed line" relationship to the quality department, to perform this function. Companies experiencing problems in this area are better advised to tackle the problem of managing information on *internal* performance indicators before tackling *external* benchmarks. In the Southern Pacific case, attention to information management plus a history of comparable data collection within the industry made it possible to move forward with benchmarking in the first year. Organizations in other industries may find it desirable to make benchmarking a second- or third-year activity.

Another chronic problem in CQI is "holding the gains." It may still be a bit early to give a grade to SP in this dimension. Where new technologies were a part of new procedures, they certainly have held the gains into 1993. Problems of holding gains have occurred in areas where new managers have been appointed. The staff is sometimes eager to slip back into their old ways and the new manager has no commitment to the new ways.

Progress to Date

A prudent reporter of the Southern Pacific story should make clear that the railroad hasn't made it yet. Continuous quality improvement is their survival strategy, but its success has not been proven. We do know that if it continues at the present pace, it will be successful. Top managers who had come up through the railroad are now believers. They see things happening—and happening faster than they would ever have believed possible. They see a culture change that has enfranchised employees and made everyone customer driven.

In the first two years Anschutz owned the railroad, he became convinced CQI was the strategy to bring about this culture change, and that turnaround would not be possible without it. At this point, it appears he was correct. The evidence can be seen in the performance improvement between 1991 and 1993. 1992 was the first year of the program and a recession year that was particularly severe in the West. Nonetheless, there was a $43 million improvement in operating profit compared to 1991. Despite the midwestern floods, the company will get to breakeven in 1993.[10]

In terms of other KPI benchmarks, the SP still is about two years away from reaching industry averages. No one is talking yet about entering the Baldrige competition.

To return to the conflicting philosophies of business management identified at the beginning of this chapter, lenders may learn from this experience that a culture change that can be accomplished in five years is worth the wait. Most important, SP is growing the business, not shrinking it, as is more common in limited buyouts. It is hard to overstate this point in a service business. A service business cannot be saved from disaster by reducing the amount of service provided. It is necessary to provide as much or more service at higher quality levels. That is exactly what Southern Pacific Lines has been able to do.

Notes

1. Subsequently, a rather successful joint quality improvement program has developed with Monsanto. The latter's CQI program required vendors to have a CQI program. If SP had not been moving in this direction, they might very well have lost a major customer simply because they weren't involved in CQI. SP began its own supplier quality certification program in 1991.
2. Indeed, because the company was privately controlled, this same group made up a majority of the Board of Directors. Such equivalency renders a separate designation of "quality council" unnecessary.
3. Some nontransportation divisions have not been pressured to develop programs.

4. Even though about 70% of these consultants have received facilitator training, it is difficult for them to be as "nondirective" as would be desirable to develop an empowered workforce or not to be perceived as efficiency experts from corporate headquarters.

5. Reduce the cost of nonconformance; improve safety; improve locomotive reliability; decrease derailments.

6. SP produced positive operating income in 1993 and the first quarter of 1994 despite a $60 million charge for repairing damage caused by summer 1993 Midwest floods. In addition, SP in 1993–94 is investing in locomotives, technology, and other equipment at a rate that is unprecedented in the industry.

7. Until 1993, the top award to teams, beyond the honor of presenting their project, was "the President's Cup," which is, in fact, a coffee mug on a walnut base.

8. In 1993, SP purchased the billing system used by CSX rather than develop the software recommended by the CQI teams. SP billing now ranks with the best in the industry. This is an example of a "breakthrough quality improvement strategy" that complements continuous process improvements.

9. Jacobson sees *continuous* quality improvement as requiring *continuous* learning. His goal is for each of his staff to have twelve hours of formal training each year.

10. More needs to be said about events of 1993 that impacted the CQI program. SP's business across the Mexican border had been growing. NAFTA may have already accelerated that growth. The company had a very successful public stock offering in 1993 and is planning another. It placed orders to buy 283 new or upgraded locomotives and to rebuild 700 of its existing locomotives. On a pulling power basis, these two numbers represent 60% of their fleet. Anschutz significantly expanded the responsibilities of Vice President Sterett. A new CEO, with a reputation as a cost-cutter, was brought in. He has ordered better accounting for the total direct and indirect costs of the quality department and CQI team activities. The integration of the DRGW into SP has been completed.

10

Vision, Values, Milestones: Paul O'Neill Starts Total Quality at Alcoa

PETER J. KOLESAR

> It is really quite impossible to be affirmative about anything which
> one refuses to question; one is doomed to remain inarticulate
> about anything which one hasn't by an act of the imagination
> made one's own.
>
> JAMES BALDWIN, *Notes of a Native Son*

In November 1987, Paul H. O'Neill, the new Chairman of the Board and Chief Executive Officer of the Aluminum Company of America (Alcoa), appointed a task force of a dozen senior managers to explore the issue of quality management at Alcoa and report to him and the company's senior management Operating Committee with concrete recommendations for change. Over a period of about six months, this Quality Task Force and the Operating Committee labored first to identify the challenges and opportunities, and then to design and begin implementation of Alcoa's "Excellence Through Quality" initiative. This is a somewhat personal account of this startup of total quality management at Alcoa.[1]

Our story details the best answers that Alcoa could fashion in early 1988 to two fundamental questions that must be answered by any enterprise embarking on a broad and intensive corporationwide total quality initiative. In no particular order, they are: "How do you gain the commitment of your senior management to total quality and to the change effort it requires?" And "How do you carry out the early stages of design of the TQM program?" Surely there are other models, but I must note that a remarkable similarity exists across the approaches of many companies to these issues. The reader will quickly see how

Alcoa was influenced by other leading quality companies—perhaps most notably by the experience of Xerox. Although five years have passed since the Alcoa initiative, the story is still timely, for the issues faced on a TQM startup haven't changed so very much.

One caution is in order, however. In early 1988 the Malcolm Baldridge National Quality Award did not yet exist. Had it, some of the Alcoa design and exploration process might have been simplified. I say this even though Alcoa has itself never fully embraced the Baldridge framework. It is my opinion that the Baldridge framework is a, albeit imperfect, very useful framework for anyone undertaking a total quality initiative. Chapter 2 by George Easton in this volume is very useful in that regard because it provides a manager's checklist of strengths and weaknesses of TQM implementation organized from a Baldridge Award perspective.[2] If one reads the Easton piece in parallel with this story, a number of the strengths and weaknesses of the Alcoa approach may become even clearer.

The chapter by Noriaki Kano, also in this volume, provides an outside expert's view—a Japanese perspective—on the practice of quality management in U.S. firms.[3] The Kano piece can also be read in parallel with this chapter. Many of the concepts, techniques, and vehicles mentioned by Kano will emerge as elements of the Alcoa approach—but not all. It should be noted that Dr. Kano influenced Florida Power and Light and, in turn, as this chapter will illustrate, Florida Power and Light influenced Alcoa, but not always positively. Part of the FP&L program was seen as too rigid, too Japanese for the Pittsburgh-based century-old, somewhat All-American Alcoa.

Background

The forces that prompted and shaped "Excellence Through Quality" are deeply rooted in Alcoa history. Alcoa is the largest aluminum company in the world, with fiscal 1987 total revenues of $7.8 billion dollars, shipments of 2.3 million metric tons of primary aluminum and fabricated aluminum products, and 55,000 employees. Alcoa was founded in Pittsburgh in 1888 by Charles Martin Hall, the inventor of the modern electrolytic aluminum smelting process, and was seeded with venture capital from the Mellon family. From its founding until 1948, when the U.S. Government forced Alcoa to sell off some of its plants to emerging competitors, the company held a virtually complete national aluminum monopoly. Earlier, the company had been moving toward a global dominance in aluminum, but in 1928, under the stress of becoming truly multi-national from its domestic base and culture, Alcoa divested its international holdings. These became Alcan, the second largest aluminum company in the world. Over Alcoa's century plus of life, the company has had an enviable record of success and adaptability. Starting from scratch, it created the processes, the products, and the markets for aluminum. Alcoa meant aluminum. Alcoa meant quality.

Yet by the early 1980s, many inside and outside the company believed that the aluminum industry was now mature and the outlook poor. The reduction of trade barriers under GATT had opened North America to competition on aluminum more successfully than had the earlier anti-trust maneuvers of the U.S. Government. Third-world governments that held the principle sources of raw material became themselves manufacturers of primary aluminum, often at sharp subsidies. Aluminum, a precious metal when Alcoa was founded, had now become a commodity and its international supply, demand, and pricing system was out of Alcoa's or anyone's control. Another troubling trend was seen: exotic substitute materials appeared in the market.

In the 1982 Alcoa Annual Report, then Chairman W. H. Krome George observed these dilemmas and suggested that effective responses must imply very big changes in "the Aluminum Company." Shortly thereafter, in 1983, his successor, Charles W. Parry, articulated a new diversification strategy that would take Alcoa into the production and sales of the emerging materials that many feared would replace aluminum—highly engineered laminates, polymers, ceramics, composites, and the like. Alcoa would become "The Engineered Materials Company" and, according to this corporate vision, by the turn of the century more than half the company's revenues would be from non-aluminum products. To carry off this strategy, Parry dramatically increased and refocused the company's research and development expenditures and embarked on a program of acquisitions.[4]

Only four short years later, apparently unimpressed with their Chairman's ability to clarify and execute his diversification strategy, the Alcoa Board of Directors in a quiet internal revolution requested Mr. Parry's early retirement. Thus, Paul H. O'Neill, then President of International Paper, became the new Alcoa Chairman and CEO in April 1987. In his introductory communications to employees, to the financial community, and to stockholders, this first-ever outside CEO spoke about safety, about quality, and about the people of Alcoa as a valued resource. He also signaled a fundamental shift of strategy: Further business diversification would be put on hold while he concentrated on improving the performance results of the base business. It was back to aluminum basics.

The options available to O'Neill and Alcoa in pushing an agenda of improving the base aluminum business would be shaped by two facts about Alcoa and the industry. First, truly *fundamental* process change had not happened in the industry and appeared to be infeasible. The smelting of aluminum was still done by the century-old Hall-Heroult electrolytic process (notwithstanding very substantial efforts by Alcoa and Alcan to make major smelting innovations in the 1970s and early 1980s). Of course there had been a century of continual refinements, and by many measures Alcoa was still a world leader in aluminum process technology. Second, *revolutionary* new aluminum products did not appear to be coming along quickly either. Alcoa was no Hewlett-Packard or 3M, companies for which very significant percentages of current revenues result from products that did not exist five years ago. As of 1987, the last significant new product introduction was still the all aluminum beverage can that had been developed twenty-two years earlier—by Alcoa. Again, this product had been refined over the two decades since its introduction and by 1987 accounted for about a third of Alcoa's aluminum revenues. Where was the next such innovation coming from? Perhaps it would be the aluminum intensive automobile that Alcoa was working toward?

Thus, it made sense that a back to the *base business strategy* would also mean a back to the *basics of the business* strategy. While serving as International Paper's President, Paul O'Neill had been an observer and participant in the significant total quality management initiative undertaken by IP between 1985 and his departure for Alcoa in April 1987. Despite millions of dollars invested, a well-thought-out plan, attractive icons on the walls, thousands of hours of training, and the energies of many dedicated individuals, the results at IP failed to match the private expectations or public promises of the program's initiators. Neither Paul O'Neill nor any number of other observant and frustrated IP employees were able to get IP's quality program on track. Nevertheless, O'Neill was still convinced that quality could be made a central part of his strategy at Alcoa. "But," he said," it has to produce real value." How would the Alcoa quality effort be different? What follows is the story of what Alcoa did and why.

The Task Force Starts Work

In November 1987, Paul O'Neill and C. Fred Fetterolf, Alcoa's President, jointly commissioned the Quality Task Force to undertake a study of quality management and to recommend a course of action to them and to the Operating Committee (the seven senior Alcoa officers who, since O'Neill's installation as CEO, increasingly acted as his cabinet in running the company).[5] The 12-member Quality Task Force had six members of vice presidential rank and six members just one level below who were seen as "up-and-comers." Because Alcoa was rather niggardly with the VP title—there were only 27 in the 55,000-employee company—this was a high horsepower group. The Quality Task Force Chair was the Vice President of Engineering, Thomas L. Carter.

The first meeting of the task force in late November was not a success. An outside expert had portrayed quality as essentially a statistical issue and painted a grim picture in which real progress would not be made until a whole generation of managers died off. At Paul O'Neill's suggestion, Tom Carter called on me in December to help. Mr. Carter asked me to organize a follow-up. He requested a seminar on the statistical design of experiments for the task force. It seemed clear to me that focusing on such complex statistical material for this group of high level executives at such an early stage in their explorations of quality management was premature. Together we formulated a new set of objectives for an initial quality *education* experience for the task force. We began early on to speak of education instead of *training*, which connotes specific task-oriented learning. The task force, at this stage of the total quality initiative, did not yet need specific skills. They needed to acquire information and *understanding* on which to make strategic choices.

Tom Carter voiced his perception of the needs: "What I'd like is that within 3 weeks the task force should have a more sound factual and experiential basis for understanding TQC, understanding what it could be at Alcoa, and understanding the potential impact on the company. I'd like them to have the beginnings of a plan for how to get there." Then, in response to a question about likely barriers, Carter ticked off, "They don't know what they don't know. They think it doesn't apply to us, and that at Alcoa we're different. They'll fear a loss of power and autonomy. Lastly, in reality the Alcoa culture is not very fact-driven. Decisions are made around here on the basis of decibel level."

We began by holding an intensive three-day introductory seminar away from the job site, Alcoa's Pittsburgh Corporate Headquarters. The material was presented in a manner that encouraged critical consideration and evaluation as well as assessment of relevance to the realities at Alcoa. From the outset and repeatedly throughout the sessions, we stressed two essential points. First, we stated: "Around the world companies like yours are at this very time convened in similar seminars, digesting similar ideas, and are evolving similar quality strategies and systems. There are no secrets in total quality. In rather short order, everyone will know the essentials of what needs to be done. Success will go to those who are superior at implementation—to those who *execute* well." Second, "Diagnosis must precede and shape the specific actions and design to fit this company in this industry at this time. What are the specific organizational and performance problems at Alcoa for which total quality is an alleged solution? Any effective TQ design for Alcoa must be appropriate for the most important of these challenges, and must recognize this company's history and culture."

Day 1 was an overview of the best thinking in quality management circa 1988. To set the stage historically and philosophically, we started the seminar with a summary of the opening day of W. Edwards Deming's now legendary 1950 Tokyo lectures to senior Japanese industrial executives and scientists.[6] Other material included various definitions of quality, the economic impact of quality and the concept of quality-related costs, the strategies of prevention and continuous improvement, Juran's ideas on quality management implementation, and the philosophy and implementation of kaizen in Japan.[7]

After dinner on the first day, we performed Deming's famous red bead experiment. In this simulation, Dr. Deming illustrates the devastating impact of variation on managerial decision making through sampling beads from an urn. Red and white beads are mixed in the urn and the players sample beads by dipping a paddle into the urn. The white beads are acceptable production and the red beads are defectives. Deming urges the employees (participants) to try not to produce red beads. Of course they can't—the red beads are already in the bowl. They are inherent in the system and, try as one might, red beads can't be avoided in the sampling. As the simulation proceeds, Deming harangues the workers, displays the data on an overhead projector and makes some telling points about "management by the numbers," and at the end of the experiment describes the sources and solutions of quality problems. We played out the bead experiment with the Alcoa managers as the "willing workers" and with me as the "foreman," imitating Deming's unique abrasive style as closely as I could.[8] I fired employees, rewarded the employee of the month, and threatened to close the plant. A run chart of the red bead "defect" data was plotted on an overhead projector as we proceeded.

However, we added a special twist. Prior to the seminar, I had requested from Mr. Carter some Alcoa time series data on product quality, process reliability, sales, safety performance, and the like. I came to Pittsburgh with graphs of these Alcoa data that I had plotted on a scale identical to that I would use during the seminar in plotting the red bead data. My Alcoa plots were done in two versions, one labeled and one not. After the bead drawing, I displayed the unlabeled versions one at a time on one overhead projector while the red bead data plot was projected simultaneously on another. The question was put to the participants, "Here are some data on an important Alcoa process. Over there are the red bead data. What is the difference?" In most cases, it was indeed impossible to see what the differences were, if any. When the identity of the Alcoa plots was revealed, the room echoed to some soft gasps. These data were all very important Alcoa performance measures and their similarity to the red bead data was apparent. So was the relevance of Deming's points about process control, capability, and management's proper role.

Most telling was the plot of safety data, which pushed an Alcoa hot button. This plot showed that Alcoa's safety performance was quite variable and not satisfactory. Yet, according to the control limits, it was in "statistical control" and was not improving despite the company's long-standing safety program. It must be remarked that Alcoa was then, and is now, the best performer on safety in its industry. But Paul O'Neill was not content and he was targeting safety levels equal to those of Dupont, the U.S. national benchmark on industrial safety. To reach that level would require a reduction in the Alcoa serious injury rate by nearly a factor of five. The task force members immediately saw the analogy between the Alcoa Corporate proclamations about improved safety performance and the exhortations of foreman Deming about "no red beads."

All in all, the red-bead experiment proved to be an "aha" experience that transcended ordinary classroom learning. Over the course of the next nine months, the bead experiment was repeated in quality awareness training sessions around the company augmented with performance and safety data specific to the business unit being trained. It entered into Alcoa corporate folklore, and later on managers would spontaneously remark, "there go the red beads again" or "no red beads"—a testimony to the appropriateness of this part of the Deming philosophy. Almost immediately the Quality Task Force took onto itself the assignment of looking into safety at Alcoa from a statistical process control and Deming Plan-Do-Check-Act (PDCA) problem-solving cycle point of view. That hands-on work would prove an important part of the learning and maturation of the group on quality management.

On the morning of Day 2 of the seminar we continued with an overview of statistical control and process capability ideas, and with an introduction to the Japanese style of implementing the Deming PDCA problem-solving process. After lunch, the focus shifted dramatically as Columbia Professor Mike Tushman put the *content* of total quality aside for a moment and began to work on the *process of changing* to total quality. He introduced a framework for problem diagnosis and problem solving at a macro organizational level and made a direct analogy to our earlier discussions of the Deming style of analysis on the factory floor.[9] It was, in effect, PDCA all over again but at a higher organizational level. We reminded the task force that though Deming's Cycle was first employed on the factory floor, by 1967 the Toyota Board of Directors had adopted it for analysis of all corporate problems at all levels. Later, in a case study of Toyota Machine Tool's march toward the Deming Prize the task force would see how the master planning process that Toyota employed was just an elaborate PDCA Cycle. In his chapter in this volume Dr. Noriaki Kano discusses at some length the latest Japanese implementation of these ideas for strategic and operation planning that has come to be called "Hoshin Planning" or "Management by Policy."

The afternoon's work dealt with a number of case studies, and in each one, as soon as the main problem symptoms were displayed, these Alcoans would leap

into action and propose solutions with little orderly analysis. When this tendency was contrasted to the orderly (and apparently slower) Deming PDCA
cycle, the task force members reminded themselves, and us, of the Alcoa corporate slogan "We can't wait for tomorrow!" Our own joking rejoinder was to
describe their actual implementation of the Alcoa slogan with an alternative:
"Ready! Fire! Aim!" Along with "no red beads" this phrase would also enter the
new Alcoa lexicon.

On the first evening, discontent and uneasiness among many task force
members became apparent. It surfaced that perhaps a majority of the task force
was uncertain about their mission, about why *they* had been chosen, and about
what was actually expected of them. The day's course materials seemed quite
interesting, most averred, but "to what purpose? Why are we here?" O'Neill
and Fetterolf joined the task force on the second evening for dinner. They were
alerted to the emergent issue and encouraged to help get the task force (back) on
the rails. The dozen task force members sat around the outside of a large
U-shaped table and the Chairman and President took chairs in the opening of
the U. O'Neill started rather softly, "Safety is my number one priority with
quality right behind it . . . all-consuming quality. Quality in the broadest
possible sense. I'm asking this group to help us think about it and shape what we
as a company do about quality. Tell us candidly what we need to know so that
together we can make quality a reality—and quickly. I want our relationship to
be interactive." After about 10 minutes of remarks along these lines, President
Fred Fetterolf spoke, "I fear what will happen if we don't do something dramatic on costs. Experts say that 25% cost reduction is available through quality.
That seems credible to me . . . I became convicted of it on the Japanese
trip.[10] It is an absolute necessity. We are getting a better picture of what is good
and bad manufacturing. I'm concerned about the unevenness of commitment on
quality across the company, about the lack of common language and understanding. Tell us what the impediments are. Tell us what the operating committee needs to know and needs to do. I believe we have no choice if we are to be
the kind of company we want to be. We are willing to spend the time and money
needed to do this and win."

For perhaps an hour task force members directed a series of questions at the
Chairman and President: "What do you want to be different at Alcoa 5 years
from now?" "Why isn't the Operating Committee doing this themselves, instead
of us?" "Paul, what were the quality barriers at International Paper?" "Fred,
what about timing?" and on and on with more questions and answers. And then
the 64-million-dollar question: "Will we still be focusing on our aluminum
activities?" (Only one member of the task force was from a non-aluminum part
of the business.) Paul O'Neill replied, "I've not seen any data that shows me
that this industry is doomed. . . . You can make a great success by being the

best in an industry in which others make excuses for their poor performances. The business that you are not in and looks easy to you is a business you don't know much about."

The performance of Alcoa's two most senior officers was ostensibly persuasive. They were clear about why they were interested in quality, they were clear that they saw a long process ahead and that they were willing to invest in it. They were also clear in their charge to the group that it investigate total quality on behalf of the Operating Committee. However, after O'Neill and Fetterolf left the room and the task force debriefed what it had heard and how it now felt, some members were still uneasy about their mission. This discomfort had several sources including the members' unfamiliarity with O'Neill himself, an ongoing uneasiness about the basic strategic balance between the aluminum and non-aluminum parts of the business, and most important for those on the task force who reported directly to the four Alcoa Group Vice Presidents—the "barons" on the Operating Committee—an uncertainty about their bosses' support of the quality initiative. It was widely intimated among the group that the most powerful baron thought that total quality was bull, and that two others were at best neutral. Moreover, the task force commission had not been made all that explicit to anyone. The task force was working for and would report to the Chairman and President, yet most of its members still worked for the barons in whose hands their careers completely rested. It was also becoming clear that carrying out this task force mission would be a bigger job than they anticipated, but nothing was being taken *off* their plates.

The seminar work continued all through Day 3 with an analysis of the Xerox Corporation's efforts to install its own "Leadership Through Quality" version of TQM. This case was our main vehicle for exploring the magnitude of the change involved in moving to TQM. At this time, January 1988, the details of the development and implementation of the Xerox version of total quality were only beginning to emerge in public. Tushman had done some consulting work in the Xerox effort, and his intellectual partner David Nadler had been a central player in the Xerox "Leadership Through Quality" effort.[11] Tushman relayed to the task force the thinking and tactics employed by the senior management at Xerox in managing what they had planned as a four-year massive change effort. To get a feel for the personalities involved we showed videotapes of two of the key players at Xerox: David Kearns, the CEO who instigated the total quality effort, and Fred Henderson, who was the first Xerox Corporate Vice President for Quality. We examined the general framework of the Xerox total quality implementation plan and the levers that senior management at Xerox proposed to use in managing the companywide change effort—including how Xerox had actually used or failed to use them. These ranged from Xerox's cascading training program for all 200,000 employees worldwide, to micro management of senior managers' own personal behaviors (role modeling), to changes in the corporate organization structure itself, and on to changes in the corporate reward system.

The seminar closed down with the task force making their own assessment of what parts of the TQM ideology appeared to be of value and which did not. In addition, they took the first steps in what would eventually be a very detailed assessment of the state of quality management at Alcoa. This assessment, once started, would take on a power of its own and propel the task force into an even broader critical inquiry into the general management of the company. The work was done over several weeks. To create a reference point, the participants made a checklist of the beliefs, behaviors, systems, and processes of a total quality enterprise. Many components on this list were at considerable variance with existing practices in most U.S. companies and specifically in Alcoa. The task force prioritized them according to what appeared to be most important and appropriate for Alcoa. They also made an appraisal of how big they felt the gaps were. Opinions varied, of course, but most in the group felt that the components of total quality were appropriate and that many gaps were substantial. This work, done in groups, helped consensus to emerge. Quality management, the task force concluded, was now looking much broader than statistical control, it was bigger and more important than they had thought, and it could not be neatly separated from the rest of management.

Benchmarking

A week later the traveling began. Over a two-week period, the entire task force visited companies that had acquired reputations as leaders in quality management, including Allen-Bradley, Corning Glass, Xerox, and Florida Power and Light. An internal visit was made to PEP Industries, an Alcoa subsidiary whose main business is manufacturing wiring harnesses for the automotive industry. PEP had been propelled and helped into Total Quality by Ford Motor Company[12] and had been an early recipient of Ford's Q1 Award. A little later, there would also be influential visits to Preston Trucking and the Tennessee Eastman Division of Kodak.

All this work was done before the Baldrige Award existed and before the term "benchmarking" had been popularized and so well codified. These highly structured benchmarking visits, organized and planned by Task Force Chairman Tom Carter, were used to identify both overall quality management frameworks and specific quality management systems and tools that could be adopted and adapted at Alcoa. They were also used to test the reality of the theory. These trips were an opportunity for task force members to "kick the tires and slam the doors" of TQM at the host companies. Carter's staff prepared a briefing book in advance of each visit containing basic background on the visited company and as many specifics on its quality management approaches as were publicly available. Using this material, the task force identified in advance the key issues to learn more about or to test at each visit. These trip objectives were communicated in advance to the host firm and specific task force members were assigned to acquire information on them during the site visit. Each task force member produced individual debriefing notes on his or her specific assignment as well as on overall impressions. These data were assembled on the corporate plane on the way back to Pittsburgh and a typed summary report was frequently available the next day.

Among the general questions and issues explored on the benchmarking visits were the scope and definition of quality and quality management. Specifics that were asked included: How and why did the TQ program get started? What was the role of corporate leaders? What were the specific TQ goals? What were the specifics on quality training, on the TQC organization, and on the external and internal resources required. What were the success stories, progress to date, and proof of success. A very important question on all visits was: "What would you now do differently and what would you advise Alcoa to do differently, and why?"

Now the task force work proceeded in high gear. In addition to their real jobs, members worked about half-time on formulating an Alcoa quality mission. Momentum and engagement were building. A report to the Chairman, President, and the Operating Committee was set for the end of February. In preparation, the task force also visited three other Alcoa facilities, and individually or in pairs task force members visited Ford Motor Company, LTV Steel, IBM, and AT&T at Oklahoma City. Input and data were solicited and obtained from 11 other Alcoa locations, and all Alcoa 1988 Business Unit Operating Plans were reviewed.

Two visits were particularly influential. The first was to Xerox, a company that we had already studied during the initial seminar. Xerox, like Alcoa, was a manufacturer, had invented an industry and had held a monopoly. Xerox had been propelled into quality management in the early 1980s when, under attack from the Japanese, it had lost half its market share and saw complete disaster looming. While this had not (yet) happened to Alcoa, the Alcoa managers identified with and were moved by both the struggles of Xerox and the apparent success of their TQM counterattack. Xerox—and this was two years prior to its winning the Baldrige Award—proclaimed itself the first American company to win back market share from the Japanese, and without government assistance. Alcoa was a supplier to Xerox of aluminum cylinders—the photo receptors that copy machines use to form an image. A year earlier, there had been quality and cost problems at the Alcoa plant and a threat of loss of the account. But Alcoa had worked hard to improve and in the process Xerox had taught the plant in question some statistical process control tools.

Xerox had been motivated to use quality as its change and survival theme by the success some years earlier of its Japanese affiliate, Fuji-Xerox. The task force read and analyzed Fuji-Xerox President Kobayashi's recounting of his push for the Deming Prize.[13] Xerox had gone about its quality transformation in a particularly studied way. The role of Xerox Chairman David Kearns in the change process, the design of the "cascading" Xerox total quality awareness education, the parallel quality management organization that Xerox created and added to the existing corporate structure, the Xerox six-step version of the PDCA problem-solving process, the Xerox formalization and refinement of its competitive benchmarking process, and the overall Xerox total quality management change plan delineated in the famous "green book" that the Alcoa task force examined but could not copy—all these elements had an influential impact on the ultimate Alcoa design. Even the Xerox name for its effort, "Leadership Through Quality," would be mirrored by the name Alcoa ultimately chose for its own program. None of this suggests that the Xerox story or program was bought uncritically. On some aspects, the evidence showed Xerox talked a better game than they played. Xerox had also been an Alcoa supplier and inquiries around the Alcoa system on Xerox quality performance did not always match the "Leadership Through Quality" rhetoric. The Alcoan's theme was: learn from Xerox, applaud them, and do still better.

The first visit to Florida Power and Light—eventually, Alcoans would make three visits there—was influential in different ways. The task force quickly saw that the quasi-military management style at FP&L and its wholesale and rather slavish adoption of Japanese total quality control techniques would not find ready acceptance at Alcoa. Yet a number of FP&L elements were adopted. The FP&L quality improvement storyboard method of running improvement teams was much admired and would be licensed by Alcoa. (This is the "quality story" format described by Dr. Kano in the last chapter in this volume.) The Alcoa senior managers were quite impressed with FP&L's adoption of the Japanese style of Policy Deployment to give focus and accountability to the massive quality effort underway. There was a downside too. The thrust of much of the quality management effort at FP&L—then a year prior to their winning the first Deming Prize awarded outside Japan—appeared to focus too hard on "winning the prize" and there were suspicions among some on the task force that FP&L was doing some things primarily to look good to the jury.

All in all, the benchmarking visits had an impact on the twelve Alcoa senior managers that no amount of reading, lectures by professors, or harangues by gurus could possibly equal. Whenever possible on these visits task force members paired off with their peers. (It became one of our standard requests prior to a visit.) They verified whether total quality had actually had an impact on their peers' lives and management styles. Later on, we would expose the Operating Committee to similar experiences for that very reason—we wanted person-to-person transfer of experience. In a typical commentary, a senior Alcoa manager remarked on a flight back to Pittsburgh from a visit, "You know, Professor, we didn't see anything different from what you had told us about weeks ago, or than what we'd read in Deming and Juran. But when Joe Blow, my peer at ABC Corporation, showed me what he's been doing, the light really went on for me. Before, I understood it with my mind. Now, I believe it in my gut."

The Safety Problem: Learning by Doing

One other experience had a deep impact on the task force: their hands-on examination of the issue of safety at Alcoa. Recall that in the introductory seminar, I had used Alcoa safety data displayed as a control chart. The data used were monthly serious accident rates over a 24-month period at a major Alcoa mill, and with the labels removed it had been impossible to tell the difference between it and the Deming red bead plot. For dramatic effect I had walked slowly over to the tray of beads, leaned over it, cupped my hands to my mouth, and stage-whispered into the tray, "No red beads! No lost time accidents!" The group decided on the spot that it wanted to examine the issue of safety at Alcoa from a total quality perspective. More safety data were collected and processed TQ style: Pareto charts, run charts, control charts, and the like. The task force spent a day defining specific safety problems and examined data linking cause and effect. The two-decade long history of the safety program at Alcoa was recounted.

The task force seized on several points: how little data analysis was typically done on such problems; how improvements in safety had tapered off at Alcoa when management attention had waned; how easy it is to talk about, but how hard it is to actually get to the root causes of a social and technical phenomenon as complex as safety; the futility of managing via exhortation. They experienced firsthand their own deeply ingrained tendency toward a "ready-fire-aim" style of management. They also experienced the frustration of trying to improve a process where the special causes had largely been eliminated and where the remaining faults "were in the system" (as Deming would put it) or were "designed that way" (as Juran would put it).

This analysis of the safety issues at Alcoa was particularly striking to the task force because Paul O'Neill—since his first day on the job as CEO—had stated publicly that safety in the workplace was his number one priority. At a January 1988 meeting with financial analysts in New York, while the task force was in session, he had said, "Alcoa's most important human value is that its employees work safely. Some things are negotiable. Excellent safety performance is not. When you pay attention to all the details associated with achieving excellent safety performance and housekeeping, good economics will result." Similar remarks had been made continually inside the company since O'Neill's appointment in April 1987. But it was now nearly the end of January 1988 and no systemic attack on safety had yet been mounted. This extended and painful self-analysis on the safety issue would color the thinking of the majority of the task force on quality. Several members recounted that some years back the safety program at Alcoa had produced real improvements and then had leveled off when an important leader retired. They mused: "What would keep a total quality program from duplicating this experience?" "What happens to quality if O'Neill leaves or if his attention gets refocussed elsewhere?"

Report to the Operating Committee

By February 18, 44 days after the initial seminar, the task force was ready to fashion its conclusions and assemble a set of recommendations for O'Neill, Fetterolf, and the Operating Committee.

A particularly insightful aspect of the task force's internal company assessment was its review of the Alcoa 1988 Business Unit Operating Plans from a freshly acquired total quality perspective. This work defined serious gaps between where Alcoa was currently and where a total quality-driven Alcoa would have to be. The task force found that quality was not an explicit component of the business-unit mission statements, strategy, or philosophy. Overall, the understanding of quality was limited and, when it was included in planning, the focus was exclusively on a limited set of such physical quality characteristics as surface finish or dimension. Tracking and monitoring of customer returns, product specs, and scrap were just beginning and measurements of rework, good parts per hour, and flow times were not routinely monitored. The business-unit plans did not leverage improvements that had been made at one plant to other plants across the system. Little evidence existed that suppliers were being brought into the Alcoa quality process. At most business units, specific quality goals were absent from the plans. Following on the century-old traditions of a capital-intensive industry, the task force observed that where there was a push for quality it was typically cast in terms of capital expenditures to replace older equipment. The business plans also revealed that generally quality improvement appeared to be a bottom-up process. Only in a few noteworthy cases was there a top-down process driven by senior management. Moreover, Alcoa appeared to be all over the map on philosophy and approach, with different units influenced by different outside gurus whose messages were at times in conflict.

Among the misconceptions about quality management that the task force found in the business plans were the following:

- Random production upsets that hurt Alcoa in the past will not happen in the future.
- The identification and prioritization of cost improvement projects can be done independently of quality considerations.
- Everyone *knows* that Alcoa's products are generally higher quality than the competition, and we can guarantee our quality without bringing our processes under control.
- SPC (statistical process control) can be "turned on" for specific customers who require it, and it is primarily a matter of running off some charts to help in marketing.
- Multiple sourcing by our customers is a way of life that our quality cannot change and our customers' changing needs do not include higher quality from us.

In November 1987, just after the task force had been commissioned, Tom Carter had taken a survey of the members' opinions on the level of quality in Alcoa. Graded on a scale of 1 to 10 (with 10 being excellent and 1 being terrible), the mean Alcoa overall score had been 4.6. Now, at the end of February, as the task force completed its initial quality education and benchmarking visits, they repeated the self-evaluation and the mean score moved down to 4.0. The individual evaluations also moved closer to one another. A framework for self and external evaluations was standardized and applied to several individual Alcoa business units, as well as to all the companies that had been benchmarked. In those pre-Baldrige Award days, the Alcoa Quality Task Force had to create their own framework for this evaluation.

Of the outside companies visited, Xerox and Florida Power and Light scored highest overall. Of the Alcoa business units studied, PEP Industries scored highest, nearly as high as the two leading outsiders. This fact was to prove important to many Alcoans as evidence that quality management at its best was demonstrably possible inside the company.

While the task force members formulated their final report to O'Neill, Fetterolf, and the rest of the Operating Committee, their thinking was dominated more by imagined reactions of those Committee members who were their direct bosses than by concerns about the Chairman and President. The latter already shared a strong commitment to a new quality initiative, but how to convince the still disengaged Group Vice Presidents weighed heavily on the task force members' minds. Ultimately, the strategy they adopted was not to try too hard to convince them but to have the report simply state in effect: "We have done what you asked and examined quality inside and outside Alcoa. We have also studied quality management theories and practices as described by leading thinkers and as practiced in Japan. *It, 'quality management,'* is bigger and more important than we imagined when we started. It is vital to the future of Alcoa. Moreover, we have changed personally as a result of what we have seen and *others* need to change too. Although we can describe the main things we learned in the last two months, we do not expect our description to be convincing or sufficient. For you to understand what happened to us and what Alcoa should do, our most important recommendation is that you experience a process similar to that we just went through."

The body of the report was a series of points that summarized the activities of the task force and then listed the main findings in four categories:

- *Culture*—Quality is a rallying point around which an entire company can be energized. It is appealing to most people, building on their innate desire to excel and control their destiny. It is more inspiring than pure financial goals. Quality can be a win-win proposition vis-à-vis the union. The quality management view that 80% of the problems are with the "system" is a key contributor to this.[14] Most of the quality gurus testify to the large proportion of problems that are due to the system. See, for example, the books of Deming and Juran. There has been no scientific documentation of this contention. The author is tempted to make his estimate far higher in some industries and far lower in others. In part the issue is whether processes are "in control." On the cautionary side, quality is not a quick fix and those companies that see it that way fail. It will not become "real" until it permeates the values, norms, and culture of the organization.

- *Impact*—Quality is a differentiator that can be harvested in price and market share if it is perceived by the *customer*. In the short term, there are costs to beginning a quality effort—for example, training, facilitators. Getting beyond the symptoms of quality problems to root causes and solutions is critical. Quality emphasis and metrics are quickly moving beyond detection to full product-life-cycle indicators and into staff and support functions.

- *Enablers*—Implementation of quality requires substantial changes and additions to the organization including training, creation of top-down commitment, and the creation of broad-based involvement. Distinct attitude changes are required, including: a focus on never-ending improvement against quantitative metrics; attention to and respect for detail at all organizational levels; a fact-based orientation in decision making; and granting appropriate authority to worker teams. Successful quality efforts seem to involve substantial investments in people versus things. A change is required in supplier relations with the burden on us to understand our own needs, a thrust toward fewer suppliers and shared gains, early supplier involvement in product and process design, and a need for a formal supplier certification program. There is probably an 80/20 rule on the impact of quality management tools.

• *Strategies*—Quality can be used as a weapon to gain share; to produce a unique product; to set a pace competitors cannot sustain; and to reduce cost. Quality can be used to reduce barriers to progress and improvement in the organization—horizontal, vertical, supplier/customer, union/management, and staff/line. Quality can be used as a vehicle for focussed top-down deployment of an overall strategy/policy and as a vehicle for overall change of a broader scope. Quality can be used to close the gap between our performance and our goals or values on things that matter to the organization—for example, *safety*.

The task force saw that their most important mission was to get a gut commitment to quality by the Operating Committee, and, second, to continue their research and design work as that commitment was developed. To these ends they recommended:

• The issue of quality is so central to the business and its overall management and the magnitude of the changes needed around it are so great that a corporate quality office and officer are needed.

• You, the Operating Committee, should get educated on total quality. We will design for you an intensive study and travel program based on the best of our experiences.

• In the interim, we will continue to serve as a design team and will develop a quality implementation plan and structure for the company. Some elements of the Alcoa quality initiative must remain your responsibility and we will call these to your attention. *One of these responsibilities, which remains uniquely yours, is the development of a corporate strategic objective statement, values, and guiding principles. An effective quality initiative cannot be mounted without this.*

The Operating Committee Gets Educated

The Operating Committee agreed to all the task force recommendations and prepared to begin their education while the task force itself continued its exploration and design work. Later, O'Neill, Fetterolf, and the Operating Committee would admit that they undertook this education grudgingly since they did not understand "why they needed additional education on a topic to which the group was so committed." In mid-April, a three-day Operating Committee quality awareness seminar was held at a retreat in the mountains outside

Pittsburgh. There was an atmosphere of high stakes and high expectations on the part of the task force and all involved in the design and delivery. These were the men who *ran* the company and the conventional wisdom of total quality ideology was that the success or failure of quality management at Alcoa would depend on their engagement.

For Paul O'Neill this was another opportunity to put his own stamp on the emerging quality initiative, but he would have to do so without inhibiting his team's ability to discover it for themselves and thereby make it their own, as well as his. This group was his cabinet in formation, but they were not yet used to functioning as such for that was not the way Charlie Parry had run the company. Nine months earlier, these same men had run the company under a different leader, with a very different style, and with a very different strategy. Only Paul O'Neill was different. To date, not a single new face had been brought into the senior management ranks nor had anyone left or been removed. We knew of no precedent for O'Neill's strategy of changing the fundamentals of corporate mission and management style without at the same time changing at least some of the people at the top. Thus, this seminar and the field trips that followed were also supporting a parallel agenda of changing the outlook and style of the senior management of the company—and of molding them into more of a team.

To start off the awareness seminar, participants were asked to lay out concerns, issues, and questions about quality management they felt should be addressed. Several items on their list were the concerns of senior managers everywhere who face implementation of a quality initiative. One in particular was a most direct expression of a concern of many American managers. It was one of the Group Vice Presidents who asked, "How is quality different from metallurgy? I run a business in which metallurgy is at the core of all our products and processes. I know very little metallurgy and I have experts for that. It works well. But I'm told that quality is different and that I have to be directly involved. Is this true and if so, why? And exactly how do I have to be involved?" Another Operating Committee member asked, "I've been around this company long enough to have seen many programs come and go, including some quality programs. Most made sense on their face and had some initial impact, but for the most part the promises were never really fulfilled and eventually—in fact, not too long after their flamboyant introduction—these programs just fade away and we are back to the same old Alcoa we were before. What is going to make this 'total quality thing' any different?" A third member asked, "I've been to Japan and I've seen it in action there and I know it works, but that is a very different culture. Can we make it work here without becoming Japanese, without losing who we are and without losing our own distinct American and Alcoan advantages? I don't think we can or should try to make Alcoa into Toyota."

These issues and others were squarely faced and explored, but clearly not settled outright. The prime seminar objectives, however, were achieved: An ecumenical framework of contemporary quality management was developed and critiqued. The magnitude of the change from traditional management practices was articulated, and the process and problems of such a large scale organizational change discussed. At all points in the deliberations, the relevance to specific Alcoa situations was at the fore. We again did the Deming red bead experiment and the Xerox case study. By the end of the three days, it was the judgment of our attending coach representing the task force and most important of our chief customer, Paul O'Neill, that the seminar—the first step in the Operating Committee's education process—had "worked." Now the whole Operating Committee—including O'Neill and Fetterolf and accompanied and supported on each trip by several members of the Quality Task Force—went benchmarking to Tennessee Eastman, to Florida Power and Light, and to Alcoa's own PEP Industries. Paul O'Neill visited one-on-one with David Kearns, the CEO of Xerox. Fred Fetterolf would visit with Dr. Juran.

A consensus was forming and enthusiasm was growing, and there was a sentiment that Alcoa "is probably doing this 'just in time' for we are at best half a step ahead of the competition, if that." In early May, the Operating Committee and the Quality Task Force participated in an event that would prove to have a very high impact and further solidify what the responsibilities of the senior management in leading quality management really were. It was an "Alcoa Quality Day" and it enabled the Operating Committee to generate a good part of their own answer to that month-old question, "How is quality different from metallurgy?" Tom Carter identified and brought to Alcoa's Pittsburgh headquarters eight successfully implemented quality improvement projects from around the company. The goal was to show some of the best of what was already happening inside Alcoa and to illustrate with homegrown Alcoa examples many of the quality improvement themes that had been discussed in the seminar, encountered in the readings of Deming, Juran, and Imai, or seen on external benchmarking visits. We included projects that spanned a broad range of applications: internal supplier-customer relations; cooperation with external suppliers; and satisfying an external customer. They had projects that utilized a complete set of problem-solving tools and methods ranging from the simplest of Pareto charts through more complex statistical process control and sophisticated designed experiments.

There was an air of excitement in the Alcoa Corporate Conference Room at Pittsburgh Headquarters that morning. A score of presenters had been flown in for the occasion from all over the Alcoa system. The first speaker, with a boxer-like build and ruddy complexion wearing a suit that was neither Brooks Brothers nor Armani, stood with very apparent nervousness in the corner of the room. The primary audience was more than a score of Alcoa's most senior managers including the CEO and President—enough to make anyone a bit nervous. The master of ceremonies welcomed everyone and then simply said, "We'll get started with the presentation by the Warrick Mill." Our man stepped to the podium and introduced himself: "I'm Ralph Box. I'm a baking room operator from the Warrick Mill and this is not my usual Monday morning." The room exploded with laughter, but quickly hushed attentively as Ralph detailed his role in a project that had made significant quality and financial improvements. He spoke with obvious knowledge of technical issues such as gauge capability, and interpreted complex statistical control charts for his audience. His business sense and his pride of these accomplishments were evident and impressive. This was high-power employee involvement already in place somewhere in Alcoa. And so it went: from improved process control in anode baking, to better relations with a major carbon supplier, to the elimination of over-control in smelter tapping, to use of complex statistically designed experiments carried out to reduce the cracking of ingots as they are cast.

After five hours of project presentations and follow-up questions and answers, all the presenters and observers save the Operating Committee left the conference room. The Operating Committee debriefed. Several questions went up on the flip chart: "What are the most important things we have heard and learned?" "What does this imply for what quality management should be at Alcoa?" "What does this imply for *our* roles in quality management at Alcoa?" They homed in on several conclusions. First was that individually and collectively they, the Operating Committee, were remarkably ignorant that there was this level of quality improvement activity and competence at Alcoa—even in their own businesses. Second, it was obvious that Alcoa as a corporation had done little to create, sustain, and encourage this activity—to date quality at Alcoa was a bottom-up, grassroots, almost underground movement. Third, there was very erratic performance overall—excellent as these examples were, they were isolated pockets of excellence. Moreover, there had been no meaningful dissemination of the results of these improvement projects to other locations or businesses, not to speak of dissemination of the quality improvement methodology itself. Fourth, although several projects dealt with complex technologies, there had been no involvement of corporate R&D resources at any stage. A major conclusion that would shape the actions of the Operating Committee emerged from this several-hour discussion and working session: *"It is our responsibility to create an Alcoa in which this excellence is the rule rather than the exception—an Alcoa in which excellence is shared, systematized, and rewarded."*

Bringing It All Together

With the first wave of the Operating Committee's education and benchmarking completed, and the task force coming to closure on its recommendations for specific quality management systems, tools, training, and the like, an extraordinary day-long joint meeting of both groups was held on May 27, 1988. The day was structured to bring the thinking of the Quality Task Force and Operating Committee together, to see if they were congruent, and to make important implementation decisions. Each group had a specific set of issues to report on and was to spend the morning by itself putting the final shape to its findings and recommendations. The Operating Committee was to present its long-term goals and its image of what it wanted quality management to be at Alcoa, while the task force was to provide the specific "enablers" it had been developing. The day would end with the Operating Committee again closeted to review and act on the day's proceedings.

The Operating Committee reported first. They were now deeply involved in quality and were particularly excited this morning, having just spent the previous two days on a variety of quality-related tasks, including the last of their benchmarking visits. They were eager to share what they had done and learned, to hear from the task force, and to get on with the job. The Operating Committee now understood why the task force had been so insistent about the need for them to get educated and to travel. They too had changed. During their long morning session, the Operating Committee had framed their conclusions as follows: "What," they asked, "would we want a visitor from space, who descended into Alcoa five years from today, to see with respect to quality management?" Several flip charts were filled in freewheeling brainstorming style and these were then critiqued and organized. Their image of quality management was:

- A commitment to be the best. Aggressive benchmarking with trending. A consistent definition and processes across the company.
- A strong focus on the customer. An Alcoa that knows who its customers are, what they need, and how satisfied they are. Systems in place to elicit data and feedback on this.
- Quality processes, systems, and culture are institutionalized. These should be unifying and motivating and relate to both individual and team improvement efforts.
- A quality culture that produces 59,000 "Larry Birds" [referring to qualities that the Operating Committee saw epitomized by the great Boston Celtic basketball star] excellence, teamwork, selflessness, competitiveness, and hard work.
- There should be an Alcoa scientific problem-solving process deployed and used across the company—on the pattern of the PDCA, Xerox, or FP&L systems.
- Wide use of teams as appropriate. Teams should be fact-driven, flexible in structure and mission. Teams should be guided and managed. [There was a strong aversion to the concepts and name "Quality Circles."]

- A formalized Alcoa set of guiding principles is required, including Alcoa vision and values statements.

Having been "charged" by the task force with working on a set of guiding principles for Alcoa, the Operating Committee at this point simply acknowledged that they too shared in the assessment of how important was this need was for a new focus and stated that they had begun the work. They closed their presentation with a list they had generated of 14 prioritized characteristics of excellent companies. The Committee had also given their own appraisal of where they felt Alcoa stood. Thus, with this list they had come a long way toward jointly defining their problem. (Again, had the Baldrige framework existed at the time, some of this work might have been simpler.) All that remained now would be execution.

The Operating Committee's Characteristics of Excellence

Priority	Characteristic	Importance	Alcoa Score
1.	Being the best	100	48
2.	Safety	95	64
3.	Quality process	84	43
4.	Importance of the individual	74	51
5.	Meaning to employee	71	53
6.	Ethics and integrity	65	81
7.	Excellence in manufacturing	54	47
8.	Execution, attention to detail	54	37
9.	Good corporate citzenship	49	78
10.	Growth and profits	46	32
11.	Technology	33	60
12.	Innovation	32	31
13.	Shareholder value	26	30
14.	Knowledge and education	20	42

The task force was pleased with the congruence in the Operating Committee's report and their own thinking on these issues. They could have written this report themselves. Now it was the task force's turn, and Tom Carter presented their recommendations. His opening remarks were passionate and startling to the Operating Committee. "We have worked diligently at this quality charge you put before us. We thank you for the opportunity. We have been changed and convinced as a consequence of what we have done. We are taking up this quality mission and you cannot take it away from us. We will proceed regardless of what you do!" The Operating Committee members glanced sheepishly and perplexedly at one another—who was denying anyone anything?

The content that followed that challenge was straightforward, given where everyone now stood:

- More education and training for both groups and the design of a quality awareness training for the "top 100 in the company." (This would soon become the top 300 or so.) Topics like benchmarking, team processes, reward systems, and the like remained to be explored in depth.

- The work of the Operating Committee on values and guiding principles was urged on, and it was recommended that it be augmented by an Alcoa Quality Policy.

- A senior Corporate Quality Officer was called for and it was recommended that the person be made a member of the Operating Committee. A list of desirable characteristics for this person was offered.

- Specification of top management roles and accountabilities were to be defined by the Operating Committee with primary attention given to the roles of the CEO, the COO, the Corporate Quality Officer, and the Group Vice Presidents. The task force offered very specific recommendations on these roles.

- A set of quality management enabling mechanisms and tools were identified for development and deployment; these included a variety of quality related training, a problem-solving process, and an Alcoa Quality Book or master implementation plan (patterned on the "Green Book" quality process definition and implementation plan of Xerox).

- The task force declared their jobs done and resigned as a body, but they recommended that a standing-senior level Quality Steering Committee be created to serve as an advisory body on the implementation. They then all agreed to serve on this body, if appointed.

After some joint discussion, the Operating Committee went into session by itself to consider the recommendations. All were accepted in principle, although some needed to be worked on over the coming weeks and months. By the end of the afternoon they had selected Alcoa's new Vice President for Quality. He would be Thomas L. Carter, the Quality Task Force Chairman.

Vision, Values, and Milestones

During their external benchmarking visits, the task force had been very impressed with how tightly the quality programs at the host firms were linked to a larger sense of corporate purpose. Whether it be Xerox, Toyota, Florida

Power and Light, or Tennessee Eastman, the quality strategy, goals, and methods were always contained within a larger all-encompassing mission and value statement. Such linking with a larger purpose also came up in their readings. Perhaps at first, reading Deming's opening comments to Japanese business leaders in Tokyo in 1950 may have seemed corny—"International trade is an essential component of peace and prosperity. International trade depends on quality . . . quality leads to productivity, to competitive position . . . to jobs, jobs, and more jobs for the Japanese people." His first point, "strive for constancy of purpose," may have seemed a platitude until CEO Donald Peterson of Ford stated that focusing on corporate purpose was the single most important thing that Deming had taught the world's second largest automaker. The task force quickly became convinced that the level of extraordinary quality achievement that they envisioned for Alcoa would simply not be attainable unless the quality effort was linked to a higher sense of purpose for their company as well.

There was, however, no Alcoa corporate mission statement that any task force member was aware of. On investigation they would later discover one tucked away in the archives and, indeed, it seemed that every ten years or so a new Alcoa values statement would be articulated by someone at or near the top of the company and then filed away. Alcoans had long thought nobly of their company, of its ethical behavior, and of its contributions to society and to the nation. To many the company had been a kind of family, literally and figuratively—remarkably, one of the officers on the task force would shortly occupy the same vice presidential position as his father had. In only a few companies would employees at all levels refer to themselves with a term like "Alcoans" and really mean it. Though some said these feelings were weakening, and cynics said they were completely gone, one could sense how strongly the task force felt these sentiments. What's more, a psychological void had been created by the sudden transition from CEO Parry and his diversification strategy to CEO O'Neill and his back-to-aluminum strategy. The task force had not been pleased when, during their initial deliberations in January, they had seen a newspaper account of a speech O'Neill had given to New York security analysts expounding on Alcoa values—values that had not been discussed or affirmed within the company. The concern was less with the substance of the remarks as with a feeling that "nobody told us, nobody asked us" and a fear that a possibly fleeting opportunity would be missed to reach out to bring all Alcoans together again and get the company refocused.

The task force recommendation met with a favorable response from the Operating Committee, and once the mission issue was put before them they too felt a strong need for clarification and focus. At meetings with the rank and file and mid-level managers, Operating Committee members were confronted with confusion about what parts of the old Charlie Parry strategy were still valid, about how significant the changes really were, and about which of the old Alcoa values still held. Many Alcoans were saying, "We're confused, we need to know where we are going." The Operating Committee saw inconsistent behavior with respect to the company's implied values. And there was real concern, even fear, among some business unit managers about a new set of demanding financial targets that O'Neill had set for the company.

An enormous research, formulation, feedback, and revision effort was unleashed that would go on for months. Though the Operating Committee undertook the responsibility of formulating the mission statement, the Quality Task Force stayed involved doing background work, benchmarking the vision and mission statements of other leading firms, and serving both formally and informally as a sounding board for the long series of drafts that the Operating Committee would produce. By my tally, the Operating Committee spent at least 11 full days in plenary session on discussion, drafting, redrafting, and the like. And that does not count the very considerable time spent singly or in small groups working on support tasks.

As this work was going on, the Operating Committee was getting closer to its own articulation of what quality management should be at Alcoa. Indeed, the two tasks became inseparable. The work began in May and the final articulation of the "first draft" was not arrived at until September. With communication to other senior level managers and reaction to their feedback, the final product was not ready for roll-out until January 1989. During those months, there was hardly a time when the Alcoa mission statement was not being actively worked on by the Operating Committee. "Forged" is the operative expression, for every single word and phrase was hammered out with great care. When they were finished, this group of the nine most senior Alcoa managers would have a document that each had a tremendous investment in, one that they expected would be the compass to guide Alcoa into the future. It would be called the "Alcoa Vision, Values, and Milestones." The *Vision* was to be the target, a setting of the corporate sights on where Alcoa wanted to be in the future; the *Values* were to be the standards the company and its employees would live by, and the *Milestones* would be the measures and checkpoints along the way that would both mark out progress and specify what remained to be done. A year later, Paul O'Neill would refer to the Vision and Values document as Alcoa's enduring constitution that would take it into the next century. The final articulation, arrived at after many weeks of internal debate and several rounds of feedback from business unit and other upper level managers, was as follows.

Alcoa's Vision

Alcoa is a growing worldwide company dedicated to excellence through quality— creating value for customers, employees, and shareholders through innovation, technology, and operational expertise.

Alcoa will be the best aluminum company in the world, and a leader in other businesses in which we choose to compete.

This was more a statement of intent and ambition than of fact. In fact, the company had not been growing for some time. While it had important but very selective international operations and relationships, it could not truly be called international or worldwide. The best aluminum company? Some in the company and outside clearly thought so, but as more cross-industry benchmark data on product and process performance and on management practices became available, the self-evaluations were becoming harsher. "We'll know we are really the best," said Fred Fetterolf, "when the only question left on the table is who is second, and when our performance level is world class, not just the best in our own industry." It was hoped by the Operating Committee that the phrase "leadership in other industries in which we choose to compete" would clarify the role and standards in Alcoa's emerging other businesses like ceramics in which it would simply not be credible for neophyte Alcoa to claim to be the best. "Be a player and leader now, then raise the stakes," said an Operating Committee member.

Alcoa's Values

Integrity: *Alcoa's foundation is the integrity of its people. We will be honest and responsible in dealing with customers, suppliers, co-workers, shareholders, and the communities where we have an impact.*

Safety and health: *We will work safely in an environment that promotes the health and well-being of the individual.*

Quality and excellence: *We will provide products and services that meet or exceed the needs of our customers. We will relentlessly pursue continuous improvement and innovation in everything we do to create significant competitive advantage compared to world standards.*

People: *People are the key to Alcoa's success. Every Alcoan will have equal opportunity in an environment that fosters communication and involvement while providing reward and recognition for teams and individual achievement.*

Profitability: *We are dedicated to earning a return on assets that will enable growth and enhance shareholder value.*

Accountability: *We are accountable—individually and in teams—for our actions and results.*

Who could disagree? Was there, is there substance here? These statements might appear at first reading like "motherhood and apple pie" platitudes. But not so to the Operating Committee who labored mightily over them and who proposed to run the company by them, to live by them, to be personally accountable on them. Each word and expression included was evaluated from the standard, "Can we fully commit to that?" As an example, the Integrity value at one time included the word *fair* as in "we will be fair and honest." There was a long debate on the point that while Alcoa might want to be fair, and indeed strive to be fair, it could not guarantee fairness. So, out went "fairness." At the end of this process, the Operating Committee had words to live by. The quality thrust that had initiated this work was further amplified by a quality policy statement which became an integral part of the package.

Alcoa's Quality Policy

We are committed to quality in everything we do. It is Alcoa's policy to:
- *Provide products and services which consistently meet or exceed the needs of our external and internal customers through the efficient use of resources.*
- *Involve all Alcoans in never-ending improvement in the quality of products, processes, and services.*
- *Provide every Alcoan with the training and tools necessary to contribute to the quality effort.*

Our success will by measured by the satisfaction of our customers.

Both the task force and the Operating Committee had been strongly influenced by the frequent appearance in TQ readings of the theme of management-by-fact, by the repeated emphasis placed on the importance of specific *measurable* goals at each of the companies benchmarked, and by the policy deployment technique that was used at some of the benchmarked firms to assist in answering the most crucial question: "All right, now that we have articulated these noble aspirations, how do we propose to make them happen?" They moved part way toward an Alcoa response with the development of the "Alcoa Milestones."

The work started from the question "How will we know when we are there?" An exercise the Operating Committee used to develop responses was to imagine that a visitor from outer space would descend on Alcoa in five years. "What would you expect him to see as he walked the halls of our offices, the aisles of our mills?" Such a visitor wouldn't be fooled, he would be naive but intelligent and perceptive. All agreed that, like Deming, this visitor wouldn't be impressed by slogans, ambitions, or other quality management "artifacts." He'd have to see specific behaviors, systems, and performance to demonstrate that Alcoa had already made progress toward the vision, values, and quality policy, and was really on the road to world-class excellence. In the spirit of the total quality ideology that states that if you can't measure, it you can't manage it, he'd need measures of progress and performance—or, in the jargon of total quality, "metrics." So began the development of "The Alcoa Five-Year Milestones."

While the task force played a key role in proposing them, the Operating Committee, after more feedback from the middle management ranks, made the final definitions. (Actually, the Vision, Values, and Milestone statements were all rolled out simultaneously.) The task force laid important groundwork by defining a set of desirable characteristics for milestones which included that they should be: measurable, actionable, enduring, significant, encompassing a sense of "best" and of "stretch," limited in number, simple to understand and use, and owned. They should also be communicable, motivational, and *enabled*. This last word was meant to capture the idea that attainment of the milestones must be supported by the investments and actions of the company and its most senior management. (Echoes of Deming again. His Point 11 states: "Stop giving arbitrary targets, goals and quotas to the work force without the means to achieve them.") There was a strong aversion to throwing up a wish list to the rank and file and hoping for miracles to happen.

This work was tough going, the list of criteria was awfully long and the drafters were getting tired. After many rounds of discussion within both the Operating Committee and the Quality Steering Committee, the successor to the Quality Task Force, communications to selected members of the next level of Alcoa management, and revisions based on the feedback received, they produced the final Milestone list (see below). By now the Operating Committee had put in at least 22 days of work in plenary sessions—and still more on their own or in small subgroups—getting educated on quality, doing benchmarking, and designing the Alcoa quality constitution. It would be understandable that fatigue was setting in. The final list was arrived at perhaps as much by acquiescence as by active consensus.

Five-Year Milestones for the Alcoa Vision

Customer Commitment

- *Establish interactive relationships with internal and external customers and suppliers based on understanding of real needs and performance to targets with evidence of continuous improvement.*

Employee Involvement

- *Everyone clearly understands their customer needs.*
- *Clear definition of accountability for each team and individual.*
- *A team approach to problem solving and continuous improvement.*
- *Provide the training and education to enable all Alcoans to excel in their jobs.*

Excellence

- *Over the next five years, achieve a 50% reduction in serious injury and lost workday incidence rates as we move toward our goal of an injury-free workplace.*
- *For each process, activity, and technology, benchmark our position against best in the world. Close the gap where advantage can be gained.*
- *Critical Processes in control and capable.*

Financial and Growth

- *Average 15% return on shareholders' equity, not less than 10% in any year (and corresponding return on assets and return on investment.)*
- *Achieve growth objectives through improved asset utilization and approved expansion plans and pursue additional corporate growth as required to realize a 20% real growth in revenue above 1988 levels while achieving corporate financial return objectives.*

Five-Year Milestones for the Alcoa Values

Integrity

- *Be completely aware and committed to our conduct and behavior. (High now, same in five years.)*

Safety and Health

- *A 50% reduction in lost work days and Serious Injury Frequency.*
- *Stress [reduction]*
- *Housekeeping better*
- *More involvement of hourly [employees]*

Quality

- *Know and meet more customers' needs*
- *More processes in control*
- *More benchmarking*
- *High level of awareness*
- *More partnerships with (less) suppliers*
- *Internal customer needs met*
- *Facts used and available*

People

- *More minority and females in management positions*
- *Higher selection standards*
- *More involved in high school preparation of students for Industrial Jobs*
- *Greater number of cross-functional teams and involvement*
- *More apprentice training and development*

Excellence

- *Objectively understand world standards and gaps closed/closing*
- *Win the Malcolm Baldrige Award*
- *Be the Benchmark*

Looking at the milestones in the light of the task force's own criteria, what is an observer to make of them? On their face and as a package they are directionally appealing, yet individually some clearly violate the defining criteria. Importantly, only a few were measurable. A suggested solution was to put "metrics" on each—a complicating "fleas on the backs of fleas" suggestion. If these milestones were to be the central thrust of the company, there were some gaps that might be perilous: There were *no* milestones on innovation, *no* milestones on technology. What would be the impact on the morale and behavior of Alcoa managers. Some of the metrics were definitely "stretch objectives," so much so that some managers argued that they were demotivating. There was much inconclusive debate on this vital point, and two milestones that got particular attention in this regard were O'Neill's 15% ROE target and the critical processes in control and capable milestone. Would the marketplace— the price of aluminum ingot on the London Metal Exchange—permit the former, and would the time span of 5 years and the resources in place enable the latter? Matters of opinion surely, and how this would play out remained to be seen. To one senior Alcoan, the milestones looked like a score of crushing new priority "ones," while to another they were his Magna Carta for the next five years. To an outsider, they might violate Kano's stricture not to "chase too many rabbits."

So in January 1989, one year after the task force began its work, this first part of the job was done. The new Alcoa constitution was written with quality at its core and Paul O'Neill, Fred Fetterolf, and the Operating Committee felt that Alcoa was poised to *start* its quality journey. Many saw the Alcoa quality effort—at this time still unnamed as the company sought to avoid the "quality management is another project" stigma by refusing to have it labeled—as the key to its future. But not having a name proved too awkward and in a short while, it would be named and its spirit portrayed with a variant on the Alcoa stylized "A" logo. "Managing for Quality" sat at the apex of the A, with "Continuous Improvement" on the left leg of the A, and with "Employee Involvement" at the right leg. In the white space under the A's crossbar sat the "Customer."

Under this banner, the good ship Alcoa would sail off to the quality wars. A few on the renamed and restaffed Corporate Quality Steering Committee imagined that one destination along the way might be the Malcolm Baldrige National Quality Award.

They and the new Corporate Quality Group were already hard at work creating the enabling mechanisms and resources for the quality journey— designing an Alcoa Problem-solving Process, rolling out the first wave of quality awareness training to the "top 100," codifying a benchmarking process, and the like. As the process continued it was looking less and less simple, but more and more important to most Alcoans involved. There no longer appeared to be any serious question of whether Alcoa would do total quality or what the broad parameters would be.

Epilogue

If the replacement of CEO Parry by CEO O'Neill was the dropping of one shoe, the other shoe dropped at Alcoa on August 9, 1991, when on short notice Paul O'Neill summoned some 50 of Alcoa's senior executives from around the world to an extraordinary meeting at Pittsburgh headquarters. No agenda had been announced, and tension and rumor were rife since all present knew that President Fred Fetterolf had resigned two weeks before "over differences in policy." No explanation of what those differences were had been offered.

Opening the proceedings, O'Neill announced that the meeting was to discuss "change, but that two things would not change—the Alcoa Vision and Values." The changes he then announced were sweeping. In addition to the departure of Fetterolf, three other members of the Operating Committee had suddenly taken early retirement along with the Vice President of Engineering. There would be no replacement for the departed President, and the Operating Committee would cease to exist, as would the Group Vice Presidencies. All 25 business-unit managers would be given broader authority and bigger responsibilities and would henceforth report directly to the CEO. Paul O'Neill envisioned the new organization as an inverted triangle or pyramid with the business units and their customer relationships—the value-creating activities—forming the broad base of the triangle at the top of his diagram, the pooled corporate resources that service the business units one level below, and the CEO below that, the apex of the triangle at the bottom of the diagram. Two layers of the organization had been cut away.

Equally striking, the complex and arguably fuzzy milestones were replaced with three intense and focused imperatives:

1. Cause your operating assets to perform at world-leadership rates. If someone else is doing it better, you are not meeting the standard.
2. Live by the Alcoa Values and Policies.
3. Adopt quantum-leap improvement objectives that will at a minimum close 80% of the gap between current performance and the world benchmark on those few measures critical to your business.

The last of the above objectives would be the one that O'Neill would lean on particularly heavily as he impelled Alcoa management to accelerate the pace of change. Ironically, it is less stringent in this 1991 articulation than in its original version in the 1988 "Milestones," but the charge now appeared more forceful when put in isolation from the rest, and when the CEO made it his *primary* focus. It was as if Alcoa had said it before, but hadn't really meant it. How strongly he now felt about the benchmark performance issue was reinforced by the other central change in O'Neill's thinking. "I believe we have made a major mistake in our advocacy of the idea of continuous improvement," he said. "Continuous improvement is exactly the right idea if you are the world leader in every thing you do," he explained. "It is a terrible idea if you are lagging behind the world leadership benchmark. It is probably a disastrous idea if you are far behind the world standard. In too many cases, we fall in the second and third categories. In these cases, we need a rapid quantum-leap improvement . . . [else] we will never be the world leader."

What inspired these changes? Over the more than two and a half years since "Excellence Through Quality" and the "Vision, Values, and Milestones" had been rolled out, and while he was convinced that the Alcoa constitution and direction were sound, Paul O'Neill had become increasingly frustrated with the pace of improvement at the company. There had been real improvement and the financial markets and the business press had recognized it, but in private O'Neill's impatience showed through. [15] He was not about to wait for wrenching change to be imposed on him and Alcoa by external forces, as had happened at Xerox in the early 1980s and as was occurring now, in the early 1990s, at General Motors. O'Neill was aware of painful shortfalls in Alcoa performance relative to the best of its competitors—even on some processes that Alcoa had *invented.* He also knew of substantial process performance gaps between Alcoa mills carrying out identical operations. The Alcoa quality effort was not addressing these gaps fast enough, he thought, and it never would "if we persist in our use of the traditional command and control system of management where many thousands of people believe their only responsibility is to do what they are told to do."

At the August 9 meeting, Paul O'Neill drove home his points with sharp observations and some disquieting facts. He said, "I am no longer willing to accommodate myself to the pace and direction of the organization when my own observations and instincts tell me we should be doing something different."[16] The examples he cited began with the issues on which he had been focusing since his first morning as Alcoa CEO: safety, the environment, and customer satisfaction:

> While we have reduced our serious injury rate from 5.48 in 1987 to 3.80 [currently]; Du Pont is at 1.08 and even more alarming is that 19 Alcoans have been killed over the last four and a half years [of my tenure as CEO].

> While we have always been committed to environmental protection, we have just paid a record $7.5 million [environmental] fine to the State of New York.

> We operate some of the lowest cost alumina refineries in the world, but the levels of fines and soda [a pair of chronic quality problems in that industry] are not providing customer satisfaction.

He also cited a number of other crucial operational and financial issues, one of which particularly merits attention here as it simultaneously illustrates an issue that for some time had been a key irritation to O'Neill, relates to one of the central of the "Alcoa Quality Milestones," and brings us full circle back to principles emphasized in Deming's 1950 Tokyo lectures. He said, "We have constructed more Hall cells[17] than any other company in the world, yet our pot life is below the industry average; and this process, which we invented and have operated for over 100 years, is not in [statistical] control and [is not] capable [of meeting specifications consistently]."

To many observers these announcements were jarring discontinuous changes—changes that some interpreted as O'Neill's repudiation of total quality. A red flag to orthodox TQMers was his rejection of that arch TQ theme "continuous improvement." But not so to the man himself. In a 1993 conversation, he said "Back there in '88 and '89, we were learning to do quality, now we are really doing it. We have gone through a shifting of the gears, and perhaps the last shift up was, well, quite a bit bigger than the others."

It seems me that the package of changes Paul O'Neill implemented in August 1991 is consistent with the philosophy and goals he had articulated from the outset, and with his own personal very hands-on style. While the changes also can be seen as fitting within the quality framework that Alcoa had developed, they do significantly bend that framework. And, there are issues here worthy of some reflection. One can question whether it was necessary—indeed, whether it was dysfunctional—to dismiss and bad mouth "continuous improvement" to emphasize, as needed to be done, the requirement for breakthrough improvements. Some observers and students of change and innovation processes propose that continuous improvement and breakthrough change are ideas in conflict, that an organization that emphasizes the former will inhibit the latter. My colleague in much of the Alcoa work, Michael Tushman, is of this persuasion and we have argued the matter often. When Tom Carter raised the issue even before the task force work began, I took a "Japanese position"—agreeing with the kaizen philosophy that continuous improvement should enhance a firm's ability to carry off breakthroughs by adding greatly to its storehouse of product, process, and customer knowledge, and by adding to its ability to implement and maintain the breakthrough changes.[18] If this is true, then a false choice has been posed, and one needs both. Moreover, the "Excellence Through Quality" initiative had invited all 60,000 Alcoans to participate in continuous improvement, had trained them to do so, and had at great effort organized countless improvement teams that were already working at the time of the August 9 announcements. What were these Alcoans to make of their Chairman's statement that this continuous improvement concept to which they had just been wooed was a "disastrous idea." Most of these people would have no opportunity to participate in a quantum-leap improvement on one of the "few measures critical to your business." In the total quality roll-out, they had been told that they were part of a new team approach. Was that part of the "Excellence Through Quality" pact still intact?

Second, in these August 9 changes at Alcoa, one can see an intensification of the tension between competing long- and short-term goals. Even before this meeting, there were a significant number of Alcoa managers who felt and acted as if the quality talk was well and good, "but when you get down to it, you'd better make your numbers." "Do I hit my 15% ROI target this year, or invest in my breakthrough improvements for two [and more] years out?" Answer: "YES." Managing the tension that exists here will test the maturity and patience of Paul O'Neill and Alcoa and the integrity of their quality process.

Some Closing Remarks

The events described here are after all only the opening of the Alcoa quality management story. The process at Alcoa still unfolds and another chapter at least remains to be written. In closing, we raise a few issues that are relevant to how the quality initiative at Alcoa does, in fact, unfold. They are worth thinking about by persons outside of Alcoa for they relate as well to most companies engaged in TQM implementation. In discussing these issues, I'll take advantage of Alcoa's study of Xerox and of what is known about the Xerox quality effort.

The first issue relates to the frequent conflict between short- and long-run performance goals. This was the closing point of the previous section. Philip Crosby is wrong.[19] Except in some trivial cases, "Quality is *not* free." It pays eventually but the investment—particularly of management time and effort—is substantial. The dilemma surrounding the required investment was expressed nicely for the visiting Alcoans when their Xerox host said: "This store is open for business while under repair!" Or, in other words, "How do we do all this improvement 'stuff' and still make and sell product?" Xerox, its Baldrige Award notwithstanding, recognized the problem but never resolved it. It took Xerox senior managers years to recognize that major elements of its very well-designed "Leadership Through Quality" program were not being effectively implemented, that it was not fulfilling the grand design. Under pressure for quarterly results, many business unit managers at Xerox had gone back to business as usual and quality management processes had been, in effect, shelved. Xerox was finding that, strenuous as they are, quality program design and quality training are the easy parts of total quality. The implementation—getting and sustaining improvement—is what is really difficult. Four years after the roll-out of its quality initiative, when Xerox did a rigorous self-assessment as part of its preparation for the Baldrige Award Application, it created an extensive list of the shortcomings and required enhancements to its quality efforts. Xerox discussed this "Warts Report" in public forums and was lauded for doing so. Here was evidence, after all, that the Baldrige process was healthy and could contribute to a company's actual improvement. Yet, to date, the shortcomings in the Warts Report have only partially been addressed, and yet Xerox announced that it was moving "Beyond Total Quality." (This was the title of Xerox CEO Paul Allavie's address at a quality conference in Pittsburgh in 1992.) Perhaps this is the American way. How long can we Americans keep our attention focused on one issue?

What is the relevance for Alcoa? During 1993–94 Alcoa was being stressed as perhaps never before in its history. The collapse of the Soviet Union and the concomitant weakening of its domestic economy coupled with the almost complete loss of the Soviet defense industry as a major aluminum customer created an avalanche of aluminum on the world market. This drove down world aluminum prices to the point where not a single western aluminum producer remains profitable.[20] In late December 1993 Alcoa announced a 3% reduction of its workforce and Paul O'Neill had to deal with many discouraged Alcoans who had worked so hard over this last five years only to see the fruits of their labors eaten up by the world aluminum glut. At the earliest working sessions of the Quality Task Force in January 1988 members questioned whether the company and the new Chairman would sustain the quality effort if aluminum prices were to fall precipitously. That has now happened—aluminum prices fell from $1.10 per pound in 1989 to about $0.50 at the end of 1993. The fate of the Alcoa quality effort in the light of this stress remains to be seen. This concern is hardly confined to Alcoa. Early in 1994 the popular press contained reports that under the stress of Japan's recession its companies are also abandoning total quality.

The second issue relates to the importance of assessment of the effectiveness of a total quality effort. I take the Deming/Shewhart Plan-Do-Check-Act paradigm as central to TQM. Without the "check" phase the cycle is emasculated. Indeed, the importance of evaluation, review and correction is one of the central tenets of the management-by-policy (hōshin) system described in Kano's chapter.[21] In early 1988 the Alcoa task force had been very critical of Xerox for mounting such an elaborate quality effort and then waiting three years to evaluate its effectiveness. When I used the Xerox case study during the quality training of Alcoa's top 100 managers and asked them what they would do differently from Xerox, they invariably responded, "Early, frequent and rigorous evaluations of progress." Yet, to date, Alcoa has not done its own broad self-evaluation. Indeed, Alcoa has stepped back from several opportunities to do so. It does not seem likely that the deep culture, systems, and technology changes that the highest levels of quality management require can be sustained without a substantial feedback and review process.

Paul O'Neill believes that Alcoa continues to make substantial progress. His new and flatter organization is in place and is moving in the direction he had hoped. Alcoa has a new fact-based planning system that sets goals based in part on world benchmarks and theoretical limits of perfect performance. A large number of quantum leap projects are underway and in some areas very substantial progress has already been reported. On just one specific—the pot life issue—premature smelting pot failures fell by 83% between 1989 and 1992.

And so the Alcoa story continues. It remains to be seen whether the August 9 changes, the "Excellence Through Quality" Architecture, and, most important, Alcoa's continuing follow-up will propel it to the world eminence and outstanding performance that are its CEO's goals. Alcoa has never adopted any particular company as a TQM role model, but once, when questioned about which other companies he specially admired, Tom Carter, the Alcoa Vice President for Quality, said, "Well, I don't know if there are any 10's out there, but Toyota Machine Tool sure is a 9 + ." He went on to add, "And Toyota got to where they are by 40 years of relentless work. At Alcoa we don't have 40 years."

Notes

1. For about an 18-month period, the author served as the chief outside consultant to both the Quality Task Force that designed Alcoa's quality initiative as well as to the senior management "Operating Committee" that directed the implementation. During the early part of this work he was joined in this work by his Columbia Business School colleague, Professor Michael Tushman. Peter Kolesar's research and teaching background is in engineering, operations management, and applied statistics. He entered the world of quality management through that avenue. Michael Tushman's work, by contrast, is concerned with organizational design and change, and the management of innovation.

2. We refer here to the chapter by George S. Easton, "A Baldridge Examiner's Assessment of U.S. Total Quality Management." It also appears in the *California Management Review*, Spring 1993:32–54.

3. We refer here to the chapter by Noriaki Kano, "A Perspective on Quality Activities in American Firms." It also appears in the *California Management Review*, Spring 1993:12–31.

4. For a detailed history of Alcoa up to this time, see George David Smith, *From Monopoly to Competition: The Transformation of Alcoa, 1888–1986* (New York: Cambridge University Press, 1988). The articles of Michael Schroeder and Thomas Stewart carry the story forward to the appointment of O'Neill as Chairman and CEO and his redirection of the company. Michael Schroeder, "The Quiet Coup at Alcoa," *Business Week*, June 27, 1988, pp. 58–65; Thomas A. Stewart, "A New Way to Wake Up a Sleeping Giant," *Fortune*, October 22, 1990, pp. 90–100.

5. The Operating Committee included the Chairman and CEO, the President, the Chief Financial Officer, the General Counsel, the Vice President of Human Resources, and four Business Group Vice Presidents. When we write about the meetings and activities of this group we mean all these participants.

6. The content of Deming's 1950 Tokyo lectures is contained in W. Edwards Deming, *Elementary Principles of the Statistical Control of Quality—A Series of Lectures* (Tokyo: Nippon Kaguku Gijutsu Rommei, 1951). This out-of-print monograph is an edited version of lecture notes transcribed by Japanese participants. Proceeds from sales of this book were donated by Dr. Deming to the Japanese Union of Scientists and

Engineers, the group that had sponsored his visit. The funds were used to establish the Deming Prize. A detailed analysis of the Deming lectures is contained in P. Kolesar, "What Deming Told the Japanese in 1950," *Quality Management Journal*, 2 (1), 9–24, Fall 1994.

7. The quality education of both task force and, later on, of the Operating Committee itself involved a considerable amount of self-study. The following is a list of the main books and articles we used:

> Deming, W. Edwards, *Out of the Crisis*, MIT-CAES, Cambridge, 1986. (Particularly Chapters 1 through 3.)
>
> Garvin, David, "Quality on the Line," *Harvard Business Review*, September-October, 1983, 66–75.
>
> Imai, Masaaki, *Kaizen: The Key to Japan's Competitive Success*, Random House, New York, 1986.
>
> Jacobson, Gary and John Hillkirk, *Xerox, American Samurai*, Collier Books, New York, 1986.
>
> Juran, Joseph M., *Juran on Planning for Quality*, The Free Press, New York, 1988. (Particularly Chapters 1 through 4 and Chapter 11.)
>
> Kobayashi, Yotaro, "Quality Control in Japan: The Case of Fuji-Xerox," *Japanese Economic Studies*, Spring 1983, 75–104.
>
> Nadler, David and Michael Tushman, "A Model for Organizational Diagnosis," *Organizational Dynamics*, Autumn 1980.
>
> Port, Otis, "The Push for Quality," *Business Week* (Special Report), June 8, 1987, 131–135.

8. For an accurate description of the Deming red bead experiment and his interpretation, see Mary Walton, *The Deming Management Method* (New York: Dodd Mead & Co., 1986), Chapter 4; and Andrea Gabor, *The Man Who Invented Quality* (New York: Times Books, 1990).

9. The particular framework used for the diagnosis was an organizational model of Nadler-Tushman. David Nadler and Michael Tushman, "A Model for Organizational Diagnosis," *Organizational Dynamics* (Autumn 1980). During the seminar we made the point that alternative diagnostic frameworks existed and that it was more important that one be used rather than which one. Our main purpose was to methodically expose all the elements of the enterprise that affected quality and that conversely would be affected by a move toward total quality management.

10. Some months earlier, Mr. Fetterolf had been on a benchmarking visit to Japan to review advanced manufacturing techniques. While he and the other participants learned and were inspired by the experience, nothing concrete had resulted from the Advanced Manufacturing Task Force. This failure was indeed well known to, and on the minds of, several Quality Task Force members.

11. The history of the Xerox effort is now reasonably well documented in the public literature. See, for example, the story as recounted by two of the key participants, David Kearns and David Nadler, *Prophets in the Dark: How Xerox Reinvented Itself and Beat Back the Japanese* (New York: Harper Business, 1992). Jacobsen and Hillkirk describe in detail the challenge from Japan and some of the personalities

involved. Gary Jacobson and John Hillkirk, *Xerox, American Samurai* (New York: Collier Books, 1986). For more on the Xerox quality effort, see Chapter 7 in Gabor, op. cit., which is, by the way, much more critical of the Xerox approach.

12. The reader will probably be aware that several of the companies visited by Alcoa went on to receive national or international honors for the excellence of their quality efforts. Florida Power and Light was the first non-Japanese winner of the Deming Prize. Xerox and Eastman Chemicals (Tennessee Eastman is a division) both won the Baldrige Award. Today, one could augment the list of companies whose quality programs should be studied. Among the candidates from whom one could learn particularly valuable lessons about total quality implementation are Motorola and Milliken among manufacturers and the Ritz Carlton Hotel Company, Federal Express, and the AT&T Universal Credit Card Services among service companies. Each of these organizations has been a winner of the Baldrige Award; they make it a practice, as do all Baldrige winners, to share their quality systems quite openly with others.

13. Yotaro Kobayashi, "Quality Control in Japan: The Case of Fuji-Xerox," *Japanese Economic Studies* (Spring 1983), pp. 75–104.

14. Most of the quality gurus testify to the large proportion of problems that are "due to the system." See, for example, the books of Deming and Juran. There has been no scientific documentation of this contention. The author is tempted to make his estimate far higher in some industries and far lower in others. In part the issue is whether processes are "in control." W. Edwards Deming, *Out of the Crisis*, MIT-CAES, Cambridge, 1986. Joseph M. Juran, *Juran on Planning for Quality* (New York: The Free Press, 1988).

15. A sense of the public response to the Alcoa quality initiative and to Paul O'Neill's leadership can be gotten from Stewart, op. cit.; Thomas F. O'Boyle and Peter Pae, "The Long View: O'Neill Recasts Alcoa with His Eyes Fixed on a Decade Ahead," *The Wall Street Journal*, April 9, 1990, pp. A1 and A4. Over this period, Alcoa was repeatedly listed as first among the Metals Industry in *Fortune* magazines's annual "America's Most Admired Corporations" beauty contest. (About which a senior Alcoa manager observed, "That's real nice, but the industry sucks.") Over the two-year period 1989 to 1991, Alcoa's common stock earnings were 28.5% as compared to -28.3% for Alcan and 12.2% for Reynolds.

16. Here, Paul O'Neill is predicting a dire future unless significant anticipatory action is taken. One is reminded of a 1939 address by Winston Churchill to the House of Commons castigating the British government for its tardy and ineffectual response to the threat of Nazi Germany. It was a much more crucial and historical issue that Churchill faced then, but his words ring true in this contemporary industrial context as well. He said, "When the situation was manageable it was neglected, and now that it is thoroughly out of hand, we apply too late the remedies which might then have effected a cure. There is nothing new in the story. It is as old as the Sibylline books. It falls into that long dismal catalogue of the fruitlessness of experience and the confirmed unteachability of mankind. Want of foresight, unwillingness to act when action would be simple and effective, lack of clear thinking, confusion of counsel until the emergency comes, until self-preservation strikes its

jarring gong—these are the features which constitute the endless repetition of history."

17. A Hall cell is the electrolytic device in which the smelting of aluminum is done. It is essentially a large carbon lined bathtub. An operating efficiency issue is how long such a pot can be run before it must be shut down and relined with carbon—this time is called "pot life." Because relining is an expensive and time-consuming process, short pot lives are a critical economic issue. Alcoa was founded by the cell's inventor, Charles Martin Hall.

18. For a development of this line of reasoning, see Masaaki Imai, *Kaizen: The Key to Japan's Competitive Success* (New York: Random House, 1986).

19. The troubles of Alcoa and of the rest of the worldwide aluminum industry are documented in Timothy Aeppel, "U.S. Aluminum Makers Find World Market a Scary Place," *Wall Street Journal*, November 9, 1993, p. B3, and "Alcoa Sets Charge Totaling $70.2 Million for Fourth Quarter," *Wall Street Journal*, December 21, 1993, p. C22.

20. See his articulation of this appealing philosophy in Philip Crosby, *Quality Is Free*, (New York: McGraw-Hill, 1979).

21. Op. cit.

11

A Perspective on Quality Activities in American Firms

NORIAKI KANO

Since 1963, when I was an undergraduate being supervised by Professor Kaoru Ishikawa at the University of Tokyo, I have been a student of quality management and engineering. Over the years, I have done research and taught in the field, widely disseminating its findings. I visited the United States for the first time in 1977. In over thirty subsequent visits, I have engaged in plant visits, seminars, conferences, and presentations; counseled nearly twenty firms; and taught and lectured at several universities. This chapter draws on these experiences in evaluating recent quality trends in the United States.

My Personal View on TQM

To evaluate TQM in the United States, I need to clarify how I arrive at my judgments. The following three sections lay out my analytical framework.[1]

Generalizing an Individual Observation

It is reasonable to ask how an observer synthesizes a specific observation from Workplace A, Factory B, or Company C into a view that allows generalization from the specific area to the whole unit. I adopted the following approach for generalizing my observations. I would explain to the managers of the factory what I observed in a workplace and what generalizations I derived from these observations. Then I would ask them whether each of these views was applicable only to the workplace I visited or whether it applied to the factory as a whole. If the views coincided, then I would conclude that they were characteristic not only of specific workplaces but also of the entire factory.

For example, in one case I observed that in the final inspection area, all the inspections were properly conducted, with the detected defectives being properly reworked. Then I visited the production workplace where one of the defectives had been produced. While the workplace supervisor had been informed of the defectives, I observed that the supervisor provided little more than a warning to the worker who had assembled the defective component. Moreover, he failed to analyze why this defective had been produced. As a result, the worker had difficulty knowing what preventive action to take in the future. I generalized these observations into a view, noting that the final inspection had been properly conducted, with the detected defectives being properly reworked, but the feedback was not properly analyzed to prevent future defects. If the managers agreed with my view that this was a common problem, then it could be accepted as a generalized pattern for the factory.

I would then sum up the views of the factories that I visited in a particular area, such as a region or country, and would incorporate their common elements into a hypothesis, a tentative general view, for the area. I would then ask the local quality specialists whether the hypothesis was generalizable to the factories in the area or applied only to the specific factories visited. If they agreed with me about the common elements, the generalization would be considered valid for that area.

The views selected did not necessarily encompass every feature of the area. It can be said, however, that these features were at least partially represented in each portion. The degree to which this is true can be determined by local experts with a thorough knowledge of the factories in the area.

The House of TQM: Structure of TQM[2]

I use "The House of TQM," which shows the structure of TQM, as the touchstone for identifying the evolution of TQM's implementation in the United States (see Figure 11.1). The portion from the floor up to the roof is TQM, where the floor symbolizes "motivational approach" and the roof shows "customer satisfaction/quality assurance"—the purpose of TQM. The base is the "intrinsic technology," which refers to the driving technology specific to an industry. For example, electrical engineering is the technology intrinsic to the electric industry; chemical engineering is intrinsic to the chemical industry. Intrinsic technology provides the necessary foundation on which TQM is built.

Given the existence of intrinsic technology, it is still necessary to carry out "sweating work" (hard work such as promoting standardization, educating and training, and collecting and analyzing data) to obtain good quality. The problem is this: how to create the conditions that will impel management and employees to take up such sweating work. This "motivational approach" is shown as the floor in Figure 11.1.

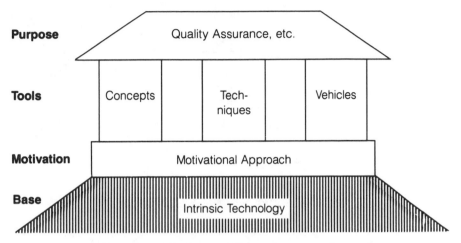

Figure 11.1.   The house of TQM—structure of TQM.

"Concepts," one of the pillars of the house, shows how to proceed from a particular perspective when a given intrinsic technology and motivation already exist. "Concepts" consists of both a theory of quality (such as "quality is the satisfaction of the customer" or "the next processes are our customers") and a theory of management (such as the "PDCA Cycle" [Plan, Do, Check, Act], "build quality into the processes," or "management by facts"). Figure 11.1 depicts this as the column on the left.

When actual activities based on these concepts begin, some "techniques" (the second pillar) for collecting and analyzing data become necessary. The seven QC tools and "The QC Story" procedure are typical techniques for this purpose, and statistical methods can also be applied here.

At this point, some methods for effectively and efficiently promoting all these activities within the organization become necessary. Management by Policy, Daily Management, and QC Circles are methods that can be called "vehicles" (the third pillar) since they quicken and facilitate promotion.

Quality Sweating Theory

The process of introducing TQM can be explained by the "Quality Sweating Theory."[3] It states that TQM is an effective tool for improving quality, but its success depends on making many employees sweat. The quality sweating theory encompasses two alternative approaches: CLSQ (Crisis consciousness and Leadership make people Sweat for Quality) and VLSQ (Vision and Leadership encourage people to Sweat for Quality). (See Figure 11.2.)

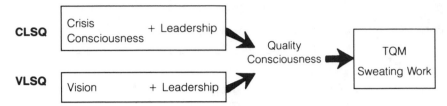

Figure 11.2. Model for TQM introduction based on Quality Sweating Theory.

Change of Quality Activities in the United States over the Last Decade[4]

In 1980, NBC aired a program, "If Japan can, why can't we?" It might be said that this TV program symbolized the historical shift of the American quality movement. Around 1980, quality circle activities began booming in the United States. By the middle of the 1980s, however, the quality movement had come to emphasize the necessity of management commitment, stressing the importance of top management's leadership. Subsequently, many companies tried to promote companywide quality activities by motivating executives and managers. This contrasts with past American practice where quality professionals played the primary role in quality activities. In recent years, this trend has been increasing. Consequently, some companies have successfully introduced and implemented Japanese TQC. A nationwide quality improvement campaign has been spearheaded by the Malcolm Baldrige National Quality Award (MBNQA). "TQM" is called "TQC" in Japan although its activities can be better explained by TQM (Total Quality Management) than by TQC (Total Quality Control) because both "management" and "control" are foreign terms for the Japanese, who understand them as synonymous.[5] Hence, in this chapter, the term TQM is used to avoid confusion except when specifically discussing Japan, in which case the term TQC will be used.

Where They Were 10 Years Ago

On my desk, I have my 1982 lecture notes on "Overseas Quality Activities"[6] as well as an article of mine based on an interview with Dr. J. M. Juran at his New York office during July 1979.[7] They show the state of quality activities in the United States during that latter half of the 1970s and the beginning of the 1980s. My views on that period are as follows:

- The education of top management is less focused on quality.
- Some proponents of the quality circle movement simplistically believe that quality circles can solve all the quality problems of a company. This

characteristic tends to make management neglect the necessity of committing itself to quality.

- Cross-functional communication is so weak that it is difficult to solve quality problems, which demand cooperation among departments.
- The cost of quality is too often overemphasized.
- Strong resistance to the introduction of quality improvement activities is manifested by the "NIH" syndrome (resistance to that which was "Not Invented Here"), even though these quality improvement activities seem to be effective in solving quality problems.
- The "AQL" (Acceptable Quality Level) practice of parts procurement as well as a short-term view for "achieving best quality at lowest cost" become obstacles to improving quality. Instead, managers need to make purchase decisions based on a long-term approach to continuous improvement.

Changes over the Last Decade: Two Episodes

In 1977, I visited the United States for the first time, staying for a month. In the production shop of a certain factory well known for its good quality management, I found a percent-defective graph on the bulletin board. Since I hadn't seen such a graph in any other factory that I visited during the trip, I took a closer look at it. I found that the last data point plotted was in July 1976, eight months before my visit to the factory.

It was not until 1984, when I visited an American factory of a multinational corporation, that I felt things had begun to change in the United States. To my surprise, a considerable number of quality slogans and quality indicator graphs were displayed throughout the factory. One of the graphs carried data points for a control indicator at a certain process plotted hourly; the last data point was plotted at 11:00 of the day I was visiting. (I happened to see that graph around ll:30.)

Several other factories that I visited later also had many quality indicator graphs, including control charts. They were practicing "SPC" (Statistical Process Control), and data points were accurately plotted. Of course, I am not going to say that simply plotting data on graphs makes quality better, but this observation does illustrate a change in quality consciousness in the United States by the mid-1980s.

The Impact of the Malcolm Baldrige
National Quality Award (MBNQA)

It could be said that the MBNQA precipitated the broad-based promotion of quality improvement within American companies. More important, it presented national quality leaders with opportunities to discuss the direction of the American quality activity systems through the formulation or revision of the guidelines for the MBNQA. They could do this during both the intensive training course for examiners and during the examiners' site visits as they audit the finalists. The successive revisions of the guidelines illustrate this development. Through this process, I believe that the institutional consensus among the experts is deepening and the American approach to quality is solidifying. Before the MBNQA was established, the consensus for nation-wide quality activities had neither been very strong nor well-organized, even though there were many excellent quality experts.

Change in the Quality System

In any country or organization, total quality activity can begin only if top management is conscious of the critical need for companywide commitment to quality and its own responsibility for introducing such activity. As testimony to the leadership that top management is exercising today in some American companies, in lectures at quality-related conventions, top managers have begun to include specific examples of their own practices, instead of just sprinkling their speeches with such phrases as "quality first," "customer satisfaction," or "do it right the first time." Also, the top managers of leading U.S. companies were influential in establishing the MBNQA. Furthermore, although formerly only a few companies had Vice Presidents in charge of quality, in recent years their number has increased. In some companies, Senior Vice Presidents and Executive Vice Presidents in charge of quality have appeared. Finally, top managers of many American companies are visiting Japan to study TQM, a reflection of their positive attitude toward the study of quality. In summary, over the last decade in the United States, what has changed most is the leadership of top management. Whereas before, quality activities were only implemented by the quality department, top management is now initiating corporatewide quality activities.

As mentioned, a criterion that formerly dominated quality efforts in the United States was quality cost. Today, this criterion is increasingly less relevant and is being superseded by "customer satisfaction." In the audit for the MBNQA, this has become evident. Although "customer satisfaction" is only one of many audit categories, it is given the largest weight of all: 30%.

In U.S. companies that have introduced quality activities in accordance with Japanese methods, their implementation differs slightly from the original Japanese version because of their different backgrounds. For example, there is an emphasis on team activities in the U.S. version, which can be seen as an effort to break through departmental barriers resulting from a strong chain of command. The term "cross-functional," which is frequently heard in the United States, reflects the consciousness of barriers between departments.

General Trends of Quality Activities in the United States[8]

Based on the House of TQM, the current status of quality activities in the United States can be analyzed using the categories of motivation, concepts, techniques, and promotion.

Motivation

As Dr. Juran said in 1979, "Top management believes that the situation is not so bad yet, and that is a problem of American firms."[9] After the economic recession of the early 1980s, however, America came to face growing trade and financial deficits. This seems to have given many people, especially top management in some leading companies, a crisis consciousness. As a result, top management has begun to play an important role in leading the quality movement. This explains why American firms have become so enthusiastic about quality in recent years.

Concepts

There are four criteria for implementing TQM:

1. *Customer satisfaction; putting quality first.*
2. *The PDCA cycle; process-oriented production; doing it right the first time.* Although the PDCA Cycle is well known, many people have difficulty applying it to their jobs. Therefore, many facilitators try to implement this concept via management by policy and daily management. Often, when they do this, employees ask managers to improve their own way of working. Some resistant employees play with the acronym PDCA, turning it into "Please don't change anything!"
3. *Emphasis on the use of data.* Along with the diffusion of the SPC method, the concept of management based on data is widely used. It is easy just to collect data and apply the method mechanically. In each case, however, what physical phenomena the data represent and what the analytical results actually mean need to be individually investigated and discussed, to determine whether the method used adequately reflects the significance of the data. In general, people are not taught to recognize the tangible phenomena based on the data. In most areas, managers and workers alike tend to do their jobs depending on their gut reactions, not on the data.

Consider the following example. On my first trip to Florida Power and Light, we discussed the reduction of service interruptions. The FPL people made a presentation with a Pareto diagram of interruptions by causes showing that lightning was the largest cause. To my question of why the groundings or arresters had not prevented the interruptions, they answered that Florida had the most frequent and severe lightning attacks in the United States and that groundings or arresters would not have prevented service interruptions produced by strong lightning. I again asked, "Please show me the data which explain that intense lightning caused interruptions so severe that groundings or arresters could not prevent them." They could not show me any data, but promised to collect data by my next visit. Nearly half a year later when I visited again, they had collected the data and found that interruptions occurred even when they did not have such strong lightning. In addition, they found a certain percentage of poles with absent or insufficient groundings, which they had not recognized until they collected the data.

4. *Employees' commitment; management is not a monopoly of managers.*

Techniques

The most popular techniques are the Pareto diagram, cause and effect diagram, and the histogram which are among the "Seven QC Tools." This is the same phenomenon I observed in Japan. Some American companies are also starting to show an interest in applying the "QC Story," which is a standard procedure for problem solving developed in Japan.

Because of the popularity of "SPC seminars," production lines are often flooded with control charts. In many cases, however, I observed that actions had not always been taken when the charts showed out-of-control situations. When I asked supervisors how they examined such facts and what actions they had taken, in most cases they could not explain their specific measures. Nevertheless, I have heard from the quality facilitators of the companies that have introduced control charts in their workplaces that their quality has been rapidly improved by the introduction of SPC. One explanation for this is that the very process of collecting data and plotting points on the charts causes foremen and workers to pay more attention to quality. Thus, even poorly used control charts can contribute to the process of improving quality by making workers more conscious of quality.

In addition to control charts, other statistical methods such as analysis of variance and multiple regression analysis have been taught to engineers and managers. I have not yet, however, found many successful applications of these techniques in U.S. firms. In the factories I observed, a remarkable number of problems were solved by combining intrinsic technology with simple methods such as the Seven QC Tools.

In the Toyota Motor Company, which is renowned for its enthusiastic devotion to quality, when management discusses how much quality has been improved and how much they should stress further improvement, it is often said, "People make efforts to squeeze a dry towel drier." This towel metaphor means that in its early stages, a company with a dripping towel gets rid of a lot of water with just a little squeeze, without any tools. As the company evolves, a wringer might be needed. In an advanced stage, an electric vacuum drier is required. If asked how much the United States has improved its quality so far, I explain that at present the United States is using a wringer, such as the Seven QC Tools, to bring about effective results. I assume that more sophisticated methods, on the level of the electric vacuum drier—such as analysis of variance or multiple regression analysis—will be required for U.S. firms to progress further.

The Taguchi Method and "QD" (Quality Deployment, sometimes called "QFD"—Quality Function Deployment) also seem to have become somewhat popular. People are also beginning to show an interest in the "Seven New Management Tools for QC." Some people seem to find somewhat flamboyant ways to demonstrate certain tools, instead of using them to solve problems. This is a common phenomenon at the early stage of TQM's introduction into any country. As TQM develops further in the United States, this phenomenon should disappear. It is nothing to worry about.

Promotional Vehicles

Promotional Organization

Who will ultimately be responsible for promoting companywide quality? The answer to that question is the key factor to successful implementation, especially in the United States. In companies that promote company-wide quality activities, I find the rank of the executive responsible for this job differs. In one company, the Executive Vice President is in charge; in another it is the Vice President or Director. Those companies that elevate someone from personnel to become the responsible director seem to have a great deal of difficulty. The new director faces such problems as how to persuade high-level line managers such as the Vice President of Manufacturing or the Division General Manager to take necessary action. I recall the late Dr. Kaoru Ishikawa mentioning that he used to think that the staff function remains strong in Western companies. But, in reality, the situation is the same, as in Japanese companies, where the line function is stronger than the staff function, so that interdepartmental barriers are very dense.

When it comes to promoting quality in implementation units—such as a division, factory, and branch office—successful results depend on whether or not their heads, general staff, and managers are actively leading the promotion. On this point, I found no differences between American and Japanese companies.

Education and Training

In classrooms and workshops, American companies promote very extensive, and sometimes very intensive, training programs in quality management philosophies, management tools, and statistical methods. It seems to me, however, that they have difficulty in adapting these philosophies and techniques to their workplaces. This is partially due to the shortage of able and seasoned quality experts who can support and encourage both executives and managers to promote companywide quality management by counseling them in actual situations as they occur.

In the United States, the exchange of ideas between companies has increased along with the number of companies promoting companywide quality activities. Given the brief history of such quality promotion, dependence on information from other U.S. companies suffices neither qualitatively nor quantitatively. I assume, however, that the exchange of quality information will improve in the future.

Quality Circles

In the mid-1970s, Wayne Rieker at Lockheed Aircraft Co. first introduced quality circles to the United States. By the 1980s, the "IAQC" (International Association for Quality Circles), which was organized to promote the concept, was actively diffusing it. At the end of 1987, IAQC was reorganized and renamed "AQP" (Association for Quality and Participation). In addition to promoting quality circles, it holds numerous seminars on matters relating to quality and participatory management.

Quality circle activities seemed to peak around the middle of the 1980s. This peak points to the end of one phase of the quality movement. Companies had initially defined quality problems in relation to workers' morale and workmanship, so they believed those problems could be solved by quality circles. In the early 1980s, many American management study teams came to Japan. Most of them were interested in nothing more than quality circles. Gradually, however, many learned that promoting quality circles alone was not sufficient to achieve quality. So they began, sometimes hesitatingly, to emphasize companywide implementation of quality activities.

These movements may also have been affected by the article "Quality Circles After the Fad," published in the *Harvard Business Review* by Professor Edward Lawler III and associates.[10] The authors sharpened my own reflections on what happens to a company if it introduces quality circles without promoting companywide quality activities.

Although the quality circle boom has been declining, it is clear that group activities of workers, such as quality circles, are essential to a comprehensive implementation of quality. I believe that U.S. companies will need to reactivate quality circles as part of the future development of TQM.

Team Activity

Several different types of team activities exist in the United States. One type is similar to quality circle activity and involves a voluntary problem-solving group made up of workers in the same workplace. On completing one theme, the same team will work on the next one in an on-going activity. These teams are sometimes called functional teams since each group at the bottom of the organizational hierarchy shares one operational function.

In a second type of team activity, a Japanese and American joint venture company in the United States defines the team as the unit to which a set of jobs is assigned. In typical American companies, a job is assigned to each worker. In this case, a team of 10 workers is given a set of jobs to be shared, flexibly, among team members. In the unionized sector, generally, a detailed job classification is developed jointly with the labor union, and it is not unusual to see over 100 different kinds of jobs classified in just one factory. To adopt an alternate type of team approach, job classifications must be reduced to allow workers to do multiple jobs. Since this change is linked to the wage system, it necessitates negotiating with the unions. Because these teams are formed primarily to build quality into a product during the assembling process as specified rather than to improve it, they can be called "quality building-in process teams." Several workers in a plant where this team method has been adopted told me that their transformation from single-skill to multiple-skill workers has made them more interested in the job and more aware of quality.

A third approach involves initiating a team comprising staff or line managers, usually formed on orders from management. It is often called a task team or a project team. Once the task is completed, the team is disbanded. Participation in such teams, just like participation in quality circles, depends in principle on the free will of individual employees. Such teams are often formed across different departments; the nature of the task given sometimes demands the creation of two other types of teams: a problem-solving team (a team to address a particular problem arising in the process of promoting quality activity) and a task-achieving team (a team formed to implement a particular project, such as developing a new product).

Of the three types, the third one is the most standard team activity. It seems to me, however, that its content and nature varies from company to company, or even from department to department within the same company. In some cases, members of the team work on the task part-time while they do their regular job back in their own section. In other cases, members work full-time on the team activity. I also heard that the freedom to go beyond departmental barriers to do the activity required by the objective helped revitalize both staff and line managers who participated. This method is certainly useful in temporarily removing the barriers between departments. It could, however, produce new problems, such as a need for accumulated technical expertise and communication between different teams. Whatever the merits or demerits may be, this type of teamwork should not be overlooked when talking about quality activity in the United States today.

Management By Policy (Hōshin Kanri)

Of the various elements of Japanese TQC, what most interests American management is customer satisfaction activity and management by policy. "MBO" (Management by Objective) has long held a central place for American managers. But, in actuality, in many companies it has become a mere skeleton, without much substance. In contrast, management by policy looks very fresh. It has the following features:

- *The four stages of management by policy:* policy setting, policy deployment, policy implementation, and evaluation and feedback.
- *Linkage of annual company policy with longer-term plans:* Annual company policy is linked with long-term and mid-term plans.
- *Policy elements:* Each policy consists of an objective and the strategies to achieve it.
- *Setting up annual company policy:* Annual company policy (frequently called presidential policy in Japan) is nominally a top-down approach. In reality, however, top management collects the opinions of people inside the company about chronic major problems and their wishes for their company's future and uses this information to formulate the annual plan.
- *Policy deployment conducted before the fiscal year starts:* Each annual company policy is incorporated into each department manager's annual policy. That way, implementing departmental policies helps to realize the company policy. Additionally, in each department, the manager's policies are coordinated with those of its related functions. Whether the deployment mentioned above is vertical (between a superior and his or her subordinates) or horizontal (cross-functional), communication within the organization should be fluid.

- *Policy implementation:* After company policy is deployed throughout each department, each function prepares the program and schedule needed to implement specific items to achieve those targets assigned to it. After the fiscal year begins, the items are implemented according to schedule. This process is conducted through the PDCA cycle, usually quarterly or monthly, but occasionally weekly or even daily.

- *Evaluation and feedback:* At the end of the fiscal year, the implementation results are evaluated for each function, at each department and company level. This is done whether or not the implementation items have been realized and the targets achieved, and whether or not department managers' policies and company policies have been achieved. If they haven't been reached at a particular level, the causes should be investigated. The results should be reported to policy makers. That would allow some compensatory action and prevent the recurrence of similar failures in the coming year.

This system was developed to implement the concept of PDCA cycle for company policies. Before introducing the system, a company's policies are often dreamlike, with no systematic actions taken. In the 1960s, the "Integrated Management" system was created by Nippon Denso, Sumitomo Electric Industries, Nippon Kayaku, and Komatsu. It came to be named "Management by Policy" and was initiated in earnest by Bridgestone Co. around 1967.

In some American companies, Management-by-Policy has already been introduced and implemented. I observe that American top executives are involved with it in the following ways:

Two categories of strategy. So far, U.S. executives have been involved in preparing various strategies. But when asked to implement them, they have not been necessarily successful. Gradually, these executives have begun to understand that excellent strategies are not always successful. Hence, in addition to a system for preparing strategies, they must install a system for realizing them. In general, executives deal with two kinds of strategies. The first kind, which is effective immediately after decision making, involves personnel, budgeting, or merger and acquisition. The second kind is effective only with a companywide effort, such as a quality strategy. Management-by-policy is the ideal vehicle for realizing the second kind of strategy. When it comes to the introduction and implementation of this second strategy, however, U.S. companies have encountered a variety of difficulties inherent in management-by-policy, just as many Japanese companies did at a similar stage.

English translation problems. [11] American companies have encountered the problem of how to translate *"Hōshin Kanri."* The Japanese Society for Quality Control committee for the English translation of Japanese TQC terminology, which I chaired, decided to translate the Japanese term *"Hōs-*

hin Kanri" into "Management by Policy." But this translation alone is insufficient. What makes an exact translation difficult is that a considerable semantic gap exists between the English word "policy" and the Japanese word *"hoshin."* In English, "policy" implies something rather permanent. The phrase "annual policy" makes English speakers uncomfortable, for it implies that a policy might change from year to year. A detailed explanation is also in order because of the common assumption that *"hoshin"* or "policy" implies an objective and its methods. Because of this confusion, some American companies such as Hewlett Packard have begun using the Japanese word *"hoshin."* They feel it is better to use the original word untranslated and free from the misleading connotation of "policy." Some of the other names selected by American companies that have introduced management-by-policy are "policy deployment" and "hoshin process."

Chase too many rabbits.   It is very common for a company introducing Management-by-Policy to set up too many policies to implement, and I often caution companies about this. This caution, however, is generally neglected or forgotten during the first year; consequently, the results are inadequate. Then management pays attention to focusing its efforts from the second year on.

Inadequate analysis of data about the current status: a preference for pursuing dreams.   When top executives decide company policy, they are apt to chase their dream rather than analyze data about the current status. Dreams are necessary, but top executives should understand that it takes many years to realize them. I recommend that part of the introductory year's annual policy include overcoming weaknesses—reducing failure cost and market claims, for example—rather than enhancing strengths, such as further increasing market share.

Insufficient cross-functional coordination can undermine company policy.   One company, for example, set up a medium-term policy of developing a new product along with specific target for sales and profit. At the end of this period, however, the company achieved its sales target, but not its profit target. This was because of the unexpectedly high warranty costs incurred by the new product. The warranty problems resulted from poor design review and poor reliability that, in turn, arose from product failures under certain usage conditions, which had not been predicted. If service engineers had participated in the design review, the problems in all likelihood would have been minimized because these engineers would have recognized similar kinds of failures in the past. This product development policy was deployed under the auspices of the product development department, which had no contact with the service department. This is an example of poor policy deployment.

Development of a project.   I have noticed that in American organizations, policy is deployed down to lower levels and finally, in most cases, to project teams. At the implementation stage for each project, analysis is conducted to solve problems, countermeasures are developed, and the results are replicated at different departments or sections. This process seems appropriate for American culture. In some companies, in fact, the task teams execute these projects. In the case of Japanese companies, however, the team projects are deployed within the ordinary organization; the team members come from departments and sections whose chiefs have key roles in the promotion of the policy objective.

Presidential diagnosis. Some companies have introduced presidential diagnosis—sometimes called "presidential audit" or "presidential review"—to ensure that top management's policy is deployed and implemented at each department, and to provide top management with an opportunity to learn what is happening on the first line of operations. In introducing presidential diagnosis, one company made the following argument:

> Top management's role is to make decisions on various kinds of important issues, including policy making. Implementation is mainly the job of managers who report the results to top management through the chain of command. Top management, therefore, macroscopically knows what is happening in the field. Under such a system, of what use is a presidential review? Would not top management's visit at each department or workplace create confusion in the chain of command?

Once such an argument was overcome, however, and the process implemented, the company discovered the merits of the diagnosis. In particular, top management became aware of very different kinds of microscopic information. This company still continues to use the presidential diagnosis. In another company, a division general manager's review was implemented on a trial basis for about two years before the process became companywide and was eventually upgraded to presidential diagnosis.

Few companies are conducting a combined evaluation for objectives and methods of implementation. In the evaluation stage, we need to check whether objectives are achieved as well as how they are realized. The evaluation results can be categorized into the following four cases:

	Objective	Method	Comment
Case A	OK	OK	Very happy
Case B	OK	No good	God blesses the company
Case C	No good	OK	Hopeless
Case D	No good	No good	Still hopeful

These cases can be compared to students who: Case A—fully attended the class and passed the exam; Case B—rarely attended the class but passed the exam; Case C—fully attended the class but failed the exam; Case D—rarely attended the class and then failed the exam. Student A and Student D are easily understood, and Student D may be successful in the next semester if he fully attends the class, so he is hopeful about next semester. Student B and Student C are not as easily understood. Student B is overjoyed that God blessed him, but he needs to be careful, for God will not always bless him. Student C may be hopeless next semester, even though he fully attends the class as he did last semester. Student C should analyze why he failed even though he fully attended the class. He needs to improve his approach to learning to pass the exam.

Similarly, in evaluating Management-by-Policy at the end of the fiscal year, both its objectives and its methods for realizing objectives should be examined. The reasons for each individual case should be analyzed. In many cases, the problems come from the mode of policy deployment.

This combination of evaluating both the objective and its methods of implementation is an orthodox approach. Yet in the United States, very few companies conduct such an evaluation. In addition, some companies emphasize objectives; others, on the contrary, emphasize only methods of implementation (process improvements).

Daily Management

This approach is less marked among American companies than is Management-by-Policy, but it is so important that it could be defined as fundamental management. It is encouraging to find a few United States companies that have introduced this system in addition to Management-by-Policy, for it strengthens the capabilities of the first-line managers and supervisors. Florida Power and Light calls this system "Quality in Daily Work" (QIDW). In this activity, these are the major tools: a control item or a performance indicator for a job, process standards (including process flow charts and forms/files), and control charts/control graphs.

American companies seem to have the following strengths and weaknesses in this activity:

- In regard to daily management, the United States should be proud of its extensive use of computer systems, although there is still room for improvement from the standpoint of their effective utilization. I have been impressed by the considerable number of computer terminals that have been installed and the reduction of paper documents in offices. In contrast, in the offices of Japanese companies, many documents are still piled up on desks. Japanese companies are over 10 years behind the United States when it comes to promoting office automation.

- Process standards have been prepared by staff departments in headquarters in the United States. Therefore when something needs to be improved in the standards, the individual workplace manager cannot revise them. In Japan, many companies operate under a corporate standardization rule. It classifies standards into categories according to the responsible department or managerial level and authorizes each of the responsible departments or management levels to prepare and revise the category of standards they are responsible for. Workplace management can revise most operational standards on their own, and this helps management to rotate the PDCA cycle quickly.

- In the United States, the training in SPC or control charts is not being linked with training for process standardization. SPC is taught by statisticians who have limited experience in workplace management. They base their training on the notion of population, which is just a hypothetical statistical model. What prerequisites are essential to apply this model to process control in the workplace? The answer is process standardization, which bridges the statistical model and the actual job process in the workplace. Without specific standards and their operation, we can neither identify the population nor use the information provided by control charts such as "under control" or "out of control."

- It is encouraging to see that the "out of control" is based on control charts. This shows that people have based their actions on "fact," rather than "intuition." In the process of finding the causes of "out of control," however, many people still depend on "intuition" over "data." To recover from this dependence, companies need executives and managers who earn the nickname "Mr. Show-Me-Data."

- One of the popular activities observed in American companies is the implementation of "5 WHY's"; namely, if a problem occurs, employees are encouraged to ask "Why" five times, on the assumption that the answer to this question will unearth a root cause for the problem. Although this is a very good practice, in many workplaces I found employees who ask the questions without fully understanding the nature of the problem. Therefore, I recommend asking "5 WHAT's" before asking "5 WHY's," repeating "What is our problem?" five times.

Quality Activities in Each Stage of the New Product Development, Production, and Marketing Processes

New Product Development

I was very curious about the process U.S. companies use to develop epoch-making new products. I found that they take a "genius approach," in which a company, when it discovers a very outstanding person, perhaps a genius, provides that individual with the necessary resources, conditions, and work environments. The company makes it easy for the person to do his or her best, without bringing into play age, wealth, education, or experience, as is popularly done in Japanese companies. In contrast, the method for new product development in Japanese companies that implement TQM could be termed the "systematic approach."

We are frequently surprised with the outstanding originality at the core of American new products—the result of giving a genius free rein—but we sometimes encounter problems with the subsidiary parts of the product that are handled by ordinary employees. Japanese products may have fewer problems as well as less originality, although Japanese companies have made great efforts to downplay this weakness. To sum up, America is strong in its genius approach, but poor in its systematic approach. Japan is just the opposite. Companies in both countries need to overcome their weakness and further develop their strength. Although some companies are already examining this issue, it might take a considerable number of years to achieve this state. (I assume it could be done very well if a Japanese-American development center were established somewhere in the middle of the Pacific Ocean.)

Production

The discipline on the shop floor in American firms seems to have been improved considerably during the last decade. People work harder and housekeeping has been much improved. Quality circles, SPC, and team activities are becoming common tools for quality improvement. Some companies are eager to promote JIT as well.

Marketing Share

The management of American companies characteristically puts a great deal of emphasis on "amount of profit," instead of "turnover growth," "profit ratio to sales turnover," or "market share." Based on this concept, U.S. manufacturing firms have cut off the less profitable business lines or transferred their manufacturing base overseas. It might be said that this is one of the negative elements that caused the "hollowing out" of U.S. manufacturing firms. Recently, however, some companies have begun to become more aware of market share and have made comparative studies of their competitors' product quality.

Conclusion

With regard to the promotion of quality, there appear to be American companies that have been implementing quality activities enthusiastically and effectively during the last decade and are beginning to take further steps for their steady promotion. Although the pace of their efforts is sometimes slow, they are having successful results.

At the beginning of 1993, as usual, various statistical reports about the past year were released by the Japanese press. Three of the articles caught my attention. One, dealing with semiconductor production, said that NEC, which had been in first place for the past seven years, was replaced by INTEL, whose sales had increased to five billion dollars (up 26% from the previous year). The second article, relating to total car sales, showed the Ford Taurus surpassing the Honda Accord in the United States as the best-selling passenger car. The third article, using data from Dataquest, deals with personal computers and reports that, worldwide, American companies (IBM, Apple, and others) are regaining market share. These facts point to a trend: during the past ten years, American improvement efforts, including TQM, have gradually led to good results in some industries. We seem to be at the beginning of a new era in which international competition is based on quality. These facts are indeed impressive, and I want to keep my eye on how things develop after this.

Because America is such a big country, it will take much more time until it gets macroeconomic results, such as contributing to the elimination of the trade deficit. In the case of Japan, it took about 20 years after the introduction of QC before the trade balance turned positive.

As I have repeatedly said, similar problems arise in Japanese and American firms when they first implement TQM. I have often heard some American specialists insisting that it is difficult to implement TQM in the United States because of its culture. I disagree. A more important factor, I would suggest, is the degree of top management's motivation to be part of TQM, and the greatest enemy of TQM is top management's doubt. "Is there a need to do so much?" or "Do I have to do so much?" This shows that they still base their professional self-evaluation too heavily on traditional measures of their companies' standing. Quality will be improved if top management will assert its leadership to smoothly implement TQM corporatewide—and from the long-term viewpoint.

When I consider how American firms will develop TQM activities in the future, one influence is mass media. It tends to discuss the short-term effects of quality. In addition, American consumers' tend to be uncritical of poor quality products and services. Let me elaborate on both points.

One characteristic in the development of Japan's TQC is that Japanese mass media paid little attention to the TQC movement, both its merits and demerits, until around 1980. As a result, Japanese top management could concentrate on TQC from a long-term perspective without worrying about mass media commentary. A drawback is that it took so much time to diffuse TQC activities throughout the country.

In the case of the United States, at the beginning of the 1980s, American mass media began to pay attention to the quality movement, so information about it has been diffused rapidly. A considerable number of articles about it appeared in various media. There are some firms, however, that implement TQM simply because it is the fashion. So quality activities in such companies tend to be perfunctory or shortsighted. It might be said of these companies that they promote TQM for the sake of TQM. So it is not surprising that the media can find easy targets to criticize.

A friend of mine, a leading individual in the American quality world, once showed me a critical article that appeared in one of the influential newspapers and asked for my comment. The article criticized the absolute amount of funds the firm expended for its TQM implementation. I answered that my friend should calculate the average cost per employee per year as well as the rate per gross sales. Typically, such articles give little consideration to the company's size and time over which the budget was spent; rather, they take the total amount as a reference, even when it is budgeted over five years. This often shocks people into thinking, "How expensive!"

According to my experience, it costs approximately 0.1 to 0.3% of gross sales, referring to total expenses, to run a department for education, training, and quality promotion. The cost can vary depending on how intensively a firm implements it or what related costs are included. So in the case of a mammoth enterprise whose gross sales amount to ten billion dollars, the total costs could be between ten and thirty million dollars a year. In a word, that's how much cost should be permitted when a firm implements quality activity to improve its product/service and to realize the use of scientific methods.

It seems to me that American consumers are quite sensitive to the prices of products. On the other hand, they are charitable about quality unless a product becomes a product liability issue. People seem to feel that it is no use complaining because the country is so large and there is too little competition. For example, this past summer when I crossed the continent on a red-eye flight, my plane took off from San Francisco Airport one hour behind schedule. The delay was due to the late arrival of a pilot. As a result, I missed my connection at Chicago and wasted three hours. I did not notice any passengers complaining to the ground staff of the airline at the Chicago terminal. Since the delay was caused not by weather but by the airline's lack of attention, one might assume that the ground service staff in Chicago would have been waiting for us at the arrival gate, eager to offer service for in-transit passengers. On that occasion, however, I could not find any ground service staff at the gate. The airline's indifference led me to wonder if passively accepting the world as it is undermines the quality improvement of American products and services.

Many similarities exist between the development of quality activities in

American TQM and Japanese TQC. Although some differences exist, they are not critical. Therefore, this permits me to assert that the experiences and knowledge of both countries is to some extent interchangeable.

Notes

I am grateful to Robert E. Cole and Gene Ulansky for helping to clarify the English language usage in this chapter as well as the content of various ideas and also to Ms. Noriko Kusaba for assisting me in preparing this chapter.

1. N. Kano, "Business Trip to Europe after an Interval of Six Years," *Hinshitsu* [*Quality*, Journal of the Japanese Society for Quality Control, in Japanese], 12 (1982): 24–28.
2. N. Kano and K. Koura, "Development of Quality Control Seen Through Companies Awarded the Deming Prize," *Rep. Stat. Appl. Res.*, JUSE, 37 (1990–91): 79–105.
3. N. Kano, "Quality Sweating Theory: Crisis Consciousness, Vision, and Leadership," *Hinshitsu* [*Quality*, Journal of the Japanese Society for Quality Control, in Japanese], 19 (1989): 32–42.
4. Ibid.
5. N. Kano, "English Translation of the Technical Terms of TQC Implementation," *Hinshitsu* [*Quality*, Journal of the Japanese Society for Quality Control, in Japanese], 22/3 (1992): 91–99 and 22/4 (1992): 87–93.
6. N. Kano, "A Comparative Study between the Western and Japanese QC," memorandum, the 207th JSA (Japanese Standards Association) COSCO Research Meeting [in Japanese], 1982.
7. N. Kano, "The Situation Is Not So Bad Yet, and That Is a Problem of American Firms," *Hinshitsu* [*Quality*, Journal of the Japanese Society for Quality Control, in Japanese], 10 (1980): 227–232 and 11 (1980): 87–93.
8. Kano (1989), op. cit.
9. Kano (1980), op. cit.
10. E. Lawler III and S. A. Mohrman, "Quality Circles After the Fad," *Harvard Business Review*, 63 (January/February 1985): 65–71.
11. Kano (1992), op. cit.

Index

Page numbers in italics refer to material in tables and figures.